"We live in exciting times—people are pouring into the streets to demand decent wages and a union, justice for victims of police brutality, an end to racist mass incarceration and so much more. Pedagogical theory helps organizers build these struggles into mass movements of millions. *History and Education* offers important insights for those who seek to change the world."
—Walter Smolarek, the Black Radical Organizing Collective (BROC)

'For decades the educational Left and critical pedagogues have run away from Marxism, socialism, and communism, all too often based on faulty understandings and falling prey to the deep-seated anti-communism in the academy. In *History and Education* Curry Stephenson Malott pushes back against this trend by offering us deeply Marxist thinking about the circulation of capital, socialist states, the connectivity of Marxist anti-capitalism, and a politics of race and education. In the process Malott points toward the role of education in challenging us all to become abolitionists of global capitalism."
—Wayne Au, Associate Professor in the School of Educational Studies at the University of Washington Bothell; Editor of the social justice teaching magazine *Rethinking Schools*; Co-editor of *Mapping Corporate Education Reform: Power and Policies Networks in the Neoliberal State*

'Curry Stephenson Malott is a scholar committed to the global working class struggle. In this volume he fearlessly and unapologetically challenges critical pedagogy by centering the oppressed and global working class in his analysis and synthesis. What distinguishes this work in progressive education is the way in which Malott draws on important theorists and revolutionaries, most notably Harry Haywood, Karl Marx, and Vladimir Lenin, and in the process, advances radical pedagogy. In the end Malott dares to demand that the working class and oppressed deserve an educational praxis and paradigm that serves their educational needs and liberatory interests."
—Kashara White, Party for Socialism and Liberation

'Eight years after the global capitalist crisis modern societies are treading down a dangerous road. In this context Curry Stephenson Malott addresses important questions such as, what is the state and what role does it play in the revolutionary process? Do we need a Marxist theory of the state today? What has historical experience shown? What can critical approaches to education gain from Marx? In this text, Malott, with considerable clarity, scholarship, and passion contributes to the unraveling of these and other questions. Along the way, he makes crucial interventions in debates about what counts as *radical* in the academy and explores critically and insightfully the anti-communist propaganda, offering up needed clarifications to the histories of the Soviet Union, China, the DPRK, and the Black Panther Party. In the process *History and Education* opens up welcome new horizons for a communist pedagogy. One does not have to agree with every position Malott takes to acknowledge that *History and Education* is essential reading for classroom and pre-service teachers, teacher educators, and educational researchers. It is also an excellent tool for use in any course in education, sociology, and political science."
—Polina Chrysochou, Anglia Ruskin University, England

"Curry Stephenson Malott, in *History and Education*, helps us forge, sharpen, and prepare new intellectual and organizational weapons for the global class war. In this volume Malott contributes to the revolutionary pedagogical literature by carefully and thoroughly revisiting Marx's original theorizing and connecting that work to, and historicizing the work of, communist activist leaders from the Soviet Union, to the DPRK, to North America. These tools, wrought and forged from radical world history and philosophical activism, are just what are needed, now more than ever, in these perilous times. *History and Education* is a must-read for any student of radical activism, any teacher, or anyone now fighting for justice in the streets."

—Marc Pruyn, Senior Lecturer, Monash University, Melbourne;
Co-editor (with Luis Huerta-Charles) of *This Fist Called My Heart:
The Peter McLaren Reader, Volume I* (2016)

History and Education

EDUCATION and STRUGGLE

Narrative, Dialogue, and the Political Production of Meaning

Michael Peters & Peter McLaren
Series Editors

Vol. 9

The Education and Struggle series is part of the Peter Lang Education list.
Every volume is peer reviewed and meets
the highest quality standards for content and production.

PETER LANG
New York • Bern • Frankfurt • Berlin
Brussels • Vienna • Oxford • Warsaw

Curry Stephenson Malott

History and Education

Engaging the Global Class War

PETER LANG
New York • Bern • Frankfurt • Berlin
Brussels • Vienna • Oxford • Warsaw

Library of Congress Cataloging-in-Publication Data
Names: Malott, Curry.
Title: History and education: engaging the global class war /
Curry Stephenson Malott.
Description: New York: Peter Lang, 2016.
Series: Education and struggle: narrative, dialogue
and the political production of meaning; vol. 9
ISSN 2168-6432 (print) | ISSN 2168-6459 (online)
Includes bibliographical references and index.
Identifiers: LCCN 2016014709 | ISBN 978-1-4331-3399-2 (hardcover: alk. paper)
ISBN 978-1-4331-3398-5 (paperback: alk. paper) | ISBN 978-1-4539-1867-8 (e-book)
Subjects: LCSH: Socialism and education. | Marx, Karl, 1818–1883.
Classification: LCC HX526.M277 2016 | DDC 370.11/5—dc23
LC record available at https://lccn.loc.gov/2016014709

Bibliographic information published by **Die Deutsche Nationalbibliothek**.
Die Deutsche Nationalbibliothek lists this publication in the "Deutsche
Nationalbibliografie"; detailed bibliographic data are available
on the Internet at http://dnb.d-nb.de/.

The paper in this book meets the guidelines for permanence and durability
of the Committee on Production Guidelines for Book Longevity
of the Council of Library Resources.

© 2016 Peter Lang Publishing, Inc., New York
29 Broadway, 18th floor, New York, NY 10006
www.peterlang.com

Printed in the United States of America

CONTENTS

FOREWORD

Drawing Class Lines Through Critical Education: A Proletarian Program for the Current Crisis

Derek R. Ford

There is a common belief out there that capitalism is so totalizing, so all-subsuming, that even the most radical scholarship can be accommodated within its circuits of production and consumption. Curry Malott, in this book, seems to be out to disprove that belief. He succeeds, and in his success, he demonstrates that this belief reveals nothing about contemporary capitalism, and everything about what passes as radical scholarship today.

At the base of this book, then, is a critique of—and corrective to—the deep-seated anticommunism that permeates much of the Western and academic Left, especially within the U.S. Thus, it isn't just the global bourgeoisie and its representatives who will despise the contents of this book; it's likely to upset quite a few self-proclaimed and celebrated "critical scholars" inside and outside of education. One thing is for sure: after reading this book it's hard to look at the field of critical education—especially critical pedagogy—the same way. With biting critique and careful historical and theoretical analysis, Malott lays bare what he, following Sam Marcy, calls the "crossing of class lines" that characterizes so much critical scholarship. The crossing of class lines is, simply, when one finds oneself shoulder to shoulder with imperialism, shouting the same slogans ("Down with authoritarianism!") and attacking the same enemy (communism).

Bringing communist theoreticians and revolutionaries into the educational conversation, Malott begins to develop a "communist pedagogy" in this book, and this pedagogy offers the field needed clarifications, historical contexts, conceptual frameworks, organizational imperatives, and future possibilities. Malott begins by tackling a question that is, for any organizer, presently absent in academia writ large today: the state. He clarifies for us what the state is and what role it plays in the revolutionary process, reminding us along the way that revolutions are, by definition "one of the most authoritarian human actions possible." Revolutions take place when one segment of society imposes its will absolutely on another segment; there is no revolution without repression. As Marx (1867/1967) puts it in *Capital*, "Force is the midwife of every old society pregnant with a new one" (p. 703). It is only through utilizing the state and its repressive and productive powers that a new society can arise, for the bourgeoisie, as history has shown, doesn't go without a fight.

Once deposed they count their losses, regroup, find new allies, and launch campaigns of terror. The history of the communist movement has proved this without exception. Thus, to forfeit or bypass the state "is to surrender before the final battle has even begun." Just months after the exploited masses of Russia took power in 1917 they were under attack from fourteen imperialist armies, each of which was in coordination with the White Army that served Russia's former capitalists and landlords. When Cuban guerrillas overthrew the U.S.-backed Batista dictatorship in their country, it wasn't long before the U.S. invaded the island. The CIA's forces were repelled by the armed Cuban masses, but the campaign against Cuba continued with assassinations and terrorist attacks. There were plans for another U.S. military intervention, and these plans were changed only when the Soviet Union sent medium-range ballistic missiles with nuclear warheads to the country. There is a reason that imperialist politicians constantly denounce any attempt by an independent government to acquire a nuclear weapon—and it isn't because they hate bombs. They don't care that Israel has a nuclear weapons arsenal and that it has never allowed international inspection of its nuclear capabilities, and they aren't dismantling their own nuclear weapons. Instead, they are attacking the DPRK for its nuclear capability, and they are denouncing Iran's alleged attempts at a nuclear weapons program (which isn't documented). They bully countries into dismantling nuclear weapons programs, imposing deadly sanctions and threatening more war. It is interesting to note that the two governments who have complied with U.S. dictates to abandon nuclear weapons development were Iraq and Libya. Both governments were overthrown after they complied. What is the lesson here?

The establishment of the Soviet Union in 1917 and the Communist International in 1919 provided a new hope for the world's oppressed. This hope wasn't merely ideological, but was also *material*. As Malott shows, the Soviet Union was the center of gravity in the proletarian struggle for much of the twentieth century. It was the armory from which the world's oppressed drew their weapons to overthrow their oppressors, and it fertilized a counter-hegemonic bloc to imperialism, allowing the class war against the bourgeoisie to take on a truly global character for the first time in history. On the one side of the war stood the imperialist states and their puppet governments, and on the other side stood the socialist states and the anticolonial states.

This was a beautiful period of struggle for humanity, although it wasn't without its setbacks and its errors. Yet Malott argues that there is a crucial difference between critiquing the leadership or policy of a socialist state and critiquing that state's social system. And here is where his criticism of critical pedagogy is most severe: critical pedagogy turned its weapons of critique against the social systems of the proletarian class camp, thereby crossing class lines. Malott provides several historical and contemporary examples of pedagogues such as Henry Giroux who not only denounce the proletarian camp, but even go so far as to equate the Soviet Union with Nazi Germany—its literal opposite. Democracy is opposed to totalitarianism in critical pedagogy, which is exactly how Winston Churchill framed the world struggle in his famous "Iron Curtain" speech in Missouri on March 5, 1946. Talk about crossing class lines!

There is a material basis for such class collaboration, and a history of it that stretches back more than one hundred years with the betrayal of the Socialist International, which was the grouping of mass socialist parties. In 1912, the Socialist International met in Basel, Switzerland, for an emergency meeting. The outbreak of an inter-imperialist war was imminent, and the socialist movement needed an orientation. The outcome of the meeting was clear: in the outbreak of inter-imperialist war, all socialists should oppose the war and refuse to fire on workers of other countries. For those parties with representatives in parliament this meant that they had to vote against any war credits. When push came to shove, however, the overwhelming majority of the socialist parties capitulated to imperialism and united with their national ruling classes. The Socialist International collapsed.

Why did this happen? How was it that the parties of working-class revolution united with their class enemies? Lenin answered these questions in his work on imperialism (1920/1965). Monopoly profits extracted by imperialist powers, those profits "obtained over and above the profits which capitalists squeeze out of the workers of their 'own' country" made it "*possible to bribe the labour leaders and the upper stratum of the labour aristocracy*" (p. 9). These monopoly profits provided the material basis for national chauvinism and reformism, the latter of which can be defined as sacrificing the gains of the entire working class for the short-term gains of a particular section of the working class. The socialist parties that betrayed the working class, like the German Social Democratic Party, were able to keep their offices, their news-papers, their positions in parliament, and so on. The Bolsheviks, who stayed loyal to the proletarian revolution, were driven underground and their parlia-mentary representatives were arrested.

It's not too hard to see, then, why what Malott calls "antisocialist social-ism" is so prevalent in the academy. We are back at the limits of what counts as radical today. There are limits. You can be a socialist in the academy, but only after you denounce every socialist country and the history of the com-munist movement. All you need to do is add a few quick lines dismissing the Soviet Union as "totalitarian" and you will be all set, no need to worry about your tenure and promotion. It will help, too, if you stick to teaching and writ-ing about this critical stuff and refrain from organizing and agitating.

We should hope that these critical scholars will engage with Malott's ideas and arguments, and do the only logical thing: repudiate their previous writings and actions. This is what Malott has done in and with this book, which is an honest political self-critique. He writes of his "long journey of self-reflection and de-indoctrination." Malott's work has been heavily influenced by the revo-lutionary critical pedagogy of Peter McLaren. More than anyone else, McLaren has been instrumental in bringing Marx into the field of education, and this book is certainly situated within the opening that McLaren's work has created. McLaren turned to Marx at the height of the post-al era, and it was an uphill battle all the way. But, as Malott notes, the "fog and bigotry of anticommunism in the U.S. is slowly dissipating." Indeed, the crises of capitalism and imperi-alism have aroused new mass movements in the U.S., from Occupy in 2011 to today's Black Lives Matter. The campaign of Bernie Sanders has both capital-ized on and furthered the acceptance of the word "socialism." It's now safe(r) for communists to come out of the shadows and boldly organize, and that is precisely what this manuscript represents.

Malott doesn't just formulate his program through critique, however, for he also points to several examples of organizations in the U.S. that have refused to cross class lines. Chief among these is the Black Panther Party, which clearly located itself within the context of the global class war. The Black Panther Party for Self-Defense was explicitly a Marxist-Leninist Party that saw itself as part of an international communist movement. Panthers distributed Mao's little red book at rallies, traveled to the Democratic People's Republic of Korea, and aligned themselves with all foreign anti-imperialist governments. They developed their own application of Marxism-Leninism particular to the contours of U.S. capitalism, and they did not follow orders from any foreign Communist Party, but they militantly defended all social-ist formations and all people's governments. A modern day example that he gives is the Party for Socialism and Liberation, which has unflinchingly stood against imperialism.

While it is common to hear dismissals of the Soviet Union as "authori-tarian" or "totalitarian," there are also the quite puzzling designations, "state socialist," or "state capitalist," or "deformed workers' state" that pop up. They are labels that intellectuals in capitalist countries put on socialist governments because they know better. The way that one arrives at these designations is by drawing up what an ideal socialist society would look like and then comparing that to actually-existing socialism. As Malott carefully shows us, however, this is idealism pure and simple. A materialist analysis acknowledges that "the tension within the co-existence of the past, present, and future represents an unavoidable, dialectical reality that carries with it the contested curricu-lum of struggle." The Soviet Union, for example, erected socialism not out of advanced capitalism but out of feudalism. But socialism was constructed. It wasn't perfect, there were ebbs and flows, but capitalism was never restored. There were income differentials, sure, but there was no bourgeoisie in the Soviet Union; labor power wasn't a commodity to be bought and sold, and the relations of production were not relations of exploitation (see Szymanski, 1979, for empirical proof of this).

When the wave of counterrevolutions in 1989–1991 overthrew socialist governments throughout Europe, it was celebrated as an advance for democ-racy and freedom. And for the world's bourgeoisie, it was: they moved in and gobbled up the countries, making private all that was held publicly before. Isn't it odd that, whenever privatization happens in the U.S., critical intellectuals decry it as "neoliberalism," but when it happens in former socialist states it is seen as "democratization"? Malott's analysis here cuts through this mystifica-tion, helping us see that these are just two sides of the same coin, two of global capital's strategies for accumulation. We have to resolutely oppose both.

The global proletariat today is more fragmented and dispersed as a result of this freedom and democracy. With the framework of the global class war that Malott provides we can more deeply appreciate the transformations that have taken place since 1991. I propose that there are two primary phases here. The first is an all-out imperialist offensive against all socialist and independent states and peoples. Without an effective counterweight against imperialism, many independent and socialist states found themselves under the immediate threat of military and economic attack. The economic blockades on Cuba and the DPRK were immediately expanded and intensified. A new war was started against Iraq—first by military means, then by economic means, and then again by military means. Thousands of bombs were dropped on Yugoslavia, Bosnia, and Kosovo to break up the Socialist Federal Republic of Yugoslavia, sending the different nations within the federation into turmoil and chaos. Panama was invaded and its president was kidnapped and taken hostage in a U.S. prison. This is the context in which the recent wars on Afghanistan, Libya, Syria, and Yemen must be seen (in fact, the war on Afghanistan was the first step in a new war against independent states in the Middle East). It is similar to U.S. policies toward states such as Venezuela, Bolivia, Ecuador, Iran, Sudan, China, Ukraine, Zimbabwe, and Russia.

But we are in a new historical moment, and it is a vulnerable and exciting one. The U.S.-led imperialist offensive has waned; the era of uni-polar imperialism seems to be over and new counterhegemonic blocs are forming. While the war on Iraq did overthrow the nationalist Ba'athist government, it wasn't as easy as the imperialists had imagined it. The Iraqi people waged a heroic insurgency against occupation forces, and the project of installing a new puppet government ultimately failed. In 2007–2008 the capitalist economic crisis shook the world. With the U.S. bogged down in Iraq and Afghanistan, a socialist tide gathered in Latin America, bringing socialist and anti-imperialist governments into power, most notably with the election of Hugo Chavez in Venezuela. At the same time, independent powers like China and Brazil have emerged as real economic forces. True, these states are characterized by capitalist relations of production (although that's not 100 percent true in China's case), but they are not imperialist. China, in particular, has opened up an avenue for anti-imperialist and independent governments to emerge. Chinese economic relations with the Bolivarian revolution, for example, have been critical in Venezuela's independence from U.S. imperialism.

The emergence of a counterhegemonic bloc has thrown imperialism into crisis. The strategy of installing puppet governments is no longer feasible, for these governments can easily abandon the U.S., as happened in Iraq. In the face of this reality, Dan Glazebrook (2013) argues that the strategy of imperialism today is to generate failed and weakened states. This is a compelling way in which to understand imperialist strategy in Syria since 2011. When protests against the Syrian government began that year, imperialism seized the opportunity to initiate a regime change. The West had been funding opposition groups in Syria for some time, and these groups as well as radical Islamists quickly emerged as the opposition leadership (all progressive opposition groups quickly sided with the government, as they were satisfied with the reforms instituted—including a new constitution—and aware of the threat of imperialist intervention). But Russia and China vetoed a UN Security Council resolution to wage war on the country. So for five years now the West has been waging a proxy war against Syria, and in the process has created the material basis for the emergence of Daesh—or the Islamic State in the Levant—and has facilitated weapons and money transfers to them and the al-Nusra Front, which is affiliated with al-Qaeda. Russian military intervention in Syria, which began on September 30, 2015, has been essential in turning the tide of the war, allowing the Syrian Arab Army to liberate key cities from the terrorist forces. Of course, the U.S. doesn't want Daesh to get too powerful, and it can't have Daesh threatening U.S. geopolitical interests. The U.S. is flailing around trying to stay balanced on a tightrope it strung across the Middle East. If the U.S. were really interested in ending terrorism, it would immediately fall back and join in an alliance with Syria, Iran, and Hezbollah, the three groups that have actually been fighting Daesh and the terrorist groups for five years.

This is the state in which we find ourselves: imperialism is in crisis, a new counterhegemonic bloc has formed, and social movements in the United States are gaining ground and becoming more and more militant. The veil of anticommunism is lifting. What are we to do? The question, as Malott puts it, is: "Will education support the basic structures of capitalist hegemony and its domination over the Earth, or will it strive to uproot them?" This book provides us with an essential framework for understanding our history, our present, and, thus, for formulating the tasks ahead for critical educators. By drawing a clear class line through critical pedagogy he has offered up a new space in which to theorize and enact the possibilities of critical education.

Until victory,
Derek

References

Glazebrook, D. (2013). *Divide and ruin: The West's imperial strategy in an age of crisis.* San Francisco: Liberation.

Lenin, V. I. (1920/1965). *Imperialism, the highest stage of capitalism: A popular outline.* Peking: Foreign Languages.

Marx, K. (1867/1967). *Capital: A critical analysis of capitalist production* (Vol. 1). New York: International.

Syzmanski, A. (1979). *Is the red flag flying? The political economy of the Soviet Union today.* London: Zed.

PREFACE

Eugene Puryear*

In his 1872 preface to the French edition of *Capital*, Marx famously relates to a French translator that there is "no royal road to science, and only those who do not dread the fatiguing climb of its steep paths have a chance of gaining its luminous summits."[1] The context of the quote is an apology of sorts. Marx laments the difficulty of moving through some of the early chapters. Particularly regrettable, in his view, since this translation was being brought out in a serial form that "will be more accessible to the working class, a consideration which to me outweighs everything else."[2]

Marx's note strikes with particular relevance as one works their way through Curry Malott's *History and Education*. Not so much the content of the quote but its context. Marx was writing in the midst of a period of great struggle. In the wake of the Commune, emigres streamed into London from abroad.

Under the pressure of those events, 1872 also occasioned the epoch-defining split in the First International between Marx and Bakunin. A glance into the letters of Marx's *Collected Works* reveals the revolutionary as too overwhelmed to even write his daughter and grandson,[3] something confirmed by the intricate factional fighting detailed in further correspondence.

*Eugene Puryear is a member of the Party for Socialism and Liberation and the author of Shackled and Chained: Mass Incarceration in Capitalist America (2013, PSL Publications).

The split between the two was occasioned by the organizational implications flowing from Marx's central insight from the Commune: "The working class cannot simply lay hold of the ready-made state machinery, and wield it for its own purposes."[4] Marx's realization was that the International had to be "a real organisation of the working class for struggle." The bloody counterrevolutionary wave in Paris demanded a purge of any remaining romantic, adventuristic flights of insurrection.

Malott grounds his communist pedagogy in an insight: "The educational act cannot avoid an engagement with the basic structures of production and the vast diversity amongst the hundreds of oppressed nations throughout the world."

What is valuable is that Malott takes "engagement" beyond mere recognition. The "educational act," shaped by our imperialist world and mediated thorough its contradictions, can, within the same context and through the same contradictory format, play a role in consciously transforming itself. But what institutions, structures, ideas—in the concrete—would this require? *History and Education* contains concrete considerations on all these themes.

History and Education, too, was written at a time of great upheaval when the lessons that Marx was imbibing from the experience of the Commune seem particularly relevant—in the wake of the Arab Spring and the "distant cannons" of mass movements of the popular classes that have erupted in the decade previous.

As Marx did, now seems as relevant as ever a moment to revisit the circumstances of struggle that recommend the Party form. The importance of struggles that move in the direction of power, not just influence—and the incumbent necessity of overthrowing the ruling class dictatorship—has been underlined by raw defeats in Egypt, Venezuela, and Greece. This book's discussion of the Party form points to the urgent necessity for militants to study and understand the counterforce needed to overthrow imperialist power.

Malott deserves credit for transcending the anticommunist prejudices abounding in our society to engage with thinkers like Harry Haywood. Haywood is easily one of the most influential theorists of any type in the history of Black America. His theoretical work on the issue of the Negro Nation has influenced not just the left but also wide swaths of the Black Nationalist community, including the Nation of Islam. Yet in broader academic circles he is essentially unknown.

The text following this preface contains a number of challenging views that, like Haywood's, may be new to many readers. However, its clear propositions will confuse no one and, for the serious, will spark critical thinking. *History and Education* doesn't shy away from the tough implications of many of its premises, and for those of us who share its commitment to a communist outlook, that is something to be thankful for.

Notes

1. https://www.marxists.org/archive/marx/works/1867-c1/p2.htm
2. Ibid.
3. http://marx.theoccupiedtimes.org/works/1872/letters/72_03_21.htm
4. https://www.marxists.org/archive/marx/works/1871/civil-war-france/ch05.htm

ACKNOWLEDGMENTS

First and foremost, all respect and appreciation are in order for Peter McLaren. McLaren's groundbreaking work in Marxist pedagogy is the foundation from which this book stems. For this, I could never thank him enough. Many thanks also need to be expressed for the consistent support from Chris Myers and Peter Lang Publishing. In addition, I would like to thank Derek Ford for not only his support and friendship but also for his invaluable feedback and assistance reviewing and editing *History and Education*, and for his brilliant and generous foreword. Major thanks go out to Walter Smolarek for his invaluable comments on early drafts of the manuscript. I would also like to express my deep appreciation for the preface Eugene Puryear wrote. Finally, I would like to thank the Party for Socialism and Liberation (PSL) for advancing the proletarian camp of the global class war, which was the primary inspiration for writing this book. Being a member of the PSL is a high honor, making it crystal clear to me that being a member of a communist party should be viewed as a source of extreme pride.

I would like to thank the following publications for permission to reprint the following sources:

Introduction

Malott, C. (forthcoming). *Lenin, the State, and Communist Pedagogy*. New York: Hampton Institute.

Chapter 1

Malott, C. (2015). Communist Pedagogy and the Contradictions of Capital. In C. Jenkins (Ed.), *The 2016 Hampton Reader: Selected Essays and Analyses from the Hampton Institute: A Working-Class Think Tank* (pp. 113–121). Albany, NY: Hampton Institute.

Chapter 2

Malott, C., & Orelus, P. (2015). Marxist Historiography in the History of Education: From Colonial to Neocolonial Schooling in the United States. *Postcolonial Directions in Education*, 4(2), 140–194.

Chapter 3

Malott, C. (forthcoming). The Crossing of Class Lines: Confronting Critical Pedagogy in Defense of Communism. *Critical Education*.

Chapter 4

Malott, C. (2015). *Right-to-Work* and Lenin's Communist Pedagogy. *Texas Education Review*, 3(2), 32–43.

Chapter 5

Malott, C. (forthcoming). A Communist Pedagogy of *Becoming*: Centering Marx's "General Law of Capitalist Accumulation." *Knowledge Cultures*.

INTRODUCTION

Lenin and the Withering Away of the State

For some readers the first three words in the title of this book, *History and Education*, will elicit an immediate question: why history *and* education and not the history *of* education? It is a subtle yet profound difference. This is not a history of education text in either the traditional chronological sense or the more contemporary thematic format. The closest I come to advancing a history *of* education is chapter 2, which offers a history of the *history* of education from a unique Marxist framework, focusing on the colonial and common school eras. These eras are highlighted because they are key moments of expansion and control for capital's position within what was fast becoming, with the colonization of the Caribbean and the Americas in the sixteenth century, a global class war.

Overall, however, it is a book that takes Marx's contributions to the field of history as a central optic that is fundamental for engaging the global class war, because it examines the worldwide driving force, capitalism, developmentally and dialectically, where new eras are not conceived as emerging separately from the world as it exists, but always out of the contradictions of existing conditions.

Education is emphasized because it has been one of the mechanisms, both formally and informally, through which both sides of the global class war, the bourgeoisie and the proletariat, have advanced their antagonistically related causes (i.e., maintaining production relations as they exist on one side, and transforming them into qualitatively distinct ones on the other). This book seeks to advance, through an optic of division (Dean, 2012; Haywood, 1958; Marcy, 1979; Parenti, 1997), without apology or disclaimer, the proletarian class camp of the global class war through education and, therefore, offers contributions to a communist pedagogy. This is the central purpose of *History and Education: Engaging the Global Class War*.

Whereas *Marx, Capital, and Education: Towards a Critical Pedagogy of Becoming* (Malott & Ford, 2015) advances the proletarian class camp of the global class war through a detailed, systematic examination of the internal logic and dialectical development of capital through its stages of expansion and crisis, this book emphasizes the global, historical development of the antagonistic relationship between capital and those who are subsumed within its expanding social universe, with a special emphasis placed on workers' states and the Party-form. By focusing on the global class war, we are forced to confront not only the central gravitational force of the capitalist class, which has been the U.S. since at least the mid-nineteenth century, but the center of proletarian revolutionary power as well, which emerged in Britain with the birth of capitalism and then migrated East to Russia with the victory of the Bolshevik Revolution in 1917. It then continued east to Southeast Asia (Marcy, 1979), and today is much more fragmented and dispersed, with two major centers being China and the Democratic People's Republic of Korea (DPRK), as outlined in chapter 3.

Because of the focus on the global class war, it makes sense to begin this book with a brief exploration of Lenin's conception of the state, as the state-form has and continues to play a crucial role in the class struggle. Lenin's (1917/2015) *The State and Revolution* offers an experientially based approach to the role of the state in the fight against capitalism. Lenin's insights in this work are therefore the foundation from which this book's approach to communist pedagogy rests. After exploring Lenin, I offer a brief introduction to the idea of a communist pedagogy, followed by a chapter-by-chapter summary of *History and Education: Engaging the Global Class War*.

Lenin and the State

In *The State and Revolution*, Lenin (1917/2015) begins his discussion with the observation that the evidence Marx and Engels provided demonstrating that the state only exists with the presence of class antagonisms is so overwhelming that bourgeois ideologists have been forced to confront it. However, in confronting it, bourgeois ideologists, as well as anarchists, have distorted all reasonable conclusions. For example, Marx notes that the purpose of the state's coercive power is to maintain the capitalist class's domination over the laboring classes. The reconciliation between opposing classes can therefore only be achieved through proletarian revolution in which the laboring classes destroy the capitalist state and appropriate its coercive power to repress the counterrevolutionary forces of the opposing class. This insight, according to Lenin, has been distorted by bourgeois theorists who suggest that the state's purpose in capitalist society is to reconcile the antagonism between labor and capital through reforms, thereby creating harmony and balance between the two opposing interests. Marx's theory of anticapitalist revolution is, therefore, mutated into a theory of opportunistic reform. The critiques of the American labor movement in the current era (outlined in chapter 4) demonstrate this bourgeois opportunism.

The insight that because the state emerged as an instrument of class rule, its power lies in its ability to exercise physical force is extremely important for correctly building a communist party. The state, as a coercive force consisting at the base of a standing army and police, therefore occupies a position above society, alienated from society, maintaining and expanding the domination of one class over another. Bourgeois ideologists, explaining away this very obvious form of class rule, tend to argue that armed force in the bourgeois state is needed not to enforce class structures but because of the highly complex nature of modern society. What this hides is the inherent antagonism between the capitalist class and the working and peasant classes. In the bourgeois state, the armed forces serve the interests of the capitalist class, which become readily apparent when the workmen go on strike and the militias are sent in on behalf of capital. If the working classes and peasantry were to arm themselves under the leadership of a communist party, then the structurally determined class antagonism would begin to point toward war between the two competing class camps. It is during such times of struggle that it becomes increasingly clear to the oppressed that capitalist society is split between two great irreconcilable class camps. What enables the state to exist above society, alienated from productive labor, is its ability to levy taxes from producers and the system of production in general. This is certainly no less true today than it nearly one hundred years ago when Lenin wrote *The State and Revolution*.

Quoting Engels here, Lenin corrects the tendency among socialist oppor-tunists to ignore the larger context under which Engels discusses how the state will wither away. It is only after a proletarian revolution in which the working classes smash the bourgeois state—and institute a dictatorship of the proletariat, abolish private property, end the exploitative capitalist rela-tions of production, and stamp out the remnants of bourgeois counterrevolu-tion—that what is left of the state, the proletarian state, can begin to wither away. Whereas the bourgeois state suppresses the demands and struggles of the peasantry and working class, the proletarian state represses the remain-ing elements of the old bourgeoisie until they have all been destroyed. The objective of the proletarian revolution is, thus, to smash the bourgeois state, thereby transforming its power into a proletarian state, which then, through the development of communism, can wither away once the remaining capi-talist counterrevolutionary forces have been defeated. Because of the ruthless barbarism of the U.S. imperialist state and its allies, no successfully estab-lished proletarian state has ever had the security and economic stability to wither away as envisioned by Lenin and by Marx and Engels before him. Just taking the statement of how the state will wither away without situating it in the context of the dictatorship of the proletariat, the liberal reformers have contributed to the tendency that subverts the insight that revolution itself is fundamental.

In critical pedagogy this most often manifests itself in the belief that a properly funded, critical education for democratic citizenship will allow class antagonisms to more or less correct themselves, one might argue, determin-istically or automatically. A communist pedagogy, on the other hand, takes as fundamental the need for working class revolution and the creation of a temporary proletarian state, which Marx and Engels, after the Paris Commune of 1871, called the dictatorship of the proletariat. Explaining his theory of rev-olution with educational terms Lenin offers significant insight into his com-munist pedagogy:

> By educating the workers' party, Marxism educates the vanguard of the proletariat, capable of assuming power and leading the whole people to socialism, of directing and organizing the new system, of being the teacher, the guide, the leader of all the working and exploited people in organizing their social life without the bourgeoisie and against the bourgeoisie. (p. 120)

Socialist reformers, on the other hand—and, we could add, most of those grouped under "critical education"—tend to be guided by what Jodi Dean describes as the effect of the absence of communism, that is, the acceptance of capital's inevitability, an acceptance that is propped up by a vulgar carica-ture of the idea of communism, warding off and dissuading an always-present potential communist uprising. The goal of critical pedagogy, therefore, tends to be building democracy, the very system Lenin reminds us is the political sys-tem most conducive to capitalist exploitation due to its distance or alienation from production. Bourgeois democracy is based on the freedom to exploit, not on the freedom from want.

Until the Paris Commune of 1871 Marx and Engels understood, abstractly, that the bourgeois state must be replaced with vague notions of democracy serving as a loose, inadequate guide for action. The Paris Commune made absolutely clear, despite the fact that it was ultimately defeated, that the tem-porary proletarian state would not emerge with the simple, nonviolent, dem-ocratic transfer of power from the capitalist class to the laboring classes, but can only be born from the womb of the destruction of the bourgeois state. The first demand of the Commune was therefore to dismantle the bourgeois army and put in its place the empowered and armed laboring masses. It was clear that a peoples' army in power, led by direct representation and united around their diversity, will be compelled to act in defense of their own class interests and wage war against the differences of privilege that divide them and the capitalist class who stands as the primary benefactor of their former disunity. Every truly socialist revolutionary movement from this time on has taken this position as a fundamental truth and place of departure. The replacement of bourgeois democracy with proletarian democracy (i.e., communism) requires the violent suppression of the counterrevolutionary bourgeois forces. Agreeing with Marx here, Lenin argues that one of the reasons for the failure of the Paris Commune system was an insufficient focus on repressing the bourgeois class after the revolution, thereby leaving the counterrevolutionary element able to launch a successful counteroffensive.

It became clear to Marx from studying the communes that proletarian democracy or communism could not exist without a form of representative democracy. The corrupt element was, therefore, not representation, but par-liamentarianism, because it is unaccountable to the people and it makes the most important decisions behind closed doors. Proletarian democracy ties representatives directly to the people by making their positions immediately recallable. What is more, salaries of government officials were reduced to workers' wages under proletarian rule. By stopping parliamentary expendi-tures, eliminating the cost of maintaining standing armies, and reducing the wages of government officials, the financial burden of maintaining a bourgeois state was lifted from the shoulders of workers. Rejecting utopianism, these insights were not invented out of mere speculation but were the direct result of Marx rigorously studying a concrete situation.

True to his dialectical analysis, Marx, as well as Lenin, was not under the false allusion that socialism could only happen when all workers had developed a critical consciousness. Rather, Marx insisted that all forms of administration and hierarchy could not immediately be disposed of after the initial stage of smashing the bourgeois state. Only through protracted struggle and a communist education could the old forms of social control be completely eliminated, gradually withering away. Refuting anarchist claims that centralism and hierarchy are inherently oppressive to laborers, Lenin (1917/2015), following Marx, argues that centralism is in fact indispensable for crushing capitalist resistance and advancing a qualitatively distinct socialist formation:

> Now if the proletariat and the poor peasants take state power into their own hands, organize themselves quite freely in communes, and unite the action of all the communes in striking at capital, in crushing the resistance of the capitalists, and in transferring the privately-owned railways, factories, land and so on to the entire nation, to the whole of society, won't that be centralism? Won't that be the most consistent democratic centralism and, moreover, proletarian centralism? (p. 144)

Reflecting this Marxist-Leninist approach to the Party-form, the Party for Socialism and Liberation (PSL) (McInerney & Thompson, 2010) describes its "structure and operating principles" as "based on democratic centralism," which they define as "internal democratic debate combined with unity in action" (p. 56). Lenin argues that the problem with the bourgeois anarchist position, as opposed to democratic centralism, is that it is unable to conceive of "voluntary centralism" (p. 144) that is driven by the unity of the people. The anarchist can only imagine bourgeois centralism. As a result, the anarchist imagination stands as a pseudoradicalism impeding revolution wherever it gains influence. Lenin, therefore, observes that one of the most serious mistakes of the anarchist is failing to understand that "authority and autonomy are relative terms, that the sphere of their application varies with the various phases of social development, that it is absurd to take them as absolutes" (p. 153). Lenin is alluding to one of the central points in *The German Ideology*, outlined in chapter 2 of this volume. In this text, Marx and Engels (1846/1996) argue that it is incorrect to believe in "a universal principle in the existing world" (p. 41). That is, they challenged the utopian belief that the fight for a just society is primarily an ideological fight and is, thus, a battle for a predetermined consciousness and the imposition of a fixed ideology.

Lenin (1917/2015) is contesting the tendency of anarchists to be informed by a fixed, narrow ideology that rails against the authoritarian state, demanding it be immediately abolished, even before the well organized, persistent, counterrevolutionary capitalist class is defeated. Forfeiting the authoritarian tools (i.e., the state) needed to defeat one's class enemy before victory has been secured, for Lenin, is to surrender before the final battle has even begun. Marx agrees that the state as such will vanish when class structures are once and for all time dismantled. However, until the capitalist class is defeated, even after the initial seizure of state power and the destruction of the bourgeois state, the proletarian state (i.e., the dictatorship of the proletariat) must exist to fight the capitalist class.

Because they have never been free from imperialist subversion and counterrevolution, the workers' states that continue to exist—from the DPRK to Cuba—have never been in a position to see their authoritarian state apparatus wither away. The DPRK's involvement with nuclear weaponry must be understood within this context of imperialist aggression. What this contemporary example demonstrates is that not only has the proletarian state not been able to wither away, but it has had to expand, which has consumed ever larger portions of the total social product and added strains to the state's ability to satisfy the needs of its people. Of course, bourgeois opportunists—and their "critical" apologists—absurdly take these consequences of imperialist aggression as evidence of the failure and inferiority of communism.

Making this point even more concrete, Lenin draws on Engels by noting that the revolutionary act is perhaps one of the most authoritarian human actions possible since it consists of one portion of a population exerting its will by means of violent, deadly force on another portion. In conclusion, Engels argues that anti-authoritarians either do not know what they are talking about, or they are counterrevolutionary class colluders. Marx, Engels, and Lenin all agreed with anarchists that the state, as such, should not be regarded as permanent, but, contrary to the anarchist position, the proletarian state, in which workers have gained state power, must persist until all external and internal imperialist threats have been defeated. While Lenin was well aware that the end date for the elimination of the counterrevolutionary threat was an unknown factor, he correctly speculated that this could take a long time, noting, "It will obviously be a lengthy process" (p. 174).

A Brief Introduction to the Idea of a Communist Pedagogy

The communist pedagogy advanced here is grounded in the ontological insight that the educational act cannot avoid an engagement with the basic structures of production and the vast diversity among the hundreds of oppressed nations throughout the world. Because capitalism is the mode of production that dominates and influences economic life the world over, the domination of the system of nature within the social universe of capital is all but complete. Lenin's organizational framework is therefore central for developing a pedagogical project up to the anticapitalist challenge posed by the Marxist-Leninist tradition. Since humans are natural beings whose basic needs of habitation and sustenance can only be obtained externally, within the system of nature, to survive, the vast majority of humanity must, therefore, take their ability to labor to the market in exchange for a wage to access objects of their immediate needs. But the diversity of the world's oppressed nations suggests a complexity in terms of facilitating the collective access to the system of nature, which is made only more complicated by the need for organization in the face of a divisive and deadly counterrevolutionary bourgeois military industrial war machine.

No amount of communicative capitalism or immaterial labor or accumulation by dispossession can alter the raw fact that food, clothing, and shelter will always and forever be material needs that can only be obtained materially from the system of nature. Because the capitalist class currently owns or otherwise controls the system of nature, no degree of cognitive capitalism can ever displace this fundamental principle of natural life. Just as the cultural diversity of oppressed nations cannot be ignored without detrimental results, neither can the material basis of existence be neglected.

The fact that all value circulates in a capitalist economy (Marx, 1992)—even the value of fixed buildings, machinery, livestock, and crops before and after harvest—does not alter their rigid, yet forever transforming, materiality. The immaterial, fluid social substance of value does not negate the material substance it represents. This dual nature of commodities (i.e., their abstractness and their concreteness, or their exchange value and their use value) is what lies at the heart of understanding the internal logic of capital and the way it is able to employ the money relation, the abstract notion of value, to mystify the inherent exploitation within the concrete practice of laboring according to capitalist production relations. The question is: Will education support the basic structures of capitalist hegemony and its domination over the Earth, or will it strive to uproot them? A pedagogical project that names itself *communist* implies the latter. Again, without oppressed nations in leadership positions, the struggle to uproot capitalist relations will be incomplete and unrepresentative. Only through the dictatorship of the proletariat can such a pedagogical project be realized. This demands critical educators engage the Party-form.

A pedagogy infused with a commitment to communism, therefore, presupposes a theory and practice aimed at transforming capitalist production relations and white supremacist culture into communist ones based on international solidarity. Dedicated to communism, this pedagogy is grounded in Marx's critique of political economy. This engagement with Marx is marked by constant shifts and fluidity because the concrete conditions that mediate the developing divisive relationship between labor, on one hand, and capital, on the other, are forever in negotiation and, therefore, never fixed or final— until they are transformed into qualitatively distinct relations of production. Taking the historical record into account, communist pedagogy must also be fundamentally grounded in the objective fact that any movement toward socialism will always be confronted with the counterrevolutionary forces of capital, even from within the Left itself. As a result, a communist pedagogy interested in long-term survival must place special emphasis on developing a united, impenetrable front through rigorous organization, discipline, and consistency of analysis and tactics.

Chapter Summaries

In chapter 1, I build upon Lenin's theory of the state and revolution through an engagement with Harry Haywood and the Black communist tradition in the U.S. Adding to the invaluable insights of Haywood, I then engage the positions advanced within Native studies regarding the settler state and the critiques of Marx. Finally, I offer an introductory engagement with the internal contradictions of capital, thereby adding insights and further depth to Lenin's presupposition that working-class liberation from capitalism can only be achieved through armed revolutionary struggle.

From here chapter 2 builds a specifically Marxist approach to historical analysis and study. Once this new approach to educational historiography is outlined, we provide two case studies analyzing two periods in the history of U.S. education that were particularly important in the global class war, the colonial and the common school eras.

Chapter 3 explores more deeply the imperialist anticommunist propaganda that pervades our world. After this lengthy discussion, I provide a correction to the histories of the Soviet Union, China, the DPRK, and the Black Panther Party. This discussion offers the reader a closer look into the global class war and provides additional content for understanding Lenin's insistence on the indispensability of the dictatorship of the proletariat.

Taking a more U.S.-centered focus, chapter 4 explores Lenin's contributions to understanding trade unions. This analysis is used to examine both the current anti-union legislation in the U.S. as well as the dominant tendency within current U.S. labor unions. This chapter, therefore, offers a revolutionary framework for teachers and other unionized workers to rethink and transform their roles within their unions.

Finally, chapter 5 offers a systematic analysis of Marx's General Law of Accumulation as outlined in the first volume of *Capital*. This discussion leaves the reader with a theoretically rigorous analysis of capitalism, making a final statement for the resurgence of the Party-form as a necessary organizational component for smashing the bourgeois state, smashing bourgeois counterrevolutionary subversion, and for laying the foundation for communist society.

· 1 ·

THE GLOBAL CLASS WAR AND THE CONTRADICTIONS OF CAPITAL

With the colonization of the Americas, there emerged a complex war between the vast and diverse Native American Nations and the invading European colonizing capitalists and the forced and indentured European and African laborers they brought with them as imported labor power. In the 1970s, the center of Native American resistance, after many devastating eras of genocide, termination, and countless forced removals, emerged as the American Indian Movement (AIM). Native American activists have been critical of Marxist activists for advancing what they experienced as a Eurocentric worldview where one could not simultaneously be Native or Indigenous and a socialist or communist, which was attributed to Marx (Churchill, 1983). The position advocated for here follows the American Indian activists in the Party for Socialism and Liberation who simultaneously serve within their tribal leadership councils, thereby challenging the false assumption that socialism is an invasive tendency that inherently negates an Indigenous presence because it represents a lower stage in the universal hierarchy of human development. Rather, socialism represents a form of unity that allows all of the world's oppressed people to unite as a single, accumulated force aimed at the complete destruction of the bourgeois state and all elements of the capitalist class's counterrevolutionary forces, both physical and ideological (i.e., armed

anticommunist forces and white supremacy and xenophobia) while protect-
ing the sovereignty of all oppressed nations and their rights to their national
territory and to self-determination. In this way, socialism through the Party is
understood as the tool designed specifically to defeat the enemy of Indigeneity:
capitalism.

In order to build a framework that incorporates the notion of the settler-
state into the Leninist foundation laid out above, I begin by briefly introducing some of the most enduring critiques of Marx and Marxism from Indigenous
studies. I then turn to the work produced between the 1920s and 1950s by
the African American revolutionary communist Harry Haywood and explore
what his contributions to the theory of national oppression have to offer to the
notion of the global class war within the context of Indigenous studies. I then
build upon Haywood through Sam Marcy's conception of the global class war.
Finally, I turn to a number of the key contradictions of capital, which offers a
sense of the challenges that lay in front of Lenin's call to smash the bourgeois
state and institute a communist society by qualitatively transforming relations
of production through the dictatorship of the proletariat.

A Critique from Native Studies and the Concept of the Settler-State

In 1983 South End Press released an important and still unsurpassed book,
Marxism and Native Americans, edited by Ward Churchill. The text is set up
as a debate between Indigenous and Marxist scholars and activists. The volume was a response to the perceived tension between Marxist and Native
American activists during the 1970s. The underlying premise behind the volume is that there exists a fundamentally antagonistic cultural and philosophical difference between Native American activists and settler-state activists,
including both white and Black revolutionaries (although the voices of Black
revolutionaries are not represented in the book). Consequently, a consistent
theme that emerges throughout the text is that the communist alternative
to capitalism is not a vision shared by traditional Native American activists
and the communities they represent. The chapters authored by Indigenous
activists, together, send the clear and important message that any serious relationship between Marxists (both Native and non-Native alike) and Native
American activists must be based upon the recognition that Native American
Nations have an inherent right to self-determination and sovereignty.

Just as with Indigenous nations where the capitalist state has been experienced as a colonial mechanism of bourgeois expansion and domination aggressively subverting their self-determination and sovereignty, so too do nations around the world experience imperialist capitalism as a deadly, invasive, extracting predator. This perspective is indispensable for the challenges that lie ahead for the struggle against exploitation. The communist pedagogy advocated for in this book, therefore, takes the settler-state optic as critical for fully engaging the global class war.

Even though Churchill's text was published more than two decades ago, the work it identifies as in need of being done is far from complete. That work is advancing the movement that simultaneously confronts the ongoing existence of settler-state colonialism, capitalist imperialism, and the deadly anti-Black and Brown white supremacy that both justifies the super-exploitation of nonwhite workers, and lowers the overall cost of labor, negatively affecting even white workers. One highly significant development here is the emergence of the aforementioned Party for Socialism and Liberation (PSL), a highly diverse U.S.-based working-class outcommunist Party. For example, in addition to what was mentioned above, the Albuquerque, New Mexico, branch is closely connected to local Navajo and Pueblo tribes, and the PSL's Party platform explains how their vision of a socialist workers' state in the U.S. would make an immediate priority of returning or compensating all Native American tribes for stolen land, broken treaties, and five hundred years of physical, biological, and cultural genocide. This is a highly significant, important, and correct position. After the conquest of the bourgeois state, capitalist class counterrevolutionaries will not allow these measures to be carried out, rendering the dictatorship of the proletariat absolutely crucial. In other words, the changes that need to occur for humanity to be able to exist in complete dignity will require the world's peoples to physically repress the 1 percent's ability to continue to dominate the lives of nearly all of humanity. Revolution is authoritarian, this is unavoidable. It is an armed love, however, that is fueled by the love of the people, a love that understands and accepts the full magnitude of what it means to liberate humanity from the ever-present werewolf of capital.

Despite this and other important advances made by the ongoing work of the PSL, in the academic world, where cutting-edge theory has historically influenced activism, there has been a lack of progress made on the creation of a shared, mutually agreed upon vision of a world without capitalism, national oppression, and settler-state imperialism. Consequently, the best work in revolutionary approaches to Indigenous studies continues to be grounded in many of the same points that were made twenty years ago, largely because they continue to be true. While many of these charges against the work of Karl Marx, as discussed below, might not be completely accurate, they are true of some self-identified Marxists, especially in today's world, which is much more a world without Marx and with much less actually existing communism than just twenty years ago. The view of bourgeois propaganda that history has irrefutably proven that communism is a failed and inevitably authoritarian project has filled up much of the empty political space left in communism's absence (Dean, 2012). The anticommunist propaganda that has filled this void has been devastating to the Left, especially in the West, which suffers from a debilitating, knee-jerk rejection of actually existing communism. Fortunately, many of the answers to the questions posed by Native studies already exist within the works of Marx, Lenin, Haywood, Marcy, Parenti, and others.

Nonetheless, the absence of communism and the extreme distortion of Marx have made it very difficult for those of us who are committed to, and passionate about, liberation from oppression to understand Marx and resist the bourgeois temptation of crossing class lines (see chapter 3). Complicating the situation is the way this anticommunist culture has also influenced leading scholars in Native studies. Jodi Dean, in her important work on the communist horizon, observes how communism in the U.S. has come to be associated with authoritarianism as an inevitable outcome of its internal logics. The weakness of this position is treating the concept of authoritarianism as a fixed term undifferentiated in different contexts. Rejecting authoritarianism outright amounts to laying down one's arms while the counterrevolutionaries are still fully armed and committed to restoring the dictatorship of the capitalist. From the burgeoning field of Indigenous studies, Glen Sean Coulthard's (2014) important and theoretically rigorous text, *Red Skin, White Masks: Rejecting the Colonial Politics of Recognition*, reproduces the old anti-Marxist equation with a creative application of the facts. However, unlike Churchill's text, Coulthard's work is situated within an actual reading of Marx, which represents a major advance toward a unified position.

Coulthard begins by taking note of one of Marx's early errors in which he incorrectly assumed that the progressive effect that the transition from feudalism to capitalism had on the English peasantry could be universalized to every other human civilization. Dialectically, Marx commented at length on how the internal conditions and development of feudalism (in Britain in particular) had reached a crisis of limitation, which led to capitalism. For example, the highly advanced feudal division of labor and its corresponding need for a universal money equivalent, after reaching a certain stage of development, could no lon-ger advance productivity and profitability. The financial burdens placed upon the peasant proprietors were pushed beyond all natural limits, and a revolu-tionary class unity would destroy their feudal foes, leading to capitalism and a corresponding advance for former peasants and merchants. However, these two classes would continue to develop under capitalist conditions, emerging as an antagonistically related labor and capital relationship with new contra-dictions—contradictions irreconcilable under capitalist production relations.

From this point of view, British colonialism in India was initially viewed by Marx as a positive force paving the way for Indian feudalism to eventually develop into socialism after going through a universally, unavoidable capital-ist stage. However, once Marx began to realize that British colonialism was destroying Indian society, he immediately reversed his position, rejecting Brit-ish colonialism as unnecessarily destructive. Marx would eventually turn to non-Western societies, including Native American Nations, in his search for a way out of capitalism (Anderson, 2010). Coulthard rigorously acknowledges all of this. However, Coulthard seems to have retained the larger message that communism equals authoritarian Eurocentrism. Consider:

> Marx ... seemed to justify in crude developmentalist terms the violent dispossession of place-based, non-state modes of self-sufficient Indigenous economic, political, and social activity, only this time to be carried out under the auspices of the coercive authority of socialist states. This form of dispossession would eventually come to be championed by Soviet imperialists under the banner *socialist primitive accumulation*. (pp. 11–12)

Coulthard seems to hold onto the anti-Marxist-Leninist propaganda despite being aware that Marx eventually corrected his early errors regarding the uni-versal progressiveness of colonialism. His position could even be easily inter-preted as suggesting that communist regimes were oppressive dictatorships long before their creators and proponents were even born. However, what is clear is that Coulthard picks up and reproduces the old anticommunist line that refers to the Soviet Union as imperialist. In chapter 3 I deal with this charge at length, but suffice it to say that challenging the errors and mis-takes of a particular leader or bureaucracy is quite different from turning one's back on a workers' state, which represents the rights of millions of workers to self-determination and to be free of exploitation. While the outright dismissal of the Soviet Union represents the crossing of class lines, Coulthard insists that contemporary calls by autonomous Marxists for a return to the commons should be reminded that in settler-states the so-called commons are actually occupied lands that the First Nations have been struggling to recover for centuries—and this important fact serves as one of the first premises of this book. Coulthard's critique could be further developed by an engagement with Lenin's (1917/2015) *The State and Revolution*. That is, without an authoritarian proletarian state, a return to the commons remains a utopian fantasy that refuses to confront the harsh realities of the dictatorship of the capitalist.

Again, Coulthard argues, as did Churchill, that while Marx's work continues to hold invaluable insights regarding the nature and tendencies of the capitalist world that suppresses the Indigenous desire of *being* through the violent colonial occupation of Native land, the Eurocentrism that informs his rigid historical determinism is just as dangerous as that of the elites. As previously mentioned, even though Coulthard acknowledges that Marx realized it was a mistake to universalize the stages of development European societies went through, he still holds on to the communist caricature. Justifying this position, Coulthard argues that most Marxists are unaware of Marx as a real person, who developed his ideas over the course of his life, and, thus, continue to perpetuate Marx's early Eurocentrism. Unfortunately, this is likely a relatively fair position. However, there remains a framework within Marx, indispensable to the project of transforming the settler-state, national oppression, and the global proletariat into their dialectical opposites, into their own independent, self-determined becoming. The legacy of workers' states from the Soviet Union to the DPRK represents the legacy of this tradition, which would be foolish at best, and counterrevolutionary at worst, to dismiss.

To this charge we might reiterate the position that all oppressed nations and national minorities within imperialist states and settler-states have a right to self-determination. In the U.S. this includes the formerly enslaved and exploited Black nation, as well as the Chicano nation, La Raza, and Chinese, Japanese, Filipino, Puerto Rican, and Arab national minorities. Globally, this includes worker and independent states, a few examples of which are explored in chapter 3.

National Oppression and the Global Class War

We can extend the communist pedagogy offered thus far by turning to the self-identified Black Bolshevik, revolutionary activist, and theoretician Harry Haywood. Born in Omaha, Nebraska, Haywood built a revolutionary theoretical foundation for understanding contemporary capitalism and settler colonialism through his interrelated concepts of national oppression and communist revolution, which he developed in the 1920s in consultation with the Communist International, and later refracted through the experiences in what he referred to as the *Black Belt*.

After returning from World War I, Haywood joined the African Blood Brotherhood situated in Chicago, employing armed forces to protect Black workers from the white terrorism of the bourgeoisie's Ku Klux Klan (KKK). Soon after joining the Communist Party of the United States of America (CP-USA), Haywood was sent to the Soviet Union in 1923 to study revolutionary theory at two international, state-run learning institutes in Moscow— first the Communist University of the Toilers of the East named for Stalin (KUTVA), and later the Lenin School. Through his studies in Moscow Haywood was exposed to Lenin's theory of national oppression. He subsequently developed a U.S.-based theory of the Southern Black Belt as an oppressed nation (and smaller communities of Blacks in the North as national minorities), with an endowed right to self-determination by any means necessary, including armed struggle. Under Haywood's leadership, the CP-USA would play a leading role in building an antiracist, integrated Communist Party in the South fighting for the integration of labor unions as a necessary step in strengthening the working class and advancing the complete emancipation of the global proletarian class camp.

In 1958 Haywood released a groundbreaking work that outlines the parameters of "a revolutionary position on the Negro question." In this pamphlet Haywood notes that the racist white Southern terror that was spreading across the country motivated African Americans to find inspiration within the "successes of the world anti-colonialist movement in Asia and Africa" and thus sought "new, militant leadership which is internationalist in outlook" and "free from ties of white ruling class patronage." Standing in the way of the militant, internationalist communist leadership sought after by many African Americans, for Haywood (1958), was the domination of a revisionist "slightly warmed over liberal gradualism." That is, the position based upon the false assumption that white supremacy was the only barrier to social justice within capitalism, which can be overcome through a gradual process of assimilating Blacks into mainstream white society. The focus on white supremacy fails because it overlooks the fact that capitalism itself seeks profit alone, which requires the exploitation of all workers, including white workers. White supremacy is beneficial to capitalism not because it privileges white workers over Black workers, but because in bringing down the value of Black labor

power through racialist propaganda and policy, the value of all labor is negatively impacted, however disproportionally. Haywood's position was that while
capitalism degraded, through exploitation and dehumanization, all workers,
Black workers have been especially terrorized. Coupled with this was the
unfinished bourgeois democratic revolution of the Civil War and Reconstruc-
tion. The plantations of the former slaveholders were never broken up and
redistributed to either former slaves or poor whites. This betrayed revolution
prevented African Americans from joining with whites into a single nation.
Taken together, for Haywood, this all meant that Black people in the U.S.
constitute an oppressed nation that must have the right to self-determination,
which then places the organic Black revolutionary leadership in a larger leadership position within the working-class struggle more generally (as we see
in chapter 3, the Black Panther Party served this function during the 1960s
and 1970s, a time during which AIM also played a significant role). Following
the attacks on militant leadership within the Communist Party "the Marxist-
Leninist position on the Negro question" was abandoned, ending the struggle
for "the right of self-determination to the oppressed Negro nation in the Deep
South." The communist pedagogy advanced throughout this book is grounded
in this commitment to the self-determination of oppressed nations, including
the Black nation within the imperialist U.S.

This self-determination of the oppressed Black nation position, which
was adopted by the international communist movement at the Sixth Congress of the Comintern in 1928 by the CP-USA two years later, was dropped
in the 1950s as a result of two competing views. Haywood (1958) referred to
the first position as a "bourgeois liberal view" that "placed the main onus of
racial prejudice not on the ruling class oppressors but on the ignorance of the
white masses." The other incorrect position Haywood opposed was a form of
economic determinism and a right-wing deviation that regarded the oppression faced by African Americans to be class oppression and, therefore, no
different than the oppression of other working-class people, including white
workers. Summarizing the error within this position Haywood argues, "In the
name of the general class struggle it denied the special character of the Negro
question, regarding the fight for special demands of the Negro people as divisive and tending to distract workers from the struggle for socialism." Haywood
argues that both of these positions are equally incorrect in that they "conceal
the profound revolutionary and anti-imperialist character of the struggle for
Negro rights which could only be finally resolved through the land revolution
and the right of self-determination in the Black Belt."

With great concern and outrage Haywood argues that the "overwhelmingly predominant petty-bourgeois and highly skilled worker composition" of the CP-USA's leadership rendered it susceptible to the "right-revisionist" trend and external influences of the "imperialist bourgeoisie," which he attributes to the abandonment of the revolutionary position on the "Negro question." Haywood challenged CP-USA leaders for adopting the position of "direct integration" in place of "the self-determination of African Americans in the Black Belt" because he believed it to be based on the ill-founded conclusion that the situation for African Americans had dramatically improved both economically and racially.

Haywood goes on to outline the bleak situation for African Americans in terms of wages—being displaced by automation and other advances in the efficiency of production—and in terms of housing, all situated in the post–WWII economic boom where the average standard of living had increased for all workers. The situation was especially dire for Black agricultural workers in the South, which speaks to Haywood's call for a revolution in land (i.e., the farmer's primary means of production) distribution. Providing an analysis of the evidence, Haywood (1958) explains, "The 1954 Census of Agriculture showed a rapid acceleration of land concentration and monopoly, reporting that all Census farms of 1,000 acres or over, though comprising only 2.7% of all Census farms, marketed over one fourth of all the cotton sold in the U.S." Noting how the displacement of farmhands was greater in the South (32.3 percent) than in the country in general (29.8 percent), Black farm workers were disproportionately displaced (43 percent) compared to white farm workers (29 percent) (Haywood, 1958). What is more, the median annual income was nearly twice as high for white families as compared to Black families. In addition, the percent of sharecroppers who were Black increased dramatically in the same period, reaching 83 percent by 1954 (Haywood, 1958), which is significant because of the enslaving effect of the practice. Mechanization in agricultural production had also led to a 31 percent decrease in the number of hired workers in the South between 1942 and 1957, leading to a sharp increase in African American unemployment and to an overall "explosive situation" (Haywood, 1958). The Black radicals emerging from this context were the natural revolutionary leaders to be recruited into the Communist Party.

But the integrationists missed this important analysis and conclusion that the changes in agricultural production were driven by the laws of capitalist accumulation that always seek to increase profit margins by extracting ever larger sums of value from labor. The fact that all of the changes were leaving Black workers either out of work and desperate, or in a state of "starvation" and "sinking to a squatter's misery" if they were able to "stay on the farm," was creating the conditions for rebellion, which, according to Haywood, the CP-USA should have understood. Haywood condemned the Party leadership for adopting the liberal line that mechanization was destroying the old plantation system of slavery and racial hierarchy and was, therefore, erasing the "contradiction involved in the Negro question." Rather than seeing it as intensifying the exploitation and discrimination of the Black nation, the CP-USA took the position that "the semi-feudal plantation system, the historic base of Negro national oppression, has withered away" (Haywood, 1958). Haywood understood that white supremacy and racial hierarchy were not going to wither away on their own accord without the dictatorship of the proletariat.

The same bankrupt, gradualist reasoning began to be employed, especially after the 1964 Civil Rights Act, to argue that the largely assimilationist historically Black colleges and universities (HBCUs) were no longer needed because all of the barriers to integration had been removed. This analysis misses the historic role of HBCUs in the creation of the Black elite class. Making this point Haywood (1958) notes, "In order to maintain the suppression of the Negro people, Wall Street, operating through its enlightened liberal wing, has long adopted a conscious policy of building up a top stratum among the Negro intelligentsia—an intellectual elite as a buffer against the Negro masses." Situated in the context of the Cold War, Haywood then reflects upon the growing number of Black elites appointed to high level government positions, serving as global apologist ambassadors downplaying the oppression of Blacks in the U.S. Unfortunately, little has changed, rendering the Black radical tradition, of which Haywood is a major figure, however unsung, more relevant now than ever.

The election of the first Black president, Barack Obama, has also been employed to elicit the same conclusion, that is, that race is no longer a factor in determining one's opportunities for economic stability, and that if Black people are poor, it is not related to race, and certainly not to capitalist imperialism. It is instead an individual problem solved by fixing individuals through a system of education, a system that is designed to fail Black students and students of color, thereby paving the way for mass incarceration (Puryear, 2012). Making this point Puryear (2012) notes that of African American men between the ages of thirty and thirty-four who had not completed high school 52% had criminal records compared to 13% of white males who had not completed high school in the same age range. Despite the fact that much of the recent media coverage of police shootings across the U.S. has tended to portray Black victims as somehow personally responsible for their own murders, the recent explosion of outrage and protest over this state-sanctioned police terrorism aimed at working-class Black communities has been remarkably successful. However, rather than demonstrating progress toward the bourgeois ideal of a capitalism based upon fairness and equality (fundamentally impossible within capitalism even if race were not a factor) and, thus, an integrated capitalist system, recent events should be understood as demonstrating the ongoing need for a Communist Party with a revolutionary position on the "Negro question" to guide and direct the increasing instances of spontaneous riots toward the communist horizon.

For example, the material existence of most African Americans has continued to deteriorate as Black workers are being displaced and excluded from the labor market as the positions of the most exploited workers are beginning to be occupied by new Latin American immigrants as a result of shifting global migration patterns driven by austerity and capitalism's downward descent. The call for the self-determination of oppressed nations as part of the communist position against imperialism in today's world is taking on greater relevancy. Bourgeois calls for integration continue to dominate even the educational Left. The communist pedagogy here has a lot to gain from the contributions of Harry Haywood. Summarizing the importance of identifying and addressing the unique circumstances of the Black worker for the larger movement for communism Haywood (1958) explains:

> As is well known, the consequences of this national oppression of the Negro affects not only the Negro, but the mass of poor whites as well, in the South and elsewhere, pulling down his wages and reinforcing the subjection of white labor to monopoly capital. This fact is the objective reality upon which the CP established its basic principle of labor organization, Negro-white unity for equality and better conditions for all workers.

Haywood was clear here that it was the financial managers of Wall Street who were intent on keeping the Black communities in the South as super-exploited, flexible, reserve pools of labor oppressed, degraded, and abused in the capitalist interest of suppressing the price of labor throughout the market in labor in general. This Marxist analysis helps make sense of why the rapid industrialization of the South in the 1940s and 1950s excluded African Americans from the generally better paying factory jobs (as compared to the misery and low wages of sharecropping). Again, this understanding explains why Haywood (1958) was so adamant that the liberal theorists and communist revisionists in his own party were dead wrong that the industrialization and mechanization of the South represented "the solution to the Negro question," or that race was not an all-important factor that should be front and center in the struggle toward the communist horizon.

Consequently, Haywood stands firm in his belief that justice and equality are impossible goals for the working class under capitalism. Without some degree or rate of exploitation of labor power, the capitalist is not able to expand his wealth and create new capital, and the greater the rate of exploitation, the greater the accumulation of capital. Haywood, therefore, concludes that "any fundamental change in social relations in the South can come about only as a result of revolutionary struggle of the Negro and white toilers of that region." Because the constant revolution of the means of production in capitalism (driven by a desire to make production more efficient through labor-saving machines that replace human power and intellect with a mechanical automaton), and because the racialized production relations of slavery continue to serve the capitalist interest of driving down the cost of labor in order to increase the rate of profit, the liberals and revisionist communists "underplay and minimize the profound, revolutionary, anti-imperialist potential of the Negro liberation movement" (Haywood, 1958).

This analysis continues to hold true, but rather than a "land-starved agricultural population" seeking to remove "all vestiges of slavery," today, millions of African Americans across the country constitute a largely wage-starved and disproportionately incarcerated population militantly seeking to remove "all vestiges of slavery" (Haywood, 1958). The role of the vanguard Party is indispensable here as the liberal reformers constantly pose a threat to the complete liberation of the toiling and excluded masses. As it was true in the 1950s, it remains true today, that the historical development of capital will never solve the problem of immiseration since it is its primary cause in bourgeois society. It is also true in the current neoliberal era of capitalism that it is unwise to reduce the difference between the exploitation of white versus Black and Brown workers to an all-encompassing division between labor and capital because it takes out of focus the historical energy of the oppressed, downplaying and minimizing "the profound, revolutionary, anti-imperialist potential of the Negro liberation movement" (Haywood, 1958).

Similar to the argument of Ward Churchill, who claimed that Marxism is a European construct inherently out of place outside of Europe, Haywood

(1958) challenges the position that the idea of national oppression was a "foreign formula" dogmatically imported to the U.S. context. Again, Haywood argues that such positions are the result of bourgeois infiltration and an underestimation of the deep-seated white supremacist terrorism and the cynical recklessness and violence of capitalism itself. Without Marx, a full understanding of capital and a path out of it remain elusive. Haywood stresses the importance of comprehending the role of U.S. imperialism, both nationally and globally, in perpetuating the capitalist system of accumulation. Haywood, therefore, strongly objected when his Party, the CP-USA, took the position that the "Negro liberation movement" was separate and distinct from the communist movement even though the CP-USA leadership included activists from the Black liberation movement, such as Haywood himself. Haywood rejected the CP-USA's position that the Black liberation movement should evolve spontaneously without the Party's vanguard leadership, direction, and scientific analysis and corresponding position. As a result, Haywood maintained that the CP-USA was capitulating to the bourgeois, integrationist African American leadership, which eventually led to his break from the Party. Recently, we have seen Black bourgeois leadership capitulate to the integrationist rhetoric as they directed antipolice violence rebellions in Ferguson, Missouri, and Baltimore, Maryland, toward a reformist position, asking for more accountability for police and more funding for education, but saying little to nothing of the capitalist system itself that is the root cause of growing immiseration. However, whereas the Occupy Movement embraced a critique of capitalism, it has been critiqued for denying itself the necessity of leadership when confronting an enemy as powerful and well organized as capital is, due to vague calls for horizontalism and democracy (Dean). Lenin, as we saw above, is clear that calls for horizontalism or anti-authoritarianism should not be regarded as serious or well informed.

Haywood's insistence that "national oppression of the Negro people ... will not die by itself" and that "it can only be destroyed through mass, revolutionary struggle led by a Marxist-Leninist vanguard Party" continues to hold great relevance and urgency in the contemporary context of growing national oppression. The role of the Party is to advance "the full development of the Negro nation," which includes a designated homeland and "the right to decide the political future of that area." Furthermore, "socialism must tap all the resources of the population, and develop all human potential" (Haywood, 1958). This, for Marx, is the meaning of *becoming*. For Native Americans (as well as for Blacks and members of other oppressed nations) this does not mean becoming something other than Indigenous, but rather, it means restoring Indigenous culture, language, and political organization situated in the contemporary context, but free from colonial and capitalist interference. Because inequality and white prejudice took generations to develop, it will take time to eliminate so concrete actions must be institutionalized to facilitate the process. This work, of course, cannot be properly considered in isolation from the international context.

During his time at KUTV and the Lenin School, Haywood found himself studying and learning with communists in training from China, Vietnam, South Africa, and elsewhere, which reinforced his international perspective and commitment to the working class not only as a globally connected entity but also an entity with important distinctions that cannot be ignored (Hall, 2012; Haywood, 1958). The communist pedagogy advanced here is, therefore, informed by the indispensability of a communist future wherein the self-determination of oppressed nations and national minorities allows the fulfillment of the ethic of each according to her ability, and each according to her need to flourish. This work, as demonstrated above, also engages communist pedagogy in the tough practical questions of organization and how to combat counterrevolutionary, anticommunist pushback. In order to expand on the international perspective upon which Haywood insists, we now turn to a more detailed outline of the *global class war*. I then highlight a number of the central contradictions of capitalism to further contextualize what a communist pedagogy must respond to and address in both theory and in practice.

The Global Class War

The communist parties within the U.S. imperialist behemoth that lived through the tumultuous post–Great Depression and post–WWII eras, as Haywood began to demonstrate, faced many obstacles, from right-wing deviations, to a deadly FBI counterintelligence program, to an over-the-top anticommunist propaganda campaign. The success of the capitalists in normalizing anticommunism is evident in the way it has poisoned much of the Left, including some of its brightest scholars, such as Noam Chomsky, whom Michael Parenti (1997) argues possesses "an inexhaustible fount of anticommunist caricatures" (p. 46). Rather than focusing on the global pressures forcing the communists' hands, many Left, Western intellectuals portrayed communist leaders as driven by the quest for power for the sake of power itself, rather than by the revolutionary commitments they had risked their lives for.

As the primary target of imperialist aggression is no longer global communism but global terrorism, socialists are now in a new strategic position to advance the communist movement. Recent opinion polls have repeatedly found that more than half of Americans between the ages of fifteen and twenty-five have a favorable perception of socialism and prefer it to capitalism (Malott & Ford, 2015).

However, while socialism is gaining popular support, the long-term effects of Cold War–era propaganda will likely be felt for some time to come and must, therefore, be understood and purposefully challenged. One of the primary tactics of the counterrevolutionary Western propagandists that has greatly influenced Left anticommunism has been to associate communism with fascism. Parenti (1997) notes how the Italian fascists and German Nazis, who were, first and foremost, motivated by an anticommunist union–bashing agenda—which was fueled by conservative racism, sexism, homophobia, and anti-immigrant sentiments, and thus propelled to power by the vigorous support of industrial and financial capitalists in their own countries and from the U.S. and England—co-opted the massively popular use of socialist-like symbols, rallies, youth organizations, and so on to gain support in their own countries. In other words, fascists and Nazis looked like communists because communism was so popular, which enabled bourgeois propagandists to convincingly argue that communism is fascism. Fascism, at its heart, "is nothing more than the final solution to the class struggle, the totalistic submergence and exploitation of democratic forces for the benefit and profit of higher financial circles" (Parenti, 1997, p. 17). When the Nazis and fascists became too powerful and began setting their sights on Western colonies, U.S. support for Hitler and Mussolini quickly became sour, and they began to be portrayed as the monsters they always were.

Having co-opted the organizational form of communism, while waging war on its content and proponents, the fascists and Nazis were painted by U.S. propagandists as the totalitarian twins of communists. This propaganda informed policy. After WWII, for example, the communist fighters who battled fascist antiworker forces in Italy were outrageously depicted as the aggressors and were subsequently imprisoned and executed while the fascist and Nazi war criminals were largely released from prison. The most terrible of the Nazis criminals found refuge in the nerve center of imperialist power, the U.S., and many of them would assist U.S. leaders in the ongoing global class war against the proletarian camp (Parenti, 1997). The level of criminal violence demonstrated during this era provides another reminder for why the creation of communism will require a strong dictatorship of the proletariat because the level of violence and cruelties that the anticommunist counterrevolutionaries are capable of has no limits. The capitalist drive is also incapable of rest, perpetually driven to drive up the rate of exploitation beyond all natural human limits. For example, by the 1990s the neofascists in Europe would learn from U.S. reactionaries how to

> achieve fascism's class goals within the confines of quasi-democratic forms: use an upbeat, Reaganesque optimism; replace the jackbooted militarists with media-hyped crowd pleasers; convince people government is the enemy—especially its social service sector—while strengthening the repressive capacities of the state; instigate racial hostility and antagonisms between the resident population and immigrants; preach the mythic virtues of the free market; and pursue tax and spending measures that redistribute income upward. (Parenti, 1997, p. 22)

In Western countries the bourgeoisie have employed the fascist tactic of appropriating labor's collective consciousness through long-winded appeals to "hard-working Americans" while quietly selling off their futures through pro-business legislation with titles that speak to the desires of "Main Street Americans," such as Paycheck Protection and Race to the Top. Again, the anticommunist tendency became so commonplace in the U.S. that Left academics who challenge these policies and redistribution of wealth upward without being sure to denounce communism saw, and see, their credibility weakened within the Left itself (Dean, 2012; Parenti, 1997). However, this, too, is beginning to change as the socialist-like platform of Bernie Sanders—Democrat and candidate for president in 2016—advocating for free education, universal healthcare, and a livable wage gains increasing support from an immiserated working class. The socialist theme of the recent Black Radical Tradition conference at Temple University in Philadelphia, Pennsylvania, which attracted nearly two thousand attendees, is further evidence of a socialist resurgence in the U.S.

However, despite these encouraging trends, it remains difficult for the Left to fully comprehend the complex and often confusing international context where leaders of various parties, movements, and workers' states debate fiercely concerning each other's class character and their relationship with the counterrevolutionary imperialists and neofascists. Unless the complex history of the communist movement is better understood by the working class, the current surge in socialist popularity and desire could be fleeting. Indeed, communist confusion would be the cause of many disputes among and splits within communist and socialist parties in the U.S. and beyond (see chapter 3 and the Sino-Soviet split).

For example, responding to serious errors of the two major socialist parties in the U.S. in the 1940s and 1950s, the Trotskyist Socialist Workers Party (SWP) and the Stalinist CP-USA, Sam Marcy (1976b), in 1950, developed, as a corrective, the concept that this book is based upon: the global class war. Whereas the CP-USA seemed to respond to the complexity and anti-Soviet tendency in the U.S. by uncritically following every decision and position of the Soviet leadership, the SWP, of which Marcy was a member, rejected the Soviet Union as no longer a workers' state due to perceived mistakes made by its leadership, which they referred to negatively as *Stalinism* or *Stalinistic*. For Marcy, both of these positions were based on the incorrect conflation of a particular leader or administration with the organizational structure of the state system and the mode of production they were administering. This insight continues to be indispensable for bringing clarity to a complex international landscape.

Marcy's (1976b) conception of the global class war challenges the equally incorrect positions of both the SWP and CP. For Marcy (1976b), the two primary questions concerning, say, the Soviet Union, were (1) What is the class character of the organizational structure of the government? and (2) What is the class character of the leadership? This way, the workers of the Soviet Union and their state apparatus that guaranteed them the right to a job, to meaningful education, to housing, and to the system of nature in general, that is, access to the consumption fund, could be rigorously defended while any errors made by their leaders could be challenged without crossing class lines.

While Marcy's dialectical conception of the global class war is a challenge to the errors being made by U.S. socialists, it is also informed by a keen awareness of the changing global political context. Marcy is one of the first U.S. socialists to recognize the post–WWII shift in global politics. It is clear to Marcy that after WWII the U.S. emerged as the dominant imperialist power of the capitalist world. He also understands that the spread of communism to Eastern Europe and China caused the warring imperialist states to subordinate their competition among themselves over colonies (i.e., large portions of the system of nature and access to millions of people worth of potential unskilled labor hours, whose relative price had been severely suppressed) in order to establish a coalition or strategic alliance aimed at eliminating or containing the spreading proletarian revolution. This suppression includes a complex mix of highly funded domestic and foreign policies and practices. Domestically, the war against communism took the form of both counterintelligence programs (COINTELPRO), which includes secret war tactics, including the assassination of leaders, and educational reform laws such as the National Defense Education Act, to laws passed by Congress criminalizing communist organizations, such as the Sedition Act. Internationally, the U.S. led a string of terroristic military interventions that has left much of the world in a state of utter turmoil and destruction.

Consequently, Marcy concludes that the world was, in fact, dominated by a global class war, a division between two great antagonistic class camps—proletarian and bourgeoisie. However, while in the most abstracted or macro perspective, the world is divided between the bourgeois class and the proletarian class, it "is not a simple conflict between two self-contained and independent entities, suspended in mid-air and gravitating under their own impulsions" (p. 33). Marcy refuses to give in to simplistic and deterministic explanations that attribute magical attributes to internal laws of economic systems. Referring to and acknowledging the historic significance of the conflict between the two great world powers, the U.S. and the Soviet Union, during the 1950s, Marcy notes that the global struggle was not "merely two-sided" (p. 33). Alluding to the diversity of imperialist and proletarian forces and conglomerations throughout the world, Marcy notes that they are not "arbitrary entities" but "living social forces" that are neither "self-contained" nor "independent" (p. 33).

Rather, these antagonistic and semi-autonomous entities are "organically inter-connected, indissolubly anchored to and absolutely dependent upon the two great class pillars of contemporary society—the world proletariat and the world bourgeoisie" (p. 33). Even though the Soviet Union and the Eastern socialist countries, and many of the independent states that survived under their shadow, are no longer in existence, the global class war is a struggle, as mentioned above, not between countries but between classes. The sharp class division remains, but constant revolutions in the means of production, driven by competing capitalists, lead to constant shifts in the composition of capital and, therefore, to the forever increasing brutality of the relationship between the buyers and sellers of labor power (i.e., workers and capitalists). The dynamics of the global class war, therefore, ebb and flow. While a period of decline for the proletarian camp began to develop during the late 1970s, today we are perhaps at the beginning of a shift in power back to the proletarian side. If this is the case, the role of the Communist Party is to put all its energy toward crushing the bourgeois state as a first step toward communism.

The savageness through which the bourgeois capitalist class has waged its war on the ambitions and beautiful coming to be of the global proletariat has been so cruel, so merciless, so heartless, that it is difficult to find words strong enough to avoid downplaying its level of intensity. It is a war waged on the flourishing of the nascent curiosity and joy of a young child. This war is waged not only physically, through actual military interventions and police forces operating as invading forces, imposing their will on the working-class communities—especially those of color—they patrol, but it also oppresses by simply existing as personified capital. For example, the perpetually extending and deepening tendency toward the impoverishment of workers is coupled and facilitated with an extending intellectual alienation. With the advent of capital, it was just the product of a peasant's labor that he was alienated from. Very soon though, the peasant, first in England, was expropriated, violently, from the soil, and, thus, alienated from the means of production and forced, out of necessity, to enter the labor market to peddle his human commodity. The laborers' collective leverage against the employers' tendency to drive wages down came from the knowledge and skill of how to command the tools of industry needed for commodity production. Without the workers who were trained and experienced with the very specific sets of skills and knowledge of tool use, production could not take place. While the increasing division of labor and reducing tasks to shorter and shorter repetitive operations further alienated workers from their more potentially complete integration of mental labor and manual labor, they still possessed some skills indispensable to production that afforded them some leverage against the constant encroachments of capital (Marx, 1867/1967).

However, with the advent of the machine factory in the mid-nineteenth century, the alienation of the workman from his intellectual capacity was greatly advanced, to the great detriment of the proletariat class camp. That is, the machine factory not only eliminated the workman's tools, but it replaced his muscle power with machine power, and, at the same time, it replaced his intellect and knowledge with a central command center integrating a series of automated machines. Whereas before a grown, muscular man trained with specific knowledges was needed for production, now what was needed was just minders of machines, which could be anyone compelled to enter the labor market as a seller, including young children and the smallest of women. The compounding implications of this shift were dramatic on all sides—poverty and extreme immiseration on one side, and never-before-seen opulence on the other. With a workman's wife and children now able to mind the machines, the flooding of the labor market drove the price of labor down. The extreme efficiency of the machines drastically shifted the composition of capital, greatly reducing the amount of labor hours required to transform a given quantity of raw materials into useful products. If the capitalist can only create new and greater value by putting more and more labor hours into motion, then decreasing the amount of labor hours needed creates another incentive to extend the length of the workday to its natural limits. When workers win reforms that restrict the length of the workday, then capital finds an outlet for the pressure to expand by extending existing operations and intensifying work, which equates to speeding up machines, thereby squeezing more and more value or surplus out of workers within a given quantity of time. Where capital gains more profit, the laborer loses both intellectual capacity and life years. Without working-class resistance, the spirit and intent of capital will lead to the premature exhaustion and death of the laborer (Marx, 1867/1967). As we see in the next section, capital's quest for profit is also disruptive to capital itself.

Having made significant progress toward communism and, therefore, against the destructive tendencies outlined above, the USSR, for Marcy, was in fact a workers' state, even if the leadership, at times, had made mistakes and betrayed the spirit of its proletarian base. The shortcomings of such a state's leadership, such as the USSR after Lenin and Stalin, did not negate its existence as a workers' state. Marcy, therefore, argues that the Soviet Union and all worker states and all states independent of imperialism should be defended at all costs, which means critiquing their leadership when they betray the interests of the global proletarian class camp. Similarly, it continues to be important to defend the legacy of the USSR and to understand that when workers' states fall, it is a setback for the proletarian class camp in the global class war. Marcy's description of imperialism's class character, "with its nerve center in the USA," underscores the ongoing significance here since it tends to "draw together all bourgeois states and all kindred social layers and mobilizes them for war against" (p. 33) the proletarian class camp at home and abroad, and now even against independent national bourgeois states, such as Syria.

Following Trotsky, ironically enough, Marcy eventually broke from the SWP and created the Workers World Party (WWP), believing that the SWP's further deterioration was irreconcilable. For example, by refusing to engage Communist Party Stalinists in the U.S. and the U.S. working class they represented, Marcy believed the SWP was self-destructive in their belief that they could achieve communism through an isolationist policy. Marcy, rather, following Trotsky's advice, believed the correct position was to engage the U.S. CP Stalinists, according to their Marxist and Leninist global orientation, arguing that the world proletarian class camp was one class, and its leadership would emerge through an internal ideological battle. Communism could, therefore, not be created either in isolation within the U.S. or isolation of the U.S. from the larger global proletarian class camp.

While Marcy's conception of the global class war continues to be indispensable to the movement for communism, Lenin's (1917/2015) *The State and Revolution* also remains crucially important. The global, anti-imperialist context has to be connected to a program for confronting local labor issues, especially in the center of global capitalist power, lest the most savage imperialists go unchallenged in their own country. Haywood's contributions to understanding national oppression in the U.S. and Coulthard's work on the settler-state are, therefore, also indispensable for the development of a communist pedagogy.

Contradictions of Capitalism

As each day passes, the gap between labor and capital becomes wider and deeper. Generally speaking, for example, in the aftermath of the 2007 recession, the capitalist class in Britain is 64 percent richer and the poor are 54 percent poorer. Similarly, in the U.S., the amount of total wealth going to the top 1% has more than doubled since 1979. As general poverty escalates, racialized inequality also tends to expand. With growing immiseration, spontaneous working-class uprisings and rebellions occur with more frequency. But without a scientific understanding of the society we live in and a theory and method of organization, embryonic proletarian resistance is not likely to shift the paradigm, therefore, leaving the root cause of suffering intact.

In this context critical approaches to education have a lot to gain from Marx. That is, while the consequences of capitalism, such as massive wealth and poverty, are readily visible to the untrained eye, their dialectical relationship and root causes are not. Whereas bourgeois propaganda, what they call *education*, would have people believe that wealth and poverty reflect natural or socially constructed differences in ability, intelligence, perseverance, and so on, Marx, on the other hand, would have us see labor and capital as part of a contradictory whole, each requiring the other to exist as such. Both parts of the whole live an alienated existence: capital lives in opulence, whereas labor is plagued with uncertainty and growing poverty. While Marx's contributions here are vast, complex, and largely counterintuitive, I will summarize a few points that I think are most closely related to an anticapitalist communist pedagogy.

Point 1

First of all, capitalism is not a static system. It is developmental. It is its own internal contradictions that drive its developmental change.

Arguably capitalism's most central contradiction is that in its unlimited quest for the self-expansion of capital, that is, for profit, it not only disrupts the lives of workers, it also disrupts itself. In other words, the process of capitalist production is disruptive to capitalist production.

Think of the Great Depression and the stock market crash of 1929. Not only were an unusually large number of workers thrown out of work, but thousands upon thousands upon thousands of capitalist enterprises also went belly up. U.S. workers' experience of living this contradiction allowed socialist workers to recruit heavily and swell the ranks of the CP-USA from 8,000 members to more than 100,000 members during the ten years of the Great Depression. While the bourgeois state's response to this working-class agency was the savage and deadly crushing of the communist rebellion, workers still won many concessions (which are under attack to this day), from a series of new labor laws and social security to more autonomy in the classroom, which was allowed only after communists were purged from schools.

Similarly, the housing market crash of 2007 not only disrupted the lives of millions of workers by destroying the exchange value of their homes, but the wave of foreclosures disrupted mortgage lenders' ability to realize the exchange value in their investments. This led to a ripple effect, disrupting capitalism in general. Of course the capitalist state bailed out their capitalist masters, externalizing the cost to labor through crushing austerity. In education this has meant even more budget cuts and rollbacks. Following Lenin, critical educators can use these crises as schools of war, because the bailouts make it increasingly obvious that the state works not for labor, but for capital. This can foster a class consciousness among labor, including teachers, conducive to the movement needed to develop capitalist production relations into socialist ones, and to transform the state into an apparatus that represses not working-class resistance, but that represses bourgeois domination and capitalist exploitation.

Disruptions, of course, are nothing new to capital. Capitalism, as Marx explores in volume 1 of *Capital*, began with a series of deadly disruptions he referred to as the chief moments of primitive accumulation, from the expropriation of European peasants from the soil, beginning in England, to the genocidal African slave trade, to the discovery of gold and the genocidal colonization of the Americas. There are no areas of the world safe from the disruptive and devastating effects of capitalism.

The first disruption was a prerequisite for the development of the rest. That is, before the process of the augmentation of capital could begin, a class of people needed to be created who had no way to support themselves but by selling their ability to work on the market for a wage. History has shown us that the peasant will not do this voluntarily and must, therefore, be violently expropriated from the soil. In the process the conditions necessary for capitalism to take hold, such as the creation of private property, become its consequences as the dependency of labor on capital proceeds on an extending scale through the system's development.

While regulations and organized labor can slow down this process, only working-class agency can push capital to become its own dialectical, communist opposite. Critical education can play a fundamental role here. While this formulation of dialectical change should not be interpreted to suggest a clean or linear process, it is a process with a definite direction nonetheless.

Point 2

The next fundamental insight for a critical education against capital is the understanding that within every hour of paid labor there contains an unrequited or an unpaid portion.

At its most basic level we can understand this, as Marx did, by dividing the workday into two distinct portions: necessary labor time and surplus labor time. Necessary labor time is the material basis of the minimum wage. It is the equivalent value of the bare minimum cost of reproducing one's existence for a twenty-four-hour period. The minimum wage today in this country is far below what is socially necessary. While explaining the specific ways capital pushes wages below what is socially necessary is beyond the scope of this introductory chapter, it is driven by the same internal logic as capitalism in general. If it takes six hours of labor to reproduce the value of one's daily existence, then every hour the laborer works after that is surplus labor time, the material basis of surplus-value or profit. Because the products of labor power go to the buyer of this commodity and not the seller, the extra value created goes to the capitalist and not the laborer.

Again, this is the basis of capital's exploitation of labor. This exploitation is disguised or hidden by the money relation. That is, if you have a job, when you receive your paycheck, it appears that every hour of work is paid, because every hour of work is typically accounted for right there on your pay stub. Consequently, the relationship between labor and capital appears to be fair. If workers are unhappy with the paychecks they receive, we are told it is their own fault for not working harder for the kind of results they desire. What we are not told is that there is no escape from exploitation within capitalism. Without some degree or rate of exploitation, the owner of wealth cannot expand his or her money, and they cannot, therefore, create new value. Without exploitation, in other words, the capitalist cannot exist as such. Money, in other words, is not necessarily capital. Capital is the product of a self-expansive process based upon the exploitation of human labor power. Just being wealthy does not make one a capitalist. This is another counterintuitive characteristic of capitalism.

Reflecting on this larger context of capitalism, one of the purposes of a critical education is to help students understand their true class position within it, and develop the collective revolutionary agency necessary to transform it. There is no substitute for this. Even as poverty escalates and the consequences of capitalism become more obvious—over-the-top opulence on one hand, and extreme poverty on the other—the internal mechanism of how new value is created capitalistically remains hidden, and so do realistic solutions. That is, without a scientific understanding of capitalism, solutions are doomed to be focused on tinkering with the rate of exploitation: such as the current movement for the fifteen dollars an hour minimum wage, the movement to grow unions, the movement to tax capitalists more, and the movement to increase public spending on things like education. While all of these interrelated movements are important and tend to be supported by socialists, they leave the basis of capitalistic exploitation itself untouched. The history of education in capitalist society is, in large part, the history of how attention on the root capitalist cause of poverty has been diverted away from the economic structure and to the individual.

For example, dating back to the mid-nineteenth century the moral crusade for Common Schooling, led by Massachusetts lawyer turned Secretary of Education Horace Mann, has tended to be conceptualized as placing the hope for social improvement, that is, ending poverty and suffering, on the individual, ignoring the internal drive of capital itself. The more feudalistic model of educating or socializing workers was based on the Christian concept of original sin, where education served the function of keeping the inherent evil within the poor at bay.

With the development of capitalism, this theory of education began to be replaced with the more nineteenth-century concept of the blank slate, where the immoral laborer had to be molded into the proper citizen. In this context poverty is the result of improperly molded workers rather than on the drive to accumulate surplus labor hours. Schooling in capitalist society has, therefore, always tended to be based on the assumption that poverty is an individual problem, and capitalism offers individuals the freedom to overcome it. Today's rhetoric argues that unaccountable schools with low standards, created by teachers' unions that protect incompetence, have failed to mold the individual into the type of worker that is competitive on the twenty-first-century international labor market. Of course unions cannot protect workers who do not do their jobs, they can only work to ensure dismissals are not arbitrary. What is more, the individual cannot be held responsible for the poverty created by capitalism's limitless quest for surplus-value. The emergence of intelligence tests around the First World War became a central device in providing a so-called scientific measure justifying racialized and gendered class-based inequalities and outcomes.

As the enrollment of school-aged children continued to increase through the Great Depression, the curriculum steadily moved away from the Common Schooling approach where rich and poor children were supposed to be schooled together as a way to ensure workers did not grow up to hate their exploiting bosses. As capitalism expanded and developed technologically, the children of the elite were more and more groomed for leadership, and the children of labor were trained for specialized jobs through a differentiated, or socially efficient, vocational education.

Traditional educational historians argue that the emergence of vocational education was an example of how schools were providing what workers wanted, therefore, operating as a progressive, democratic institution. Responses to this narrative argued that social efficiency was really about dumbing workers down to snuff out radicalism and quell the revolutionary potential within labor as alienated existence.

The social control argument is easy to understand given the logic of social efficiency. That is, the assumption was that educating future machine minders, for example, with luxuries such as philosophy, literature, political science, among others, was a waste of resources and, thus, not efficient. Another interpretation of social efficiency was that wasting educational resources, on, say, public speaking and debating skills not required for the future mechanic was taking time away from producing better mechanics, for example. In the years before and after WWI it was argued that inefficient, common methods of education were putting America at an international competitive disadvantage.

But capital and its state apparatus, also under false illusions about the fairness of the exchange between labor and capital, have tended to be ignorant to how the competitive advantage of individual capitalists is always only temporary, and its cumulative effect, actually, tends to shift the general composition of capital so it takes fewer labor hours to transform a given quantity of raw materials into useful products and, therefore, leads to a tendency toward the falling rate of profit. Let me explain.

Point 3

Because the price of individual products is determined by the average amount of labor time it takes to produce them, the capitalist ahead of the technology race will yield a greater surplus from his products than his competitor until the new, more efficient or productive technology is integrated into that branch of industry generally, and the average amount of time it takes to produce a given commodity is decreased. This tendency drives down the price of products, the value of labor, and the rate of the capitalists' profits. This is another one of capital's central driving contradictions.

This internal drive of capital, therefore, while enriching certain capitalists in the short term, ultimately erodes its own desired effect. That is, if the only way to expand capital is by exploiting human labor power, then the capitalist is always searching for ways to put more labor hours into motion. If advances in production decrease the amount of labor hours needed to convert a particular quantity of raw materials into useful products, then the capitalist faces an internal contradiction threatening the objective of his existence as personified capital (i.e., the capitalist).

Bourgeois education policymakers fail to either acknowledge or realize that the real key to increases in the efficiency in production is not necessarily in the training of laborers, but in the means of production itself. The real threat to workers is, therefore, not their own immoral character but the internal drive of capital, and what the capitalist is compelled to do to counter the falling rate of profit.

For example, the measures capitalists enact to counter the falling rate of return are always at the expense of labor. Such measures include increasing the intensity of work, extending the length of the working day beyond all natural limits, expanding imperialistically into new regions, and when there remain no new regions to expand into, turning to each other, imperialist nations to imperialist nations, in a military competition for existing colonies, sending working-class youth of one empire to kill and be killed by the working-class youth of another empire. And when the most exploited and degraded hands of an internal or external colony resist, and especially when they engage in national liberation struggles, they are called terrorists, and ruthless attempts are made to destroy them, collectively or individually. After WWII imperialist competitors put their differences aside and united against the Socialist bloc. Today, they are united against terrorism and the independent nations of the Middle East. The communist movement, as defined by internationalism, remains imperative.

Thinking about what this means for education, Marx challenges communist pedagogy to resist attempts to reduce the necessity of transforming concrete material conditions into an exercise in transforming consciousness alone. Marx also challenges critical educators, as already suggested, to resist utopian conceptions of a new society, emerging magically separate and disconnected from the one that exists. Marx is correct, I believe, that new social arrangements can only emerge out of existing ones.

In this context of uncertainty, deadly state racism, oppression, exploitation, and contradiction, more and more organized struggle is in fact emerging. The resistance is developing not only outside of the U.S., but it is happening within the country as well. With the Soviet Union unfortunately gone and the fog and bigotry of anticommunism in the U.S. slowly dissipating, a new socialist movement, a new anticapitalist movement, is emerging. The Occupy Movement, the Black Lives Matter Movement, and the Sanders campaign, despite some significant socialist critiques, have been contextualized as harbingers of what is to come.

In the context of teachers' unions, the recent strike of the Seattle Education Association sent shock waves across the country. The strike was caused by a breakdown in contract negotiations between the teachers' union, the Seattle Teachers' Association, and the Board of Education. Following national trends in budget cuts for public education, especially in urban school districts with large minority populations, teachers in Seattle have had to fight for income, healthcare, lower class size, measures to address structural racism, and limits on standardized testing. Even though the teachers were motivated to resolve the negotiations and return to work, their negotiators felt like management was not willing to see it through. As a result, on most of these issues the two sides could not come to an agreement, which eventually led to the teachers striking. The spirit of solidarity and militancy of the subsequent strike embodies the spirit of the largely forgotten history of socialism in the U.S. That is, the Seattle teachers' strong connection and solidarity with students, their caregivers, and other unions gave them strength, leverage, and a real ability to achieve largely unprecedented concessions, including the removal of the "Student Growth Rating" clause that links teacher evaluations to student test scores. They were also able to achieve the establishment of thirty "race and equity teams" charged with identifying examples of institutional racism and recommending ways to address them. It is not perfect, but it is a great beginning. The Seattle Education Association's concrete support and victory for these and other social justice issues might be viewed as a reminder of what workers can win through their organizations and leadership.

Of course, this does not mean we can sit back and wait for things to get better. It means we have to fight harder than we ever have. It means we have to be more disciplined and organized than we ever have. It means we have to be smarter than we ever have. It means we have to be fiercer and more committed than we ever have. The future is not guaranteed, by any means. While it may be hard to imagine, things could take a turn for the worse, and it is up to us to ensure that they do not.

· 2 ·

MARXIST HISTORIOGRAPHY IN THE HISTORY OF EDUCATION

From Colonial to Neocolonial Schooling in the United States

With Pierre Orelus

Introduction

This chapter draws on Marx's scholarly contributions to historiography to examine the *history of* and approach *to* the history of education in the United States. Before delving into a Marxist historiography, however, we review the developments within the history of education beginning with Michael Katz (1975, 1987) and Bowles and Gintis (1976), focusing exclusively on the U.S., even though the goal of a Marxist pedagogy is global in nature. For example, Katz (1975) approaches the history of education in the U.S. from the tradition of historiography, which focuses on the theories, methods, and at its most relevant, the political economy of doing historical research. Many trace this method back to Marx himself. We argue that Katz's central questions behind his historiography seem to be grounded in a materialist approach not entirely unrelated to that found in Marx, such as, "what drives the politics of educational history?" (Katz, 1987, p. 1). While Katz (1975, 1987) does not identify his work overtly with Marx, he situates it as belonging to the same general trajectory as the work of Bowles and Gintis.

What is more, one of Katz's (1975) central critiques is that traditional history of U.S. education texts tend to advance the idea that the U.S. is a meritocracy and social class, therefore, plays no role in the purpose or out-comes of education, despite mountains of evidence to the contrary (Kozol, 2012). Katz (1975, 1987), however, argues that class is not only a central determinant of capitalist schooling, but it is much more than a thing or a group of categories, differentiating consumption levels and patterns. It rather is a divisive, always-in-process *social relation* between the dispossessed, the excluded, and the laborers (i.e., those who rely on a wage of some sort to survive, including teachers, inmates, and all oppressed nations) and capital (i.e., those whose wealth comes from the labor and land of others, either directly as in industrialists and imperialist colonizers or indirectly as in investment bankers). As argued below, Katz's (1975) class analysis here is undeniably influenced by education scholars who identify as Marxist (Cole, 2007; Darder, 2014; Malott & Ford, 2015; McLaren, 2004). This chapter, therefore, follows Katz on two interrelated lines of reasoning: his focus on social class (i.e., capitalism) and his historiography—interrelated because historiography itself suggests critique, which, in the case of the history of education, has led a number of educational historians to not only social class, since social class predates bourgeois society, but also to capitalism, or the uniquely capitalist process of expanding value itself. At the same time, however, the bulk of Katz's work focuses mainly on the ideological aspects of how the poor are themselves blamed for their poverty (Ryan, 1976) rather than the more Marxist critique of political economy, which is central to our understanding of capitalism and the process of historical change and development. Furthermore, we contend that, unlike Marx, the Marxist and class analysts of the history of U.S. education of the 1970s seemed to have failed to fully grasp the importance of racialization, colonialism, imperialism, and the global class war in the histories of education they constructed. This conclusion is based on the observation that in constructing the larger social, political, and economic context in which capitalist schooling is unavoidably situated, the radical revisionists (as Katz, 1987, referred to them and himself) scarcely mention slavery or the conquest and genocide of American Indians and the American continents, and they also tend to distance themselves from actually existing socialist countries while oddly supporting the idea of socialism in the abstract.

One of the benefits of historiography is that it demands such critiques because it brings the method of inquiry to the surface by interrogating the historically contextualized theoretical and political influences behind the construction of history of education texts. Attempting to capture this process, Thomas Holt (1992), in a short manuscript on doing history, argues that histories are narratives constructed through various philosophical frame-works. Following this approach, Katz (1975) argues that traditional history of education texts tend to be written from bourgeois theoretical frameworks as apologies for capital since they deny the existence of systematic or insti-tutional colonization, exploitation, and oppression, that is, of social class as either a socially reproduced category or an antagonistically related social rela-tion between labor and capital.

We provide a broad view of the historical development of education in capitalist society through the lens of how the telling of that story has changed over time and through the construction of a Marxist historiography for the history of education, drawing primarily on *The German Ideology* (Marx & Engels, 1846/1996) and *The Eighteenth Brumaire of Louis Bonaparte* (Marx, 1852/1972). The debate and struggle over the narrative of the history of edu-cation in the United States never exist in a vacuum, unaffected by the larger society in which it is situated. For example, because textbook companies in the U.S. are capitalist enterprises driven by the desire to create capital (i.e., self-expand), they gravitate toward narratives perceived to be popular, and in today's hyper-bourgeois U.S. society, where even the Left has largely abandoned Marx and the notion of a global class war (i.e., capitalist coun-tries against both socialist countries and workers and the colonized in their own countries), the prospects of major textbook companies adopting Marxist titles appear to be slim. Successful professors in the U.S., therefore, tend to be professors that reproduce the dominant ideology—the ideology of the ruling class—not because of a conspiracy, but because it has become common sense. That is, the idea that communism equals a static, authoritarian inevitability is largely taken for granted even in critical pedagogy. While Marxist perspec-tives are far less common, interest in Marx's vast body of work is experiencing a global rejuvenation as the bigotry and fog of anticommunism slowly dissi-pate. This chapter hopes to contribute to this resurgence.

However, highlighting the importance of historical contextualization, the Marxist approaches to the history of education, represented by Katz and Bowles and Gintis, emerged during the height of the global communist move-ment and national liberation struggles against colonialism that manifested themselves in the U.S. with the American Indian Movement, which was a response to the era of termination (i.e., the U.S. government terminating the official status of many federally recognized tribes) and urban relocation (i.e., moving American Indians from reservations to urban areas) and the Civil Rights Movement (i.e., the Student Nonviolent Coordinating Committee), which developed into the more revolutionary Black Panther Party. Again, this is another reason why it is unfortunate that Marxist educational historians seemed to have missed Marx's long discussions on colonization and slavery and the ways in which capitalism, for example, intensified its horrors in the American South, which point to the historical significance of Black liberation movements and the struggle of American Indians for national sovereignty.

What follows is a brief outline of three of the major approaches that tend to be employed in the creation of historical narratives: traditional, constructivist, and postmodern. This brief discussion is not comprehensive but it is essential as it introduces readers to the field of the history of education. Next, a considerable amount of space is dedicated to developing a Marxist historiography in the history of education. This section draws on Marx in unique ways and provides the theoretical foundation for the remainder of the chapter. We then briefly engage the radical revisionist challenge to the history of education during the 1960s and 1970s. Finally, we provide a critique of two major periods in the history of U.S. education, making a case for a Marxist historiography in the history of education. In the process we draw on, critique, and add to Bowles and Gintis and others. The approach to the history of U.S. education we offer is informed by a commitment to challenge the ongoing and deepening capitalist or bourgeois control over the purpose and outcome of education. That is, education continues to perpetuate and extend racial, linguistic, and ethnic inequality through unequal funding schemes, and the ongoing assumption that Black, Brown, immigrant, and English as a Second Language (ESL) students are inherently low achieving and prone to violence and criminality. Such scapegoating and state-sanctioned strategy, in the face of deepening global poverty, serve to keep the price of labor low, justifying extreme exploitation on one hand, and over-the-top wealth among the capitalist class on the other.

Bourgeois Approaches to the History of U.S. Education

The traditional approach to history in Western society treats history as the objective, verifiable, predetermined unfolding of events. At its most harmful, the traditional approach uses the notion of objectivity to hide the agenda of situating bourgeois, settler-state, U.S. society, the center of which is the capitalist mode of production, as inevitable and permanent. At its best, however, traditional history, and the traditional historian, engages the documentary evidence with a genuine attempt to uncover hidden truths as part of the process of creating texts that reflect, as does a mirror, past events. The traditional approach to the history of education seems to reflect the former tendency—it, therefore, seems to be a product of the global expansion of bourgeois society combined with elements (such as hero worship of the elite) carried over from European feudalism.

Pedagogically, traditional history of education, of whatever sort, tends to separate thinking from doing. Students, in this context, confront the history curriculum passively, expected to memorize its narrative presented not as a narrative with a worldview and political ideology (even if unstated), but just as it is, objective reality (Freire, 1970/1998; Holt, 1992; Katz, 1987). Such a pedagogical approach is particularly conducive to indoctrination. Consequently, it is not surprising that history has been used to serve the interests of the elite. Summarizing Marx (1857–1858/1973), we contend that as long as there are elite classes, from feudal lords, the enslaving plantocracy of the antebellum South, the giants of industrial capitalism to the financial investor class of late capitalism, there will be an attempt to convince the laboring classes, the dispossessed, and the colonized that their particular era is permanent, fixed, all that is holding evil at bay, the people's true salvation, and when possible, preordained by God.

A response to this approach has been the constructivist model that argues that histories are not mirror images or reflections of past events but are narratives written from different points of view informed by various analytical frameworks, serving particular interests (Holt, 1992). Perhaps the most famous of books advocating for this perspective is *What Is History?* written in 1961 by British historian Edward Hallett Carr (1961/1997), and it is still often used in England and the U.S. in introduction to history survey courses (Evans, 2000).

According to Evans, *What Is History?* "challenges and undermines the belief, brought to university study by too many students on leaving high school, that history is simply a matter of objective fact," and rather "introduces them to the idea that history books, like the people who write them, are products of their own times, bringing particular ideas and ideologies to bear on the past" (pp. 1–2). This tradition, associated with sociology, places complexity at the center, arguing that it is misleading to treat any historical narrative as the only valid story because history is so complex and can be constructed from a nearly limitless range of points of view. Katz (1987) calls Carr's approach *interdependence* and argues that it is a form of bourgeois ideology designed to thwart genuine inquiry into the nature of what drives historical change.

At its more useful moments, pedagogically, constructivism leads to deeper understandings of power and how it operates, placing students at the center of investigation and inquiry, actively engaged in the construction process of political consciousness and knowledge formation, among other things. Critical social justice and multicultural approaches to education challenge students to place their own family histories in the context of the historical narratives they construct.

Consequently, students are challenged to understand their own connection to major events, processes, privileges, and oppressions, such as colonization, religious indoctrination, genocide, manifest destiny, slavery, industrialization, patriarchy, white supremacy, and so on, as part of the educational purpose of creating democratic citizens actively engaged in social justice work. However, while these pedagogies are invaluable sources of critical education, they are not without limitations. For example, the constructivist trail to social justice can easily lead to the dead end of overrelativism, where anything goes, and nothing is concretely and systematically confronted or challenged. Jodi Dean (2012) argues that the Left's call for democracy amounts to nothing more than a call for more of what already exists, which has long since proven ineffective in eradicating capital's need for exploitation or settler-state oppression.

This is to say that the notion of social justice is so vague and all encompassing that it has arguably become safe and even a self-validating aspect of bourgeois society. The idea that a more genuine or deep democracy is the critical pedagogical path to social justice also tends to fail to push beyond the social universe of capital. Stated otherwise, a call for more democracy suggests that what is missing is more participation, therefore, ignoring the inherent antagonism between the capitalist class and the working class (Dean; Malott & Ford). Because this class antagonism is based on the fact that the capitalist can only create new or more value by accumulating the realized value provided by surplus labor hours (i.e., by exploiting the labor of workers), it cannot be resolved once and for all time without the abolition of both the self-expansive process of accumulation and the settler-states' required private ownership of the means of production in the hands of a few capitalists and investment bankers. What this analysis points to is the Marxist approach to history outlined below.

Contributing to the bourgeois attacks against a revolutionary Marxism, in the 1980s, a new pseudoradical tradition emerged from critical theory, postmodernism, which challenged both constructivist and traditional assumptions regarding the nature of truth and objectivity associated with the scientific method. Risking oversimplification, we might note that postmodernists tend to argue that language does not mimic concrete reality but only reproduces the identity-based ideology and signifiers of particular language users. In other words, human interpretation and perspective are far too varied and infinitely complex for language and narrative to be able to fulfill Western science's promise that it can be disconnected from the relative power, privilege, and biases of its users.

While both Carr (1961) and Elton (1967/2002) argue for the central importance of causes and that one should study the historian before her or his facts, the postmodernist argues that histories are nothing more than competing discourses where causal explanations for the emergence of institutions, for example, such as systems of education (i.e., social class, colonialism, slavery, etc.) are too simplistic to be regarded as anything more than primitive discourses. At the heart of postmodernism is the rejection of what is identified as the Enlightenment grand narratives of Western science, including Marxism, each of which excludes non-Western voices by claiming itself as the one absolute, objective truth. What is more, it was argued that the breakdown of Fordism (i.e., the contract between labor and capital), the further globalization of the economy, the flexibilization of labor, and the creation of computers and robotics were leading to a knowledge economy and a fundamentally new era.

That is, postmodernists argue that "the Western world ... was entering a 'postmodern' epoch fundamentally different from industrial capitalism of the nineteenth and twentieth centuries," therefore, arguing that "the classical Marxist stress upon the class struggle as the driving force of history and the working class as agency of socialist change" was outdated (Callinicos, 1989, p. 4). The postmodern challenge, therefore, includes the position that Marxism had been proven authoritarian and, thus, dangerous by so-called Stalinism and misguided as evidenced by the fall of the Soviet Union.

Postmodernism, therefore, signaled a more complete break with the proletarian global class camp by more fully denouncing the world's past and present socialist states and parties. The Party itself was abandoned as an inherently oppressive hierarchical, Western construct embracing the fragmented, more identity-based new social movement with no identifiable leaders. What is more, the emergence of a more fragmented, fractured postmodern condition relegated working-class movements irrelevant because industrial production had been replaced with a new knowledge economy accompanied by new forms of control and new relations of production. Dean argues that the result of the deindustrialization of imperialist centers, such as the U.S., as been accompanied by de-unionization and the emergence of a service sector–oriented workforce. The challenge for a Marxist history of education here is, therefore, to recover the collective sense of the Party needed to push toward the communist horizon situated in the context of a settler-state that has always been at war with the national sovereignty of Native North American tribes and confederacies. This entails a complex mix of defending, challenging, and advancing the past work of Marxist educational historians.

In the history of education, the radical revisionist work of Katz (1975, 1987) and Bowles and Gintis has, therefore, been under attack as modernist and, thus, vulgar. According to Milton Gaither (2012), the postmodern challenge has left the field of the history of education without direction or purpose, which we hope our efforts here begin to change. While Gaither argues for a free-market libertarian direction for the history of education, this chapter makes the case for the contemporary relevance of a Marxist history of education. That is, like Callinicos, we, too, believe that postmodernists are wrong in their assertion that we are in a qualitatively new era, rendering Marx's analysis of how capital is augmented and circulated, globally and colonially, irrelevant.

Following McLaren (2005), we argue that the changes mentioned above point not to a new era, but rather to a more intensified hypercapitalism, rendering the work of Marx, not less relevant, but more relevant, than ever. However, while our place of departure is the Marxist history of education work of the 1970s and 1980s, it is our intention here to go beyond it. In the process we argue that Marx's theory of history and historical work is an underused and undertheorized source of direction for the history of education. Therefore, what follows is a brief summary of a Marxist approach to history, looking specifically at Marx.

Marx and Engels's Materialism: Contributions to a Marxist Historiography

This approach to historical investigation identifies a force, *contradiction*, embodied in all entities, as driving all change and movement. The challenge is, therefore, to identify the primary contradiction (i.e., driving force) behind the movement of any historical era. Marx and Engels identify and outline this approach and source of contradiction in *The German Ideology*, and are, there-fore, worth outlining and quoting at length.

Marx and Engels's chapter on Feuerbach in *The German Ideology* offers a logical place of departure for elaborating on a Marxist historiography—*transforming the world cannot happen in the realm of pure thought alone.* Seeming so obvious, yet unfortunately, in the context of critical pedagogy in general and critical theoretical approaches to the history of education in particular, it still needs restating. If a Marxist pedagogy is revolutionary, then a Marxist historiography must too transcend the realm of pure thought, that is, it must be grounded in a materialist understanding of the world as it exists.

What follows is an outline of the premises of the materialist method as laid out in *The German Ideology*. We pursue this line of reasoning because a Marxist historiography must be firmly situated in Marx's materialism, and *The German Ideology* patiently spells it out. Like a Marxist critical peda-gogy of becoming in general (see Malott & Ford), Marx and Engels argue, "Communism is for us not a state of affairs which is to be established, an ideal to which reality will have to adjust itself. We call communism the real move-ment which abolishes the present state of things" (pp. 56–57). Communism can, therefore, only develop out of existing production relations at their pres-ent highly advanced stage of development with all its diversity and colonial contradictions—that is, the contradiction that the privilege of the white working class in the U.S. stems from its historic role serving as the exploited labor used to do the work of colonialism, and whose ultimate emancipation depends upon the unification with the very oppressed nations their labor has been employed by capitalist interests to oppress and commit endless acts of violence and genocide against.

Idealism and the Materialist Method in a Marxist Historiography

True to their critical approach to theory building, Marx and Engels start *The German Ideology* by critiquing German philosophy. However, rather than pro-ceeding as might be expected, they deliver a hefty dose of sarcasm:

> As we hear from German ideologists, Germany has in the last few years gone through an unparalleled revolution. The decomposition of Hegelian philosophy ... has developed into a universal ferment into which all the "powers of the past" are swept ... Principles ousted one another, heroes of the mind overthrew each other with

unheard of rapidity ... All this is supposed to have taken place in the realm of pure thought. (p. 39)

Marx and Engels's sarcastic reference to the dismissal of Hegel must be understood in the context of Marx's (1844/1988) correction, not dismissal, of Hegelian dialectics (see Malott & Ford). Continuing to up the sarcastic ante, Marx and Engels go on naming the German warriors of pure thought ("industrialists of philosophy") who had built their fortunes on exploiting Hegel's concept of the absolute spirit until it had been overthrown, leading these opportunistic theoreticians to begin forming commodities from the new materials, which Marx and Engels suggest are faulty critiques of Hegel. In their description of these industrial philosophers, Marx and Engels begin to allude to their correction of the German ideologists. Due to its sheer brilliance, sarcastic playfulness, and biting precision here is a sizable excerpt:

> Certainly it is an interesting event we are dealing with: the putrescence of the absolute spirit. When the last spark of its life had failed, the various components ... began to decompose, entered into new combinations and formed new substances. The industrialists of philosophy, who till then had lived on the exploitation of the absolute spirit, now seized upon the new combinations. Each with all possible zeal set about retailing his appropriated share. This naturally gave rise to competition, which, to start with, was carried on in moderately staid bourgeois fashion. Later when the German market was glutted, and the commodity in spite of all efforts found no response in the world market, the business was spoiled ... by fabricated and fictitious production, deterioration in quality, adulteration of the raw materials ... The competition turned into a bitter struggle, which is now being extolled and interpreted to us as a revolution of world significance. (pp. 39–40)

It is worth noting that the closely related constructivist and postmodern dismissals and critiques of Marx among the U.S. educational Left, including educational historians, in the 1980s and 1990s, were based on similar types of partial understandings of Marx as the industrial philosophers' rejection of Hegel referred to by Marx and Engels above. We caution against dismissing Marx (or any body of work for that matter) based on secondary sources such as Bowles and Gintis. For this reason, we are engaging Marx and Engels in a more systematic analysis to build our Marxist historiography rather than rely on other Marxist educational historians, such as Michael Katz or Bowles and Gintis. It is this approach that demonstrates the ongoing relevance of Marx despite the so-called new philosophers' (postmodern and others) bold claims of expanding beyond an outdated Marx due to the new knowledge economy.

This does not mean we endorse an uncritical acceptance of the totality of Marx, but that there is an indispensable advancement within his systematic critique of political economy. Similarly, Marx and Engels, referring to the Young Hegelians, argue that not one of them had attempted to offer a systematic critique of the Hegelian system even though they claimed to go beyond it. Marx and Engels summarize this debate arguing that the Old Hegelians accepted the idea that the alienation of humanity is the alienation of humanity from their own consciousness, which is represented as the absolute idea or the absolute spirit (i.e., God), whereas the young Hegelians took this as an enslaving consciousness to be replaced by a new consciousness. What the Old and New Hegelians had in common, for Marx and Engels, was the shared belief in "a universal principle in the existing world" (p. 41). That is, they challenged the belief that the fight for a just society is primarily an ideological fight and is, thus, a battle for a predetermined consciousness and the imposition of a fixed ideology. Notions of creating social justice through critical consciousness might be understood as informed by purely ideological conceptions of transformation and social change. As we explore below, a Marxist historiography is, therefore, not interested in only challenging the ideology and bourgeois constructions of U.S. educational history. Consider:

> Since the Young Hegelians consider conceptions, thoughts, ideas, in fact all the products of consciousness, to which they attribute an independent existence, as the real chains of men (just as the Old Hegelians declared them the true bonds of human society) it is evident that the Young Hegelians only have to fight against these illusions of consciousness. … This demand to change consciousness amounts to a demand to interpret reality in another way. (p. 41)

If our Marxist historiography is to point beyond narrative and consciousness as the target of transformation, it must also move the historian beyond the archives and the educator beyond the classroom (i.e., the shop floor of the educational machine factory) and into confrontation with the state and corporate material basis of the education industry and its managers and shareholders. If constructivist approaches to American educational history tend to take the development of narrative and critical consciousness as the sole objective for achieving social justice, then they too have fallen for the same mistakes Marx and Engels critique the Young Hegelians for. Before this task can be further elaborated on, we would be wise to revisit the premises of Marx and Engels's materialist method.

Their places of departure, of course, are "real individuals, their activity and the material conditions under which they live, both those which they find already existing and those produced by their activity" (p. 42). What Marx and Engels are pointing to here is the empirical evidence that demonstrates the specifics of the existence of actually existing human beings, their "physical organization" and "their consequent relation to nature" (p. 42). Although the point of their text is not to explore the "physical nature of man" (Vygotsky takes up this in *Mind in Society* [1978]) or the physical properties of nature, the study of history should begin with the physical properties of humanity and nature and "their modification in the course of history through the action of men" (p. 42). Such considerations point to concrete aspects of human society that should underlie any serious Marxist history of education. The error made by most history of education texts is that the connections among education, the settler-state, colonialism, and the uniquely capitalistic quest to perpetually expand capital are either loose and undeveloped, or they are treated as separate, mostly unrelated spheres or aspects of human society. These points are explored in later sections of this chapter.

In the development of their materialist system, Marx and Engels note that they are not suggesting consciousness is not important. To the contrary, they argue that what distinguishes humans from other animals is their consciousness, and as soon as humans began producing their own means of subsistence, by transforming nature, they began distinguishing themselves from other animals. Making themselves absolutely clear here, Marx and Engels note that they are not just talking about "the production of the physical existence of the individuals," but rather "a definite form of activity of these individuals" (p. 42). Marx and Engels, therefore, conclude that *what* people are, is directly related to *what* they produce and *how* they produce it. If a history of education does not capture these aspects of what makes different modes of production distinct from each other, then it will have failed to offer a complete analysis of the developing and often contested purposes and processes of schooling. Contrary to the idealists of German philosophy who take existence and nature as unchanging, Marx and Engels argue, "The nature of individuals thus depends on the material conditions determining their production" (p. 42). Such insights pose a difficult challenge to current trends in the history of education that reduce global struggles between competing classes to theories of power.

The conscious forms of activity referred to by Marx and Engels only emerge with population, with increasing intercourse between individuals.

The interaction of not only individuals within nations but also the interaction between separate nations are determined by their internal development, which is measured by the degree of their division of labor. While Marx and Engels, at this early, Eurocentric stage in their intellectual development, conceived of all societies as moving through the same stages of development, they eventually adopted a more sophisticated global analysis, as discussed below (Anderson, 2010). However, the core of their materialist method remained relevant. If the actual existence of humans and the means by which they have developed to produce their actual lives are the primary focus of concern for a materialist method, then it follows that the particular ways production has developed within nations would be of central importance to Marx and Engels and to a Marxist history of education. Of special importance to Marx and Engels here is the division of labor as an indicator of society's level of development. Whereas in *The German Ideology* Marx and Engels argue that all societies develop into patriarchies due to the natural division of labor between men and women, in the last years of Marx's life he began exploring with great joy and excitement the more egalitarian matriarchal division of labor in traditional Native American societies (Anderson). The implications of these insights for the communist horizon and for refusing to accept settler-state colonialism, and for Marxist and Indigenous solidarity, are tremendous. Let us consider Marx and Engels's insights regarding the division of labor at this point in their discussion:

> How far the productive forces of a nation are developed is shown most manifestly by the degree to which the division of labor has been carried. Each new productive force, insofar as it is not merely a quantitative extension of productive forces already known (for instance the bringing into cultivation of fresh land), causes a further development of the division of labor. The division of labor inside a nation leads at first to the separation of industrial and commercial from agricultural labor, and hence to the separation of town and country and to the conflict of their interests. Its further development leads to the separation of commercial from industrial labor. At the same time through the division of labor inside these various branches there develop various divisions among the individuals co-operating in definite kinds of labor. ... The various stages in the division of labor are just so many different forms of ownership. (p. 43)

Clearly, the materialist method outlined here is based upon the European society Marx and Engels were born into. Their framework, philosophically, stems from their correction of Hegel's system of dialectical movement and change outlined in Marx's (1844/1988) *Economic and Philosophic Manuscripts of 1844.*

That is, as humans engage their world and transform it through their activity, the division of labor naturally develops as new means of production are introduced into the growing co-operation between producers. This division of labor, in Europe, first emerges in the family and reflects differences in strength and ability due to age and sex. The father assumes the role of the patriarch, dominating the labor of his wife and children, laying the relational foundation for slavery. But what is dialectical about Marx and Engels's approach here is that each era embodies its own negation as the development of its internal logic. While not all societies develop into patriarchies, all societies develop dialectically. The significance of looking at the development of Europe is that it is within this context that the current global capitalist system developed.

Marx and Engels refer to the first form of "ownership" in the historical development of the division of labor in Europe as *tribal*, which they argue is relatively underdeveloped beyond the forms of the division of labor found within the so-called family. They identify power as patriarchal, an extension of the form of slavery found within the European family. However, as mentioned above, within the notes found in the studies Marx engaged in late in his life are detailed discussions of non-European societies. Again, Marx was particularly interested in the high degree of power afforded women and thus the gender equality found within many Native American societies, such as the Iroquois or Six Nations. We might, therefore, read Marx and Engels's universal depiction of tribal societies not as being informed by prejudice or bias, but rather the Eurocentric result of not being aware of the Native American examples. Marx himself never traveled to the Americas and, therefore, relied on anthropologists' secondary sources for his understanding of Native North Americans.

However, *The German Ideology*, like all of Marx's other major works, is primarily concerned with the development of capitalism specifically, and it specifically emerged in only one physical location, England, thus from the European model of tribal society. With that in mind, we can appreciate Marx not just as a philosopher, an economist, or a revolutionary, but as a historian as well. Following the patriarchal form of tribalism in Europe, Marx and Engels argue a form of communal state ownership emerged marked by the merger into a city of two or more tribes, either voluntarily or by conquest.

It was within this mode of production that both movable and immovable forms of rudimentary types of private property emerged but were subordinated by the communal nature of the society and, thus, the power of individuals. As immovable forms of private property began to grow in proportion to movable forms of private property, the ancient communal state gave way to feudalism. Marx and Engels move through this historical development of productive forces as part of their larger critique of German idealists:

> The fact is, therefore, that definite individuals who are productively active in a definite way enter into these definite social and political relations. Empirical observation must in each separate instance bring out empirically, and without any mystification and speculation, the connection of the social and political structure with production. The social structure and the State are continually evolving out of the life-process of definite individuals, but of individuals, not as they may appear in their own or other people's imagination, but as they *really* are; i.e., as they operate, produce materially, and hence as they work under definite material limits, presuppositions and conditions independent of their will. (pp. 46–47)

Again, what Marx and Engels are getting at here is the challenge to idealism that consciousness does not create reality, nor that reality necessarily or automatically informs consciousness, but that concrete material conditions exist despite individual consciousness, which can even work to distort consciousness. For example, for capitalism to function as such, the price of labor always has to be less than the value it produces but is hidden by the money relation, creating the illusion that every minute of one's labor is paid. That is, the unpaid portion of the workday, the source of capital's augmentation, is hidden and mystified by the material relations between labor and capital themselves, as well as by an ideology of fairness and the objectivity of the market.

Material conditions, in this instance, therefore, do not enlighten consciousness but distort it, serving as an obstacle to the full self-emancipation of the global proletarian class camp. Continuing with this example, we might note that developing an awareness of the hidden process of value expansion, which is the exploitation of labor, does not automatically change reality. Social change cannot happen in the mind alone.

Developing a correct understanding of the world as it exists and develops through history can only ever be a part of a materialist project, however indispensable. Speculative discussion of consciousness, therefore, ceases and in its place steps a Marxist history of education fully grounded within the material limits, presuppositions, and conditions that education is a part of, which should therefore be reflected in any Marxist history of education. From here, Marx and Engels specifically outline their materialist approach to history, which is of particular importance to this chapter.

Arguing that the abstractness and idealism of German philosophers have left them with virtually no premises upon which their theories are built, Marx and Engels state that the first premise of history is that "men must be in a position to live in order to 'make history'" (p. 48). In other words, "life involves before everything else eating and drinking, a habitation, clothing and many other things. The first historical act is thus the production of these needs, the production of material life itself" (p. 48). The ability to produce and reproduce life, for Marx and Engels, is "a fundamental condition of history" (p. 48). The implications of this premise for doing history is that "in any interpretation of history one has first of all to observe this fundamental fact in all its significance and all its implications and to accord it its due importance" (p. 49). A Marxist history of education, therefore, begins with considerations of how education relates to this first premise. The second premise is that in the quest to satisfy basic needs, new needs arise, which Marx and Engels refer to as "the first historical act" (p. 49). Education, in the capitalist era, we might observe, has played an increasingly crucial role, historically, in the creation of new needs.

The development of new needs historically gave rise to the development of societies of humans, beginning with the family. This occurs not with some abstract, fixed conception of family, but as they have developed in reality. Describing this third condition of history, which is intimately connected to the first two premises, Marx and Engels note:

> The third circumstance, which, from the very outset, enters into historical development, is that men, who daily remake their own life, begin to make other men, to propagate their kind: the relation between man and woman, parents and children, the *family*. The family, which to begin with is the only social relationship, becomes later, when increased needs create new social relations and the increased population new needs, a subordinate one … and must then be treated and analyzed according to the existing empirical data, and not according to "the concept of the family." (p. 49)

The final point in the above quote that abstract conceptions of the family are of little use to developing an empirical understanding of concrete reality provides the tools to critique their earlier universalization of European development. The three interrelated aspects of social existence thus far identified (i.e., the satisfaction of needs, the creation of new needs, and with them, the growth of the size and complexity of society), for Marx and Engels, are universal aspects of history that always exist despite mode of production, mode of cooperation, or degree and form of productive development.

At this point Marx and Engels introduce the significant historical observation that the reproduction of life simultaneously embodies both a natural aspect and a social aspect. Again, a Marxist approach to the history of education is concerned with the role of schooling in the development of this double relationship within the production of life—that is, as a natural relationship fulfilling the basic needs all humans require to daily maintain their existence; and the social relationship, or "the co-operation of several individuals, no matter under what conditions, in what manner and to what end" (p. 50). To reiterate, this conclusion does not equate to the dismissal of considerations of race, gender, sexual orientation, and so on, but rather encompasses all aspects of social life as they relate to specific historical periods. Offering a particularly significant observation when considering a Marxist historiography in the history of education, Marx and Engels are instructive:

> A certain mode of production, or industrial stage, is always combined with a certain mode of co-operation, or social stage, and this mode of co-operation is itself a "productive force." Further, that the multitude of productive forces accessible to men determines the nature of society, hence, that the "history of humanity" must always be studied and treated in relation to the history of industry and exchange. ... This connection is ever taking on new forms, and thus presents a "history" independently of the existence of any political or religious nonsense which in addition may hold men together. (p. 50)

It is clear here that Marx and Engels are offering another cautionary transition into their discussion of consciousness. However, before we proceed, it should be noted that it is only after elaborating on the aforementioned "four aspects of the primary historical relationships" (p. 50) that the notion of consciousness is introduced. As demonstrated above, Marx and Engels repeatedly make clear their opposition to the notion of pure consciousness because consciousness or thought arises through language, which is a response to the intercourse between individuals in the production of life itself. Language and consciousness are, therefore, always a social product intimately connected to the material conditions previously discussed.

For Marx and Engels, the division of labor is really only present with the separation between thinking and doing, that is, between mental and manual labor. In the capitalistic era in particular, the history of education offers a way to understand how this division of labor has expanded on an extending scale. At this point Marx and Engels offer another fundamental insight regarding the role of consciousness in the division of mental labor and manual labor in the history of education:

> From this moment onwards consciousness *can* really flatter itself that it is something other than consciousness of existing practice, that it *really* represents something without representing something real; from now on consciousness is in a position to emancipate itself from the world and to proceed to the formation of "pure" theory, theology, philosophy, ethics, etc. But even if this theory, theology, philosophy, ethics, etc. come into contradiction with the existing relations, this can only occur because existing social relations have come into contradiction with existing forces of production. (pp. 51–52)

Coming full circle, we then begin to gain an understanding of the ways in which historical narratives in the history of education can depart from reality and thus come into contradiction with it. As we see below, a more empirically based history of education true to Marx and Engels's conception of the four aspects of history offers a clearer path out of the contradictions of capital and settler-state colonialism, that is, out of capitalism itself.

Bourgeois and Proletarian Revolutions and a Marxist Historiography

Marx and Engels's materialist method clearly departs from any form of mysticism as it is driven by a desire to critique narratives and construct analysis around what rigorous inquiry suggests are the most determining factors or contradictions driving society's historical development. According to Friedrich Engels (1885/1972), Marx's approach to history, as outlined above, was particularly innovative:

> It was precisely Marx who had first discovered the great law of motion in history, the law according to which all historical struggles, whether they proceed in the political, religious, philosophical, or some other ideological domain, are in fact only the more or less clear expression of struggles of social classes, and that the existence and thereby the collisions, too, between these classes are in turn conditioned by the degree of their development of their economic position, by the mode of their production and of their exchange determined by it. (p. 14)

For Engels (1891/1993) then, Marx had a "remarkable gift ... for grasping clearly the character, the import, and the necessary consequences of great historical events, at a time when these events are still in process before our eyes, or only have just taken place" (p. 9). This presents a steep challenge to our Marxist history of education, for it is no easy task to grasp the full significance of current developments in educational policy and practice, which are almost always steeped in racializations, national chauvinism, and all manner of bourgeois conceptions of intelligence and worth, as actually a clear historical manifestation and expression of the division and subsequent struggle between capital and labor. Demonstrating his skills as a historian and his theory of history in the preface to the second edition of *The Eighteenth Brumaire of Louis Bonaparte*, Marx (1852/1972) provides a succinct summary of three different approaches to the history of the 1851 coup d'état. However, our interest in this chapter is less with the content of the coup and more of what Marx contributed to, by providing an example and thus expanding on the materialist premises of history outlined above. Our Marxist approach to historiography, therefore, has much to gain through Marx's analysis:

> Victor Hugo continues himself to bitter and witty invective against the responsible publisher of the *coup d'état*. The event itself appears in his work like a bolt from the blue. He sees in it only the violent act of a single individual. He does not notice that he makes this individual great instead of little by ascribing to him a personal power of initiative such as would be without parallel in world history. Proudhon, for his part, seeks to represent the *coup d'état* as the result of an antecedent historical development. Unnoticeably, however, his historical construction of the *coup d'état* becomes an apologia for its hero. Thus he falls into the error of our so-called objective historians. I, on the contrary, demonstrate how the *class struggle* in France created circumstances and relationships that made it possible for a grotesque mediocrity to play a hero's part. (p. 8)

What stands out here is Marx's reference to various versions of a historical event as constructions, which highlights his deep understanding of the implications of the division between mental labor and manual labor, or when consciousness is separated from the life activity it is supposed to reflect. Alienated consciousness, and bourgeois consciousness in particular, is therefore free to invent all manner of stories or histories to hide or distort the class antagonism and the class struggle. This is key to Marx's method. That is, Marx's approach to constructing historical narratives always takes as its place of departure a critical engagement with existing narratives refracted through the light of empirical evidence and systematic reasoning. In other words, Marx was well aware that worldviews, and especially the products of industrial philosophers, are themselves products of history serving various purposes, from justifying and perpetuating a particular practice, relationship, or society to ushering in a new one.

The challenge for the Marxist history of education, in confronting the world as it actually is, requires the ability to detect the inaccuracies and distortions that characterize bourgeois historical constructions. Without these insights the material reality of education will not be grasped, and any attempt to put the history of education to the service of a communist alternative and challenging settler-state colonialism will be nearly impossible. Making a similar point in a relatively famous passage, Marx observes:

> Men make their own history, but they do not make it just as they please; they do not make it under circumstances chosen by themselves, but under circumstances directly encountered, given and transmitted from the past. The tradition of all the dead generations weighs like a nightmare on the brain of the living. (p. 15)

Similarly, we do not make the history of education just as we please, but we construct it based on our knowledge of the world in which we confront the world as it is. Understanding this world that we are a part of, therefore, requires a thorough analysis of the traditions of all dead generations that developed into the here-and-now. This is the task of history, and the stakes could not be higher. That is, knowledge about the past shapes our conceptions about the nature of the present and possibilities for the future. Constructing such Marxist-informed narratives of the history of education in the United States continues to be an unfinished project. For Marx, the task of knowledge production is not done simply for the sake of doing it; it is part of a larger push toward removing all of the barriers that prevent the world's working classes (including teachers) from becoming (see Malott & Ford).

Contributing to a Marxist historiography of becoming (i.e., becoming communist) is Marx's (1852/1972) conception of bourgeois and proletarian revolutions. That is, if we understand education as never neutral but always political or always either serving the interests of the world system as it exists or challenging it, then education either serves the bourgeois revolution and system or it works for proletarian revolution and communism. In other words, if we view education as either revolutionary or counterrevolutionary, then Marx's discussion of bourgeois versus proletarian revolutions is highly important to our Marxist historiography for the history of education. Consider: while revolutions in general tended to "conjure up the spirits of the past to their service and borrow from them their names, battle cries, and costumes in order to present the new scene of world history in this time-honored disguise and this borrowed language," bourgeois revolutions in particular "awakened the dead" in order to "glorify the new struggles" not to once again find "the spirit of revolution" or of "making its ghost walk again" (pp. 15–17).

In other words, Marx argues that bourgeois revolutions "required recollec-
tions of past world history in order to drug themselves concerning their own
content" (p. 18). That is, the content of bourgeois revolutions (and the content of bourgeois constructions of the history of education) that Marx so often
refers to is the promise of freedom and equality, which he argues, because of
the creation of a working class of dependents it requires, can only ever be an
empty promise. As a result, bourgeois revolutions do not deliver societies new
content for themselves, but rather "the state" returns it "to its oldest form ...
shamelessly simple domination ... easy come, easy go" (pp. 18–19).

> Bourgeois revolutions ... storm swiftly from success to success; their dramatic effects
> outdo each other; men and things seem set in sparkling brilliants; ecstasy is the every-
> day spirit; but they are short lived; soon they have attained their zenith, and a long
> crapulent depression lays hold of society before it learns soberly to assimilate the
> results of its storm-and-stress period. (p. 19)

Bourgeois or traditional conceptions of the history of education serve this
same master, full of the same delusions of benevolence and hostility toward
the inconvenient facts of class antagonism and class struggle. Offering a help-
ful yardstick in which to judge the precision and effectiveness of our revolutionary Marxist historiography of becoming for the history of education
Marx's conception of proletarian revolutions is indispensable:

> Proletarian revolutions, like those of the nineteenth century, criticize themselves
> constantly, interrupt themselves continually in their own course, come back to the
> apparently accomplished in order to begin afresh, deride with unmerciful thorough-
> ness the inadequacies, weaknesses and paltriness of their first attempts, seem to throw
> down their adversary only in order that he may draw new strength from the earth
> and rise again, more gigantic, before them, recoil ever and anon from the indefinite
> prodigiousness of their own aims, until a situation has been created which makes all
> turning back impossible. (p. 19)

Paulo Freire's *Pedagogy of the Oppressed*, unlike many of his later works, is
informed by this rigorous, never-ending cycle of reflection and action tire-
lessly committed to and driven by the urgency of the global, proletarian
class camp to succeed in capturing the capitalist state and abolishing surplus labor time (i.e., exploitation), the foundation of capital's economic
existence. Internal, comradely critique (including self-critique) of Marxist
educational theory and historiography is therefore similarly informed by
the desire to improve not only our understanding but also our ability to

practice an effective Marxist historiography of becoming communist. In other words, a Marxist history of education is equally committed to an analysis of the present moment as history in the making always committed to pushing the capitalist now into a socialist future through the organization of the party.

However, rather than building upon Marx, as we have sought to do thus far, with the postmodern turn away from Marxism in critical education theory in the 1980s, the Marxist history of education work of Bowles and Gintis and Michael Katz (1975, 1987) has largely stagnated and even faded from the offerings of big publishing corporations that supply the country's foundations of education classes with textbooks. There are, however, noteworthy exceptions, such as Peter McLaren's (2007) Marxist foundations of education book, *Life in Schools*. However, *Life in Schools* is not specifically a history of education book. It is more of an introduction to critical pedagogy. If this chapter can contribute, in any way, to bringing Marx back to the history of education, then it will have been a worthwhile effort.

While we have countless brilliant colleagues around the world, and in the U.S. in particular, doing important critical pedagogy work in colleges and universities, it is probably not too far-fetched to assume that the history of education classes that have managed to survive in this hostile environment are being taught from increasingly uncritical perspectives that turn a blind eye to the massive devastation being wrought by global capitalism, especially on Black lives, in which Black Lives Matter, as a resistance movement, is arguably at the frontlines. Part of the problem, as suggested above, is that current mainstream history of education books do not do an even mildly satisfactory job of demonstrating how *the traditions of the past weigh like a nightmare on the brain of the living*, to paraphrase Marx.

However, we do not want to suggest that there are no Marxist scholars advancing this history of education work. Peter McLaren's vast body of works as well as John Bellamy Foster's (2012) "Education and the Structural Crisis of Capitals" are good examples that have advanced Bowles and Gintis's Marxist approach to the history of education. However important and insightful this work is, it is not to be found in today's history of education textbooks. This chapter is an attempt to contribute to the vast body of recent Marxist education work (see, for a very small sample: Allman, 1999; Darder, 2009; Ford, 2014; Hill, 2013; Kumar, 2012; Malott, 2012; Malott & Ford, 2015; McLaren, 2005; McLaren & Farahmandpur, 2001; McLaren & Jaramillo, 2007, 2010), which is a vital foundation for this ongoing project.

However, it is worth noting that this discussion on a few of the primary approaches to teaching history should begin to shed light on why there are competing approaches to teaching history and therefore competing historical narratives. History, we might say, is not a fixed set of facts but rather is an ongoing debate. But historical narratives are not merely neutral constructions informed by a multitude of positionalities representing the fractured, fragmented postmodern condition. Histories are either bourgeois and counterrevolutionary and, therefore, designed to serve the interests of a dominant ruling class, or they are revolutionary and, thus, strive to be part of the global class war and proletarian movement against global capitalism and settler-state colonialism.

A Revolution in the History of Education

Beginning in the 1960s the history of education, as a discipline, began to be fundamentally challenged, especially in terms of debating the historic role that social class has or has not played in educational outcomes, policies, and purposes. In *Reconstructing American Education*, Michael Katz offers a significant contribution to this history of the history of education. Reflecting on the transformation that began to challenge traditional approaches to the history of education, Katz (1987) notes:

> Starting in the 1960s, a modest revolution took place in historical writing about education. Historians rejected both the metaphor and the method that had characterized most reconstructions of the educational past. The method had divorced inquiry into the development of educational practices and institutions from the mainstream of historical scholarship and left it narrow, antiquated, and uninteresting. The metaphor had portrayed education as a flower of democracy planted in a rich loam that its seeds replenished. (p. 5)

Here Katz, employing the methods of historiography, echoes Marx and Engels's insistence on empirical accuracy and sensitivity to the politics and processes of the construction of historical narratives. Working to reunite cutting-edge developments in history with narratives on the history of education, the result was a much more critical assessment of the origins and purposes of public education. However, despite this advancement, many important developments in history proper continued to remain absent from the work of the radical revisionists referred to by Katz (1987). For example, much of the historical work pertaining to the colonization of the Americas, the genocide and ongoing subjugation of Native Americans, as well as the work documenting the African holocaust of the trans-Atlantic slave trade and slavery, and the resistance to it, as well as the militant history of African American–led share-croppers' unions after the Civil War, are nowhere to be found in the work best known as the epitome of a Marxist history of education in the U.S., that is, Bowles and Gintis's *Schooling in Capitalist America*.

Bowles and Gintis's important advancement could have contributed significantly to the relevancy of a Marxist historiography through a critical engagement with a number of fundamental texts representing an African American and Native American renaissance in throwing off the colonialist narratives of bourgeois interests and building the disciplines of African American studies and Native American studies. At the very least George James's (1954/2005) groundbreaking book *Stolen Legacy*, exploring the intellectual and scientific knowledge European slavers and capitalist society, in general, benefited. The important work of Harry Haywood (2012), building upon Stalin's position of oppressed nations within nations, such as African Americans in the U.S., as an argument and strategy for fighting capitalism within the U.S. would have added tremendously to *Schooling in Capitalist America*. Even W. E. B. Du Bois's (2001) and Carter Woodson's (2013) texts, *The Education of Black People* and *The Mis-education of the Negro*, respectively, would have provided much needed historical insight for better understanding Bowles and Gintis's discussion of the education of America's Black working class.

In terms of better understanding the conquest of America and the ongoing oppression of American Indians, Vine Deloria Jr.'s (1969) classic text, *Custer Died for Your Sins: An Indian Manifesto*, signaled the beginning of the American Indian Movement and a vast body of work. Published seven years before *Schooling in Capitalist America*, Deloria's work would have been readily available to Bowles and Gintis as they wrote their classic text. While engaging in what is somewhat of a pointless exercise, the point here is that we can look back critically as current trends in educational Marxism tend not to fall victim of such errors that wrongfully open the door for counterrevolutionaries to argue that Marxism believes the working class is a group of privileged white workers. While the so-called first-world, white working class is undeniably the most privileged subgroup of the working class, they represent only a small fraction of the global working class. Nevertheless, before the work of Michael Katz (1975) and Bowles and Gintis, the class antagonisms that have propelled the quantitative changes in specific modes of production that, when having reached a certain point of development, give way to qualitative transformations leading to the transition from feudalism, to capitalism, to socialism, have tended not to be identified as an important tendency or dialectical law of historical change characteristic of the human societies in which histories of education are situated. However, despite this important shift, the revisionists, including Bowles and Gintis, while supporting socialism in the abstract, turned against actually existing socialism. For example, in their chapter explaining capitalism and thus critiquing capitalist countries such as the U.S., Bowles and Gintis make a point to also break from "state socialist countries" in "Eastern Europe" because they "were never democratic" due to the "ruling elites" maintaining a hierarchical system of control over "production" (p. 81). Bowles and Gintis, therefore, fail to lay bare the global class war and acknowledge their lack of solidarity with the proletarian global class camp, which, during the time of their writing, represented socialist countries and millions of people of color over the world (Malott & Ford). It is a tragedy that the global proletarian class camp representing the desires of so many millions of people of color from Africa to Latin America has been propagandized in the U.S. as a movement of the white working class.

Situated within this context, we might observe that the term *critical pedagogy* was created by Henry Giroux (1981) as an attempt to dismiss socialism and the legacy of Karl Marx, first appearing, I believe, in *Ideology, Culture, and the Process of Schooling*. Critical pedagogy, as a discipline within educational theory, therefore seemed to have been constructed as a conscious break from Marx, from Marxism, and from actually existing socialism. We might therefore argue that critical pedagogy has not become counterrevolutionary, it began as a conscious betrayal of the global proletarian class camp. This is not to say that actually existing socialist governments have not committed serious mistakes. Rather, to oppose socialist countries and to celebrate their demise is to join the capitalist class's attack on the world working class's struggle against exploitation and resistance against colonialism and imperialism. Giroux's (1983) widely influential text *Theory and Resistance in Education: A Pedagogy for the Opposition* continues to serve this purpose.

Giroux (1983) argues that after World War II, in both imperialist capitalist states and countries in the so-called socialist bloc, workers suffered the same forms of increasing alienation and the suppression of political and economic freedom due to repression and authoritarianism. Giroux, in line with imperialist propagandists, contributes to the exaggerations and generalizations of the mistakes and shortcomings of various communist countries while ignoring the social gains and achievements of the workers' states, from

Eastern Europe, North Korea, Burkina Faso, China, to Cuba. However, while Bowles and Gintis and the radical revisionists sought to employ Marx in their work, Giroux sought to not only contribute to the attack on real, existing socialism, he also sought to break from Marx all together. In other words, even though Bowles and Gintis took an incorrect stance against socialist countries, they supported the possibility of a more perfectly worked out socialist alternative not yet created.

Giroux (1983), on the other hand, makes a case against existing workers' states as part of his argument against Marx in general. Giroux's work has therefore contributed to the shift from the materialism of Marx, represented by Paulo Freire's *Pedagogy of the Oppressed*, to a turn back to ideology, culture, and knowledge production similar to the German philosophers critiqued by Marx and Engels in *The German Ideology*. While a full engagement in the history of critical pedagogy is beyond the scope of this chapter, we can reemphasize the depth of the anticommunist trends operating within imperialist states, especially in the U.S., and thus found in both critical pedagogy and historiography. In other words, the fact that even within Marxist scholarship and scholarship stemming from critical theory strong currents against the legacy of worker states can be found is telling.

Again, it is not to say that serious mistakes were not made under socialism. The point is to support the millions of brothers and sisters around the world fighting imperialism and capitalist exploitation through the creation of worker states, however imperfect and unfinished. The communist challenge and responsibility is to support forward communist progress rather than sitting back while worker states are overrun by capitalists, who themselves are governed by the laws of accumulation, that is, an insatiable appetite for surplus-value, whatever the human or environmental costs. The decline of the socialist states since the fall of the Soviet Union, therefore, represents a major setback for the process of overcoming imperialism and global capitalism. This is a position that is at odds with nearly the entire critical pedagogy movement. However, if we are to take Marx's description of the proletarian revolution seriously, then such biting self-critiques must be considered.

Nevertheless, the radical revisionists offered an important advancement from the traditional narrative. For example, in 1919, Ellwood Cubberley, Dean of the School of Education at Stanford University, in his book, *Public Education in the United States: A Study and Interpretation of American Educational History*, offers a seemingly safe, nothing-to-be-alarmed-by approach to history and the role of education in the history of human societies. Cubberley's narrative is devoid of the class antagonism and struggle a genuine engagement with the messy facts of history reveals. Rather, Cubberley paints an abstract picture of relative social harmony marching along the road of progress:

> The history of education is essentially a phase in the history of civilization. School organization and educational theory represent but a small part of the evolution, and must be considered after all as but an expression of the type of civilization which a people has gradually evolved. ... Its ups and downs have been those of civilization itself, and in consequence any history of education must be in part a history of the progress of the civilization of the people whose educational history is being traced. (p. 2)

Cubberley's narrative is predictable enough: good triumphs inevitably, and the evidence, of course, resides in the very existence of the U.S. and its public education system. The story would not be complete if Cubberley had not gone on, as he did, to triumphantly trace the roots of American society exclusively to European sources, arguing that it was Christianity that preserved the civilized culture of ancient Greece following the wreck of the Middle Ages, allowing the modern era to emerge. Rather casually Cubberley goes on to explain the "discovery and settlement of America" (p. 11) as a carryover effect of the sense of adventure engendered by the Crusades.

In the process, Cubberley offers no mention of the tumultuous, violent, and uneven transition from feudalism to capitalism or the diverse interactions with, and crimes against, the hundreds of distinct Native American civilizations that populated the Americas, many of whom continue to struggle to survive in what has been referred to as the *colonial present* (Grande, 2015). Cubberley's narrative is consequently wholly supportive of not only colonization but also capitalist production relations, suggesting (by not mentioning them) that bourgeois society is either timeless (i.e., as natural as gravity and thus one of the immutable laws of nature) or is one of the great accomplishments of antiquity preserved, somehow (luckily, it is suggested), by Christianity. As mentioned below by Marx (1857–1858/1973), this is an old ideological tactic used by many elite, ruling classes from era to era, that is, to suggest their time is timeless and thus inevitable and perpetual.

Challenging the rosy picture painted by traditional historians who argue it was the transition from a rural to an urban social context that led to the emergence of public education, Katz (1987) argues a more thorough engagement with the history literature, suggesting that the most important development in the United States during the late nineteenth century was the monumental

growth of capitalism, which was the real impetus for not only public education but also urbanization and mass immigration. As we will see below the
difficulty of capitalists establishing capitalism on the Eastern seaboard of what
came to be the United States was due to the overabundance of cheap land
made available by the unintentional genocide of Native Americans, a major
barrier to establishing the necessary dependence among producers on capitalists for jobs. This nuance is missed by Katz, which greatly impedes his analysis
of the emergence of capitalism in the U.S. Consequently, once capitalist production relations appear to be more permanently established, the educational
needs of capitalists begin to change. However, as we will further illustrate,
the radical revisionists challenged the traditional narrative that depicted the
growth of common schooling and public education as evidence of the flourishing of democracy and equal opportunity, arguing, instead, that the emergence of alienating and immiserating capitalist production relations and new
dehumanizing factory-based means of production led to worker unrest and
rebellions, leading industrialists to realize workers had to be socialized into
capitalist society as a form of social control. This long-held argument, while
important for understanding how to subvert capitalist schooling practices
and policies, misses an important nuance of the factory machine and how it
accelerated the intellectual degradation of individual workers, prompting the
British government in the mid-nineteenth century to pass a series of Factory
Acts requiring the education of child laborers in an attempt to save society
from capitalism (Malott & Ford, 2015). While this discussion is important
for understanding the depths of capitalism's tendency to degrade and mangle
the human laborer, industrialists, while resisting early attempts of mandated
education in England, were soon convinced of the need to control the ideas
and beliefs of their workers.

That is, the self-empowerment of those relegated to the status of *wage-
worker* needed to be eroded and replaced by a sense (i.e., a false consciousness) that the dependence of labor on the capitalist for a job is permanent,
inevitable, and beneficial to the working class. In other words, the production relations between workers and capitalists needed to be cemented in the
minds of workers as permanently fixed and, thus, normal and natural. Offering
another insight into the changing educational needs of an emerging capitalist
class, Bowles and Gintis point out that, ideologically, feudalism was informed
by a religious interpretation of the world where one's social rank or position
was not understood to be the product of a political history of conquests and
subjugations, or even the outcome of one's own intelligence and drive, but

preordained by God, rendering any challenges to the caste system or one's place within it as an attack on and, thus, a crime against God.

Bourgeois society, on the other hand, is based upon an ideology of freedom and equality, while actually practicing a historical process of inequality and dehumanization. Consequently, unlike in feudalism, in capitalist democracies (i.e., bourgeois society), there exists an obvious contradiction between discourse and practice that has created a need for a series of cultural/ideological/political institutions (such as schools, the state, religion, the public relations advertising firm, the media spectacle, etc.) whose purpose is to both train workers in the necessary skills for productive labor as well as to manufacture consent through ideological indoctrination. Following Bowles and Gintis, we can call this the purpose of education in capitalist society, which changes over time and from region to region, depending on capital's changing needs. The dominant ideology also changes as it is met with and challenged by, the collective agency of various strata of labor and noncapitalists, from unions, settler-state environmentalists, to Indigenous revolutionaries and sovereigns, to Black Lives Matter rebels.

However, these and many other developments (some of which are discussed below) were not greeted with open arms by the history of education establishment. Katz dedicates a substantial part of his book, *Reconstructing American Education*, to discussions on the severe backlash against what were new developments in American history and the history of American education. Katz concludes that because of the new critical scholarship, the old story lines could no longer be used. As a result, new narratives were constructed or developed by bourgeois historians who seemed to be dedicated to downplaying the significance of capitalism in the history of American education. Summarizing this tendency, Katz (1987) argues:

> Even critics of the new history of education admit that a simple narrative of the triumph of benevolence and democracy can no longer be offered seriously by any scholar even marginally aware of recent writing in the field. The problem for critics, therefore, has been twofold: the destruction of critical historians' credibility and the construction of an alternative and equally plausible interpretation of the educational past. ... At their worst, the new critics have descended to falsification, distortion, and ad hominem attacks as they have tried to build an apologist case for American education. ... One major intellectual goal has animated the work of the new critics since the 1970s: as much as possible, they want to loosen the connections between education and social class in America's past and present. (pp. 136–137)

Katz is documenting here the back and forth between scholars of the history of education and the role the critical revisionists played in transforming the field.

We might argue that the 1960s revolution in the history of education failed to adequately critique the narratives and assumptions surrounding the colonization of the Americas. If traditional history of education scholars failed to engage virtually all of the latest research in history, much of which came to rather revolutionary conclusions, the critical or Marxist revisionists seemed to have missed new developments in history pertaining to the colonial era, as suggested above. The following section is, therefore, crucial in bringing to the surface the significance of the colonial era in the establishment of global capitalism and creating the capitalist need for a common system of mass education around the 1840s.

The Colonial Era

The discovery of America was another development of the desire for travel and discovery awakened by the Crusades. ... After the first century of exploration of the new continent had passed, and after the claims as to ownership had been largely settled, colonization began.

—Cubberley (p. 11)

Cubberley's quote (and the history of education book it was taken from more generally) represents a combination of what Katz (1987) describes as a pre-twentieth-century approach that seeks "direct and superficial causes—such as an unmediated link between immoral behavior and poverty" and the approach of "the first social scientists in the 1890s" who "viewed the world as an immensely complex series of interconnecting variables mutually reacting to one another" (p. 140). Katz argues that interdependence "signals a retreat from any attempt to find a principle or core within a social system," consequently, "the levers of change remain obscure and no basis exists for moral judgment" (p. 140). Clearly, Cubberley's explanation for European expansion and colonial pursuits as the result of a thirst for adventure can be described as "superficial" and "lacking in moral judgment." Cubberley's larger discussion of the history of education is unapologetically Eurocentric. We can observe this legacy of procapitalist Eurocentric apology reproduced in history of education textbooks in the decades following Cubberley. Vassar's (1965) history of American education text offers an example:

The missionary organizations were far more successful in their endeavors among the Negroes than among the Indians. ... in this great crusade. ... developing honest hard working Christian slaves. ... A large population [of Native Americans were] not slaves [adding to the difficulty of educating Indians]. (pp. 11–12)

While Cubberley's Eurocentrism stems from his glaring omission of even the mention of a Native American presence, Vassar's narrative is equally Eurocentric for implying that the assimilation of Native Americans into mainstream America represents a "great crusade." That is, Vassar presents colonialism, a process that led to centuries of physical, biological, and cultural genocide, as a positive force. What Vassar does not explicitly state, but implies, is that bourgeois society represents a more advanced stage in human social development as compared to not just Europe's feudal societies but also pre-Columbian Native American societies as well. Unfortunately, as mentioned above, the racism and white supremacy of bourgeois historians were either not discussed by the radical revisionists or they themselves reproduced it:

> The Western frontier was the nineteenth-century land of opportunity. In open competition with nature, venturesome white adventurers found their own levels, unfettered by birth or creed. The frontier was a way out—out of poverty, out of dismal factories, out of crowded Eastern cities. The frontier was the Great Escape. (Bowles & Gintis, p. 3)

We present Cubberley and Vassar next to Bowles and Gintis to demonstrate both the difference and continuity between traditional, conservative education historians and Marxist education historians on the issue of colonialism and Westward expansion. As previously suggested, Bowles and Gintis's somewhat apologetic statement on the colonization of the Americas is not a position they borrowed from Marx, for Marx was well aware of the barbaric destructiveness the expansion of capital had on the noncapitalist and non-Western societies it expanded into.

What is most obvious here is Bowles and Gintis's empathy for the children and grandchildren of the expropriated peasant proprietors of Europe who were "chastised for their enforced transformation into vagabonds and paupers" (Marx, 1867/1967, p. 734). The acknowledgement of the destructive and oppressive nature of capitalism here represents a clear break from the corporate apologist narratives that have dominated before and since Bowles and Gintis. However, at the same time, there is a haunting silence within Bowles and Gintis's narrative that is seemingly more interested in the fate of immigrant laborers than the ancient tribes and confederacies that continue to struggle to survive within a colonial present that can too easily seem perpetual or permanent. This exclusionary tendency within the Marxist tradition, despite the contrary testimony of Marx's own work, has contributed to an unfortunate misunderstanding of the contributions of Marx.

Even progressive education historians in the 1980s and beyond continued to reproduce colonialist narratives. Button and Provenzo (1983/1989), for example, after explaining the colonization of the Americas as the result of a growing middle class gaining wealth from a period of "peace, prosperity and trade" (p. 6), portray Native Americans as the helpless, primitive victims of progress:

> The Native Americans ... belonged to hundreds of tribes with almost as many different languages. In general, they had little in common with one another and did not unite to resist the settlement of their lands by the early colonists. The existence of numerous rivers and harbors, of a moderate climate, and natives unorganized for resistance, made North America splendid for colonization, if not for immediate exploitation. (p. 6)

After offering a contradictory paragraph on the next page regarding Native American resistance in what is now Virginia, Button and Provenzo seem to offer this short passage as their explanation for the disappearance of Native Americans on the Eastern seaboard—an assumption that is patently false. Even more recent history of education texts written from progressive, constructivist perspectives too often reproduce the old colonial narratives:

> Native Americans ... were a diverse and occasionally contentious population, embracing hundreds of different social and cultural groupings. The vast majority lived in agricultural and hunting societies, cast on a scale considerably smaller than European nations, even if there were exceptions in certain tribal confederations. Although the American Indian population was substantial, it was spread thinly across the landscape. Divided into relatively small and isolated tribes and without advanced military technology, the Native Americans were often unable to resist the demands of Europeans in disputes over land or other issues. As a consequence, they were readily defeated, exploited, and pushed out of the way to make room for the expanding White population. (Rury, 2013, p. 27)

It is astonishing that a book published in 2013 called *Education and Social Change* would continue to depict American Indians or Native Americans as primitive victims helpless against the powerful onslaught of Europe's superiority. If the many interpretations of Marx's work all tend to embrace the ethics of international solidarity among the world's oppressed peoples, then why have Marxists, of all people, too often been silent on the long legacy of colonialism? The most plausible explanation for this silence has to do with Marx's early work that viewed colonialism as a positive force (Marx, 2007). If mainstream Marxism tends to be based on the Communist Manifesto, which is situated within the assumption that colonialism is a positive, civilizing force because it is a necessary step toward socialism, then this confusion can partly be explained by the complexity of Marx himself. That is, because of the enormity of Marx's body of work, and because he was perpetually and rigorously advancing his ideas and deepening his insights, his positions on various topics like colonialism changed over time.

Consequently, it is easy to understand how Marx's work can lead to many different versions of Marxism (Hudis, 2012). Much of Marx's late writings (a great deal are still unpublished), which have been largely discounted as the product of a liberal turn, boredom, or triviality (Anderson), contain explorations into gender equality within non-Western societies, for example, offering a substantial challenge to the homogenizing drive of the global expansion of capitalism through colonialism. In other words, it seems as if Marx began to conclude that the challenges of creating a postcapitalist global society are so enormous, all of humanity's gifts are needed, from our intellectual endowments to our vast cultural, linguistic, and ethnic diversity. However, even in Marx's best-known work, volume 1 of *Capital* (1867/1967), a clear understanding of the destructive role of colonialism's primitive accumulation is expressed:

> The discovery of gold and silver in America, the extirpation, enslavement and entombment in mines of the aboriginal population, the beginning of the conquest and looting of the East Indies, the turning of Africa into a warren for the commercial hunting of black-skins, signalized the rosy dawn of the era of capitalist production. These idyllic proceedings are the chief moments of primitive accumulation. (p. 751)

However, while mainstream textbooks tend to continue to reproduce dominant narratives ignoring such critical insights regarding the very early roots of capitalism as a global system, an early partial exception to the rule is Joel Spring's (1986/1994) *The American School*, which dedicated individual chapters to various ethnic groups, including Native Americans and African Americans. However, Spring's engagement with Indigenous communities begins in the mid-nineteenth century, skipping the entire colonial era, thereby leaving the legitimacy of the colonial expansion of capital's bourgeois society unaddressed. Outside of the history of education discipline there exists a vast body of critical pedagogy work that addresses, in various ways, the history of education as revolutionary pedagogy challenging all that is dehumanizing from the rule of capital, the colonial present, to the new Jim Crow and racism without race. Before we move on, it is worth noting that even David Boers's (2007) *History of American Education Primer*, published in a well-respected critical education series, begins his book with a familiar story:

> The evolution of American education has occurred since our nation was founded in the 1600s. Jonathon Winthrop and his band of followers sought to avoid religious persecution in England. They sailed to America and began to set up communities in the New England area that were meant to be models for what would eventually become American society. (p. 1)

It is bewildering that well-established history of education scholars would continue to reproduce the simplistic argument that it was religious persecution alone, existing in a vacuum, that accounts for the first permanent English settlements in America. Fortunately, there exist other history of education texts offering some diversity of narrative. For example, and to their credit, Wayne Urban and Jennings Wagoner (2009), in the fourth edition of their text, *American Education: A History*, reassess the old narrative reproduced by Boers, arguing instead that the colonies were not established with the intention of building a new society but, rather, were a business venture, that is, an investment opportunity. To understand the first New Englanders' relationship with pre-existing Indigenous confederacies, it is important to remember that the colonists faced the continent and its communities as religiously mediated investors who came from a pre-existing English capitalist society that had long been primitively accumulated and normalized and naturalized traditions of private property and a market in human labor.

Established in 1607, in Jamestown, Virginia, the continent's first permanent English settlement relied on a friendly relationship with the local Powhatan Confederacy for their own survival and for the success of their investment. However, the capitalist purpose of the colony, and thus its very existence, presented a major barrier to peace. At the same time, renowned American Indian historian Robert Venables (2004) makes a compelling case that, before dissolving, the relationship between the colony and the Powhatan Confederacy was mutually beneficial.

> The London Company's investment in the highly profitable tobacco plantation business relied on peaceful relations with the local Powhatan Confederacy. Tobacco farmers supplied Powhatans with trade goods in exchange for food, which allowed colonists to invest their labor in the cash crop not worrying much about food. Powhatans' access to trade goods allowed them to grow stronger and defeat their rivals to the west thereby gaining access to trade with the copper-producing Indians of the Great Lakes. (p. 81)

Clearly, Venables does not see the Powhatan as helpless victims but as savvy negotiators committed to their own national interests. However, because of the labor-intensive nature of tobacco production and because of its profitability as a use-value, by 1619 a Dutch ship brought the first shipment of African slave laborers to Virginia to keep pace with the demand for labor. Because of these reasons, it also made more sense to focus labor on tobacco production and continue to rely on the Powhatan for food. Consequently, fifteen years after their arrival, the colonists continued to rely on the Native communities for food, which might not have been a problem, but their numbers were forever growing, therefore, placing increasing pressure on the Powhatans' food supply.

The colonists also came to the Americas with an old racist ideology stemming from an invented, Christian-related, European identity (Mohawk, 1992), which resulted in a long legacy of colonists viewing and treating Native Americans as inferiors. Consequently, it was not uncommon for colonists to disregard Powhatan national authority and settle land without compensation or consultation, leading to tension and conflict with Native communities. Perhaps one of the last straws was the colonialists' plans to establish an Indian college, in which American Indians saw for themselves no advantages. It was understood that adopting the settlers' capitalistic ways would give the elites among the new settlers a major advantage by stripping the Powhatan of their own economy and means to satisfy and expand their needs. If the foreign capitalist were to become the ruler of the land, then the American Indians would forever be subordinate in the relationship. Eventually, having their land base, food supply, culture, and very existence threatened, the Powhatan decided to terminate the colony. Commenting on this decision, Venables explains:

> In 1622 Powhatan warriors, intimately familiar with colonists' routines from being their primary food vendor, simultaneously struck 31 locations across a 70 mile area killing nearly 350 of a population of 1200. (pp. 81–82)

In the aftermath, hundreds of settlers sailed back to England. Cut off from their food supply, as many as five hundred more colonists died of starvation that winter. As a result, James I took over the London Company's investment. That is, having been operated as a private venture for the first seventeen years, Virginia "became a royal colony in 1624 and control transferred to the Crown appointed governor" (Urban & Wagoner, p. 18). While this was an important development, following Venables and other historians, the ten years of bloody war that followed and the ways Indian policy were forever transformed (from co-existence to extermination) have had far more serious implications for the fate of the Indigenous communities in North America (and the world over). According to Venables, "The 1622 attack did more than merely define future Indian policy in Virginia as one of conquest. … It encouraged an already existent English colonial attitude of racial superiority" (p. 84). For example, after learning of the Powhatan war, the Pilgrims in Massachusetts erected a fort, fearing the Narragansets. However, the struggle for the Eastern Seaboard was ultimately determined in 1633–1634 as smallpox wiped out Indians in a massive epidemic. Puritans, as might be expected, viewed this unintentional genocide as an act of God. Governor Winthrop stated:

> If God were not pleased with our inheriting these parts, why did he drive out the natives before us? And why does he still make room for us by diminishing them as we increase? (Venables, p. 89)

Following conquest and the finalization of the process of westward expansion, settler-state policy toward Indigenous communities has consistently eroded Indigenous independence and sovereignty, characterized by paternalism, indifference, and exploitative abuse. The boarding school era is a case in point. As is demonstrated throughout this section, the failure to critically engage the legacy of colonialism and expansion within the history of education is a failure to fully grasp what Marx characterized as the global expansion of capitalism and bourgeois society.

The Common School Era

As Native Americans were being pushed west into Indian Territory and the process of physically expanding the social universe of capital across the continent was underway, the middle-class, Calvinist, Massachusetts education crusader of the mid-nineteenth century, Horace Mann, worked hard to establish a state system of common schooling for all children (which, during the mid-1800s, meant white children). Educational historians, from conservative traditionalists, to progressives, to Marxists, concede the importance of the first successful common school movement to the development of the United States. That is, because of the central importance regarding Horace Mann in colleges of education across the United States (he is the equivalent of the founding father of U.S. public education who realized the vision of Thomas Jefferson's failed proposals, at both the state and national level, for a General Diffusion of Education, penned with an eye toward greater participation, at least for white males), Katz's (1975) and Bowles and Gintis's challenge to how he had traditionally been conceptualized represents a paradigm shift in the field. However, as we will see below, these new critical narratives focused on bringing to the surface the importance of social class in explaining why common schools were ultimately supported by industrial capitalists, but do not situate the process of capitalistic expansion within the context of Native American subjugation and agency, which one would expect given their silence on the issue in general. Our intention here is to highlight the important contributions of the critical education historians while simultaneously contributing to the discussion. Summarizing the dominant view of Horace Mann in their book *History of Education and Culture in America*, Button and Provenzo offer the following analysis:

> Historians have tended to look upon the Common School Movement in wholly positive terms. The traditional wisdom has been that by providing free universal elementary education, the common schools were important vehicles of social reform that provided opportunities for newly arrived immigrants and the poor to improve the conditions of their lives and those of their children. Led by idealistic and humanitarian intellectuals, an enlightened working class was able to overcome the narrow interests of not only the wealthy elite, but also the conservative religious groups. (pp. 93–94)

This traditional narrative that replaces class struggle with educational attainment as the true path to economic advancement is more or less today's rallying cry of progressive educators fighting for public education and its necessary funding. For Mann, however, as Secretary of Education of Massachusetts with a background in law, prosperity came not from education but stemmed from the rapid expansion and development of capitalism. The role of education was to provide workers and immigrants with the proper moral foundation (Cremin, 1957). Mann believed that if that the children of workers and capitalists alike attended the same schools, workers would develop a life-long loyalty for the bosses and industry. This was the basis for Mann's so-called moral education. Mann's reports and speeches were, therefore, filled with vague relationships between intelligence and poverty. For his moral curriculum, Mann held all the pedagogical sophistication of his day, conscious that a student-centered pedagogy was fundamental to the common schools' success because a child will not really learn and internalize the lessons unless he is engaged and genuinely committed to the learning experience.

As was the case with the transition from feudalism to capitalism, bourgeois society is being portrayed here as the embodiment of freedom of opportunity and, thus, equality. Marx argues that the mistake social reformers make is believing that the freedom and equality promised by bourgeois society is actually possible within the production relations of capital. Mann demonstrated no real understanding of capitalism and the way its internal drive to limitlessly expand value will always lead to the premature exhaustion and death of the laborer unless regulated by policy or slowed down by working-class resistance. But the whole legacy of education reform, especially since the Great Depression of 1929, including the Civil Rights Movement that made equal educational opportunity one of its central rallying cries, is based on the cruel illusion that enough social justice can be obtained within capitalism, thereby inadvertently working as a counterrevolutionary force against the full emancipation of the global proletarian class camp.

At the same time, popular movements, such as the Civil Rights Movement of the 1950s in the United States that led to the social movement era of the 1960s and 1970s, represent the developing sophistication of the theory and practice of a movement with very deep roots. Today this legacy can be witnessed in the riots in Ferguson, Missouri, sparked by the police murder of Michael Brown to the outright uprising in Baltimore, Maryland, as a response to the police murder of Freddie Gray, which, like in Ferguson and elsewhere, just happened to be the tipping point in a city whose African American communities have been suffering under more than forty years of savage poverty, and the centuries-old racist scapegoating and violence of a crisis-ridden capitalist system.

The Marxist history of education we have constructed views the global proletarian class camp, including labor movements, the colonial resistances of Indigenous nations, the Civil Rights Movement that developed into a more militant and revolutionary Black Panther Party for Self Defense, the teacher and professor movement against high-stakes testing, privatization, and school closures, among others, as past and present influences—even if none of our influences is without at least some critique. What all of these movements teach us is that material conditions and the dominant discourses that justify and mystify them should never be accepted or internalized passively. These conditions and discourses need to be critically analyzed. The traditional narrative regarding the emergence of common schools, for example, falsely portrays their emergence as stemming from the needs and desires of the American people, rather than a system that seems to have been imposed on labor to serve the needs and interests of capital, as argued throughout this chapter.

Offering an example of the traditional narrative of the common school era Cubberley argues that its emergence in the 1840s, beginning in New England, represents a move toward secularization, which was a response to the country's "shifting needs" from "religious" to "industrial and civic and national needs" (p. 172). For Cubberley, then, common schooling was not a response to the changing needs of the elite but rather reflected the needs and desires of the majority of the population. In the dominant discourse the people are never described as the working class and therefore not directly connected to the capitalist class in a production relation, whose productive capacity, beyond what is socially necessary for survival, is appropriated by the capitalist for the self-expansion of capital. Horace Mann, in fact, viewed this kind of class analysis that connects the wealth of the capitalist to the unpaid labor hours of workers as dangerous, and the product of uncivilized revolutionizers who do not possess the proper moral, religious foundation.

This process, whose internal drive is for perpetually expanding surplus-value and therefore tends toward the immiseration of labor, is fundamentally alienating (i.e., separating the individual from her or his very humanity), which led Bowles and Gintis to conclude that industrialists came to understand that to prevent working-class resistance, workers require ideological management. Horace Mann was fearful of the power of organized labor (remember, labor had a long history of having the ability to demand high wages because of the availability of cheap land). Mann, therefore, believed that society's salvation rested on taming the laboring masses to ensure they do not destroy God's society through strikes and other labor actions Mann considered to be crimes (Cremin). Through his work crusading for common schooling, Mann developed a series of additional arguments for why common schooling should be supported, which he seemed to employ depending upon who his audience was.

For industrial capitalists, Mann had two primary lines of reasoning. First, an educated worker, it was argued, is more passive and controllable because he will have grown up with the children of the bosses and have been more successfully indoctrinated with the idea that capitalism is inevitable and the capitalists are wise and just and thus the saviors of the peasants of feudalism, and the peoples of every other primitive society (i.e., the world). More fully expanding on this logic, Bowles and Gintis offer an important analysis noting:

> Inequality was increasingly difficult to justify and was less readily accepted. The simple legitimizing ideologies of the earlier periods—the divine origin of social rank, for example—had fallen under the capitalist attack on royalty, and the traditional landed interests. The broadening of the electorate and of political participation generally—first sought by the propertied and commercial classes in their struggle

against the British Crown—threatened soon to become a powerful instrument in the hands of the farmers and workers. ... The process of capitalist accumulation drastically changed the structure of society: The role of the family in production was greatly reduced; its role in reproduction was increasingly out of touch with economic reality. A permanent proletariat and an impoverished and, for the most part, ethnically distinct, reserve army of unemployed had been created. ... With increasing urgency, economic leaders sought a mechanism to insure political stability and the continued profitability of their enterprises. (p. 159)

Clearly, Bowles and Gintis offer a sophisticated framework for understanding the emergence of common schooling. After all, the transition from feudalism and the old apprentice system that ties many individual families to specific types of labor activity to capitalism and the rapid spread of a generalized market in labor was not just an economic transformation but also impacted the entire social universe, including the family structure, the legal system, the holdings of land, and so on. Given such monumental revolutionary changes, it is not surprising that the conscious molding of the public mind through education would come to play such a central role in these processes.

The other argument Mann had for capitalists appealed to the religious background of most, if not all, of America's New England capitalists. That is, he talked a lot about capitalists as stewards of the earth, who should give back a little in the form of taxes to fund common schools, an act God would certainly smile upon. They would also secure a positive legacy for themselves among mortals. This argument tends to be the one reproduced in history of education books, conveniently forgetting to mention its connection to social control to subvert working-class resistance against the destructive process of the self-expansion of capital. For example, Gerald Gutek (1970), in his book *An Historical Introduction to American Education*, creates a narrative that matches Katz's (1987) description of the narratives created by traditional historians to counter the new research produced in the 1960s by critical education historians:

> In framing his appeal for a tax-supported system of common schools, Mann developed a theory of humane and responsible capitalism which greatly resembled the stewardship concept contained in the Protestant ethic. ... Mann saw the abuses in the ruthless capitalism of the nineteenth century, he believed in working with the system rather than against it. (p. 56)

Where Cubberley fails to mention the working class, the capitalist class, or even capitalism, Gutek recasts capitalism from an inherently oppressive social relation to a reformed and socially responsible harmonious utopia. Before the criticalists shifted the paradigm, education historians, such as Cubberley, were able to construct a purely ideological fantasy world characterized by vast omissions. For example, Cubberley identifies the movement for common schooling as a response to Americans' push for secularization but offers no evidence that Americans were becoming less religious. Cubberley attempts to argue that Mann's response to Americans' demand for secularization was a nondenominational form of common schooling. Since Bowles and Gintis, however, it has become clear that the push for nondenominational approaches to common schooling reflected a desire to attract all segments of U.S.-born and immigrant American workers to attend schools, because issues of social control and worker militancy were escalating, striking fear in the hearts of the industrial capitalist class. This, then, is the third argument Mann used, that is, his argument to convince workers to attend his schools, especially Irish Catholics who were naturally suspicious of Mann because of his Protestant, colonizing background. It is also apparent in the above excerpt that Bowles and Gintis, following Marx, hone in on the transition from feudalism to capitalism as an important period rendering the process of formal schooling increasingly important. Speaking more directly to this issue Bowles and Gintis argue:

> In the United States, unlike Europe, market and property institutions were developed and strengthened quite rapidly. For preindustrial America already possessed essential elements of a capitalist class structure. United States capitalism sprang from a colonial social structure closely tailored to the needs of British mercantile society. Whereas, in Europe, the transformation of property relations in land from a system of traditional serfdom and feudal obligation to the capitalist form of private ownership required half a millennium of conflict and piecemeal change, in the United States, private property was firmly established from the outset. Only in seventeenth-century New England did land-use patterns approximate communal property relations of an earlier European era. In areas held by Native Americans, communal property relations also predominated. … However, the emergence of a developed market in labor, perhaps the most critical aspect of capitalist growth, involved at least two centuries of protracted and often bitter struggle. (p. 58)

It is interesting that Bowles and Gintis do not make the connection between establishing a market in labor and the interrelated, yet separated, processes of the westward expansion of the primitive accumulation of Native American land, and then the process of blocking the working class's direct access to its natural material wealth to which human labor is added in hopes of increasing its use-value. The difficulty of this process, as discussed by Marx above, contributed to both the growth of the trans-Atlantic slave trade and the elite insight that labor will not voluntarily appropriate themselves from the earth and their own humanity. In light of these comments, we can conclude that education, as well as laws and practices such as artificially inflating the price of land to prevent working-class access, assisted in the establishment of a stable market in labor.

Conclusion

The current task of a Marxist historiography in the history of education is to uncover the ways today's U.S. education policies and those around the world are an expression of the capitalist class's perpetual war waged on the working class and colonized peoples. This Marxist history of education must advance the rigorous and militant proletarian model of revolution identified by Marx (1852/1972). In other words, a Marxist historiography must be based on Marx and Engels's premises of history with an eye toward subverting the process of capital's self-expansion for communist and sovereign alternatives (i.e., a pedagogy of becoming). This means to cease to exist as alienated labor and to cease to exist as colonized subjects. This might simultaneously mean recovering what has been lost and creating something that never has been.

· 3 ·

THE CROSSING OF CLASS LINES

Confronting Critical Pedagogy in Defense of Communism

In this chapter I pose an in-depth challenge to the anticommunism trend that has dominated critical pedagogy since its emergence in 1980. This anticommunism, from a noncapitalist perspective, represents nothing less than the crossing of class lines. After outlining the major premises this chapter is grounded, I remind critical pedagogues of some of the responses to anticommunist propaganda. I then provide a brief history of the Soviet Union, the People's Republic of China, and the Democratic People's Republic of Korea, offering concrete responses to the anticommunism of bourgeois society that has infected those of us on the educational Left, especially in North America. I then offer a discussion of the Black Panther Party as another example of the communist legacy in the United States and how this legacy has been systematically under attack. The chapter concludes with a brief summary of some of the core principles of the Party for Socialism and Liberation (PSL) as an example of a contemporary U.S.-based Marxist-Leninist Communist Party that is firmly grounded in a commitment against the crossing of class lines.

Premises

The first premise of this chapter is that the struggle for global communism must take as one of its primary commitments the sovereignty of all oppressed nations, including America's First Nations. Following Coulthard (2014), this struggle for sovereignty must transcend current liberal, bourgeois conceptions of mutual recognition that occlude the position of refusal—the refusal to accept settler-state hegemony/the perpetual existence of the colonial present and the redundancy of Indigeneity—embedded within the historical Indigenous demands for recognition.

Following the first premise, the second premise of this chapter is that the agent of communist revolution is not a fixed, homogenous subject position representing a predetermined type of labor, but is the embodiment of the ongoing process of proletarianization that is a consequence of the perpetual movement and expansion of capitalist accumulation (Dean, 2012).

Again, Coulthard argues that since Native American nations, through an ongoing process of primitive accumulation, have been dispossessed of their territories, that is, of their lands, which is the basis of the means of production, most Native Americans, like all other noncapitalists, must sell their capacity to labor for a wage to survive. In this capacity, Native American workers face the same enemy as white, Black, and all other workers. However, where the non-Native worker in the settler-state only has their own settler-state from which to build communism, the Native American has their own Indigenous national territory to recover. The potential conflict over land here (i.e., between settler-state communists and Indigenous nations) can only be resolved through the elimination of the common capitalist class enemy, and the necessary insurances and time to remove, through education, white chauvinism and all manner of bigotry and structurally determined inequalities between the more privileged average white worker and the average Black, Latino, Asian, Arab, and Native American worker in the U.S. and beyond. As a result of the all-encompassing domination of capital, Coulthard recognizes that Marx's labor theory of value is relevant for all workers, including Native Americans. This is a major advance from Churchill's (1983) position that Marxism is a foreign construct and thus out of place in any capacity in Native North America, which is explained in part, by Coulthard's deeper engagement with Marx's (1867/1967) first volume of *Capital*.

The third premise is that there is an unmistakable division between the capitalist class and the working class that is fundamentally inherent within the internal logic of capital itself. This division cannot be reformed out of existence; it can only be maintained or transformed through militant collective action into qualitatively different relations of production. The framework offered by Lenin (1917/2015) in *The State and Revolution* is invaluable here and, therefore, the basis of communist parties that follow the global class war analysis, such as the PSL.

The fourth premise is that while there is a sharp line of division between labor and capital, there are important differences between white workers, Black workers, and American Indian workers that serve key functions in perpetuating the existence of bourgeois society and maintaining a very high rate of exploitation, thereby suppressing the generally higher wages of the more privileged white workers. Smashing the bourgeois state and defeating the capitalist counterrevolutionaries, therefore, require a direct frontal assault on existing inequalities within the working class.

The question this chapter (following chapter 1) picks up is from Churchill: how do the rest of us defeat our common enemy without the most privileged of us subverting the sovereignty and self-determination of the least privileged of us? Following Lenin, the communist horizon does not nullify the sovereignty of Indigenous and other oppressed nations but, rather, is grounded within their already existing potential to be without the interference of an external coercive force that has to exploit laborers to exist as such. The Marxism informing this text is therefore a Marxism informed by Marx's later developments where he looked to Native American Nations for what they might offer as an alternative to capitalism. This approach is crucial because it rejects the Eurocentrism that falsely assumes that non-European nations must pass through a universal, although specifically European, capitalist phase in order to reach the most advanced stage of communism. Marx's ethnographic notebooks, as noted in the previous chapter, point to the tip of an evidence iceberg that some non-European nations may have worked out certain social problems long before the Europeans (Malott, 2008).

While it has once again become popular to endow labor with a magical productive force, suggesting that value can be accumulated by exploiting the social substance of labor removing all material barriers to the circuit of the self-expansion of capital, the following analysis is based on the position that what has changed is not the material basis of value but, rather, the composition of capital. Even if the material element is reduced to a small amount, it cannot be eliminated completely. This is important for a communist pedagogy as it refuses to forget that humans cannot be reduced to an immaterial social substance because humans are natural beings whose life needs exist external to it within the system of nature. Even if value can be accumulated through virtual avenues, there remains, for example, a material basis within the production and maintenance of computers, servers, and electric grids based upon the extreme exploitation of human labor power and the natural environment.

Challenging Anticommunism

Jodi Dean, in *The Communist Horizon*, offers an important insight to further our understanding of the idea of communism, not as a lost dream but as capitalism's theoretical opposite and, thus, as its ever-present ontological potentiality. As the movement of the acorn is driven by its potential to negate itself by becoming an oak tree so too is capitalism driven by its simultaneously self-expansive and self-destructive and, thus, contradictory nature. That is, as capital is driven by the limitless quest for compounding growth, and maximizing the rate of return, the social substance of capital's expansion, human labor power, leads capital to forever seek new ways to increase the rate of exploitation of this commodity, and because it is the actual laborer who embodies this commodity, the drive of capital is to forever exploit the laborer. Without some rate of exploitation, there can be no new capital produced for the capitalist. That is, the value created by the laborer through the labor act must be higher than the amount of money laid out by the capitalist in wages.

The money relation here conceals the newly created value, causing the exchange between labor and capital to appear to be fair since every hour of work appears to be paid. The fact that the laborer sells his ability to labor voluntarily also conceals the fact that the laborer sells his labor because he has no choice since he has no direct, collective access to the means of production, that is, to a land base large enough to support civilization. Again, capitalism's many contradictions, such as the fact that it produces the appearance of freedom but is actually dependent on enslavement, compels, but does not determine or guarantee, that it will develop into its sovereign, self-determined, communist opposite. Regardless of the historical path it follows, capitalism nevertheless embodies its own communist opposite realized through a concrete, material process of self-negation (Malott & Ford, 2015). By self-negation I am referring to the negation of the self that is limited by the restrictions of national oppression, settler-state colonialism and imperialism, and the labor-capital relationship. The negation of a colonized self is therefore the affirmation of self-determination. What is suppressed is not the culture and sovereignty of traditional peoples viewed as a barrier to progress, but the right to profit off of the labor of others and the right of individuals to own the means of production. Again, Lenin's theory of the state is crucial here because capitalism cannot be overcome without a highly disciplined organizational structure informed by a correct analysis of global events and the challenges ahead.

Communism is the result of the manifestation of a collective desire to negate capital through the negation of the self as alienated, exploited, or otherwise repressed labor, thereby ending its negative relationship with personified capital. Communism, in other words, because it already exists within the global logics of capitalism as an unrealized potential, cannot emerge separate from the system of nature that already exists, and therefore it must emerge as a result of transforming the capitalist relations of production into socialist ones through the Party-form. Because capitalism is an all-encompassing, integrated global system, all peoples and nations will be impacted by the transformation of capitalist production, focused on exchange-value, into communist relations focused on the useful effect of meeting the self-determined, sovereign needs of all oppressed nations, and of all of those who rely on a wage to survive. Following Haywood (1958) here, the potential and actual central gravitational force of revolution resides within the most oppressed and exploited segments of the globe. The explosive uprisings that have gone through waves of emergence in African American communities and Native American Nations speak to this insight in the context of the U.S.

The communist desire is for the world's system of nature to be governed under the logic of need and ability rather than limitless exchange-value. It is a desire for all Indigenous nations to be afforded the ability to rebuild the elements of nationhood, such as economy, land, and the self-determination of the political apparatus. Humans must be in a position to collectively engage the system of nature according to their own notions of need and ability. The history of workers' states below offers a concrete perspective on what this collective access has looked like (and does looks like) in practice. Because this vision is grounded in the concrete world, the potential it embodies is similarly concrete and not fantastic or utopian.

Dean argues that since the fall of the Soviet Union and the Socialist Bloc, much of the Left, until recently, has made the mistake of turning away from communism and its seemingly paradoxical open concreteness. Rather than advancing an anticapitalist politics that points toward the communist horizon and the sharp division it suggests, a common trend in the Left is focused on the notion of postcapitalism because it is contended that communism suggests a homogeneous, predetermined monolithic structure that assumes a violent relation with the vast diversity and difference of the rest of us. Postcapitalist practice privileges the role of discourse and ideology in social reproduction. Dean, however, argues that poverty, suffering, and immiseration continue to serve as powerful levers of mobilization around the world.

Another problematic trend in the Left's contemporary position is the tendency to take democracy as its object of desire. For Dean, this is troubling since democracy already exists in bourgeois society and has not been able to protect the interests of the poor and oppressed. Unlike in slave and feudal societies where democracy does not exist, advocating for more participation in a society based upon participation makes little sense. Fighting for more of what already exists does not represent a revolutionary position and, thus, does not offer a way out of the cycle of unfulfilled desire. In this respect Dean suggests that much of today's Left is actually driven by a liberal impulse that finds common ground with conservatives and capitalists in that communism is treated as a lost horizon that history has proven will inevitably lead to violent authoritarianism. As argued in the introduction, Lenin (1917/2015) reminds socialists that a blanket decontextualized, ahistorical rejection of authoritarianism amounts to a self-imposed disarmament at the exact moment when capital's armed counterrevolution is at its most savage.

One of the more striking aspects of today's global context, for Dean, is the effect of communism's absence, as opposed to its presence. Commenting on what this absence has done to Left intellectuals in the U.S., Michael Parenti (2001) argues that they are "busy fighting the ghost of Stalin, dwelling on the tabloid reports of the 'horrors' of communism, doing fearless battle against imaginary hordes of 'doctrinaire' Marxists at home and abroad, or in some other way flashing their anti-Communist credentials and shoring up their credibility" (p. 158). Similarly, the history of what is known as critical pedagogy began in the 1980s as a conscious break from Marxist educational theory and capitalism's communist horizon, whose exact shape and logics will depend on the agency and level of class consciousness of those workers and oppressed who carry its flag forward, and expand its existence deep into the system of nature in which humanity's sustenance is irreducibly connected.

Critical pedagogy's North American founders established their credibility in the anti-Soviet fashion described by Parenti (2001). For example, Stanley Aronowitz (1989), an early collaborator with Henry Giroux, made his case against communism and for critical pedagogy's focus on what he considered to be the best aspects of American democracy, stating, "The Soviet Union is far from an egalitarian society; privilege and nepotism are rampant" (p. 23). Some years later Donaldo Macedo (1994), in his book, *Literacies of Power: What Americans Are Not Allowed to Know*, established his credentials with a surprising nod toward China's bourgeois, counterrevolutionary movement for so-called democracy, arguing, "We continually violate international laws to undermine Cuba because of its communist regime while we readily go to bed with China, which is far more oppressive than Cuba, as could be seen in the Tiananmen Square mass killings" (p. 51). Continuing this anticommunist agenda nearly three decades after his initial statements Henry Giroux (2004), in his book, *The Terror of Neoliberalism*, suggests, with stunning conviction, that Soviet communism is on par with the cruelties of neoliberal capitalism and the outright genocidal fanaticism of Nazi capitalism. For example, Giroux argues that "newer forms of authoritarianism" are "emerging under the banner of democracy" but are "taking different forms from those twentieth-century regimes of terror that marked the former Soviet Union, Nazi Germany, and fascist Italy" (p. 147). These descriptions of communism tend to mirror Dean's observation that in the United States, "The multiplicity of historical and theoretical communisms condenses into one—the USSR" (p. 23). It is not that the anticommunist propaganda only acknowledged the Soviet Union, but that it stood, and stands, as the authoritarian model from which all workers' states are inevitably molded.

The purpose of the following summary of the history of the world workers' states, focusing on the Soviet Union, China, and the DPRK, is not just to develop a more accurate understanding of contemporary world affairs, but it also is to contribute to the laying of a more solid foundation from which to build communist pedagogy (Malott & Ford). A communist pedagogy in the context of the U.S., for example, includes the subject matter required to develop a complex understanding of the creation of the current settler-state in the seventeenth century after the dawn of the capitalist era had already cast its shadow over the fall of British feudalism. As capitalism's center of gravity began to shift westward from England to America, the center of proletarian revolution simultaneously shifted from the Western European revolutions of 1848 eastward toward Russia (Marcy, 1976a). I consequently begin the following discussion with the Soviet Union, the world's first successful workers' state.

While the first workers' state did not emerge until 1917, the idea of communism predates even the work and activism of Marx and Engels. It was therefore not only the shifting global material conditions that paved the way for communism in Russia, it also was both the work of Marx and Engels, who argued that the abolition of private property should be the primary goal of communism, and the failed revolutionary movements of the nineteenth century, such as the Paris Commune of 1871, that inspired and informed Lenin and the whole of the Bolshevik Party and the mass movement for socialism. As we will see, the Soviet Union similarly served as a beacon of inspiration and guidance to oppressed people the world over. As a result, the Soviet Union would also come to be an object of obsession for the world's capitalist classes, although rather than a source of admiration, it would engender an unparalleled fear and insecurity, unleashing a similarly unparalleled counterrevolutionary offensive.

The Union of Soviet Socialist Republics

The metamorphosis of the USSR—the most striking social phenomenon in man's entire evolution—presents a living social panorama that is truly staggering. This is scarcely to be wondered at. It contains within its broad bosom such an abundance of contradictions, contrasts, and nuances—is so rich and variegated in content— combining horse-drawn vehicles with jet-propelled planes—harnessing the energy of the peasant who still draws his water direct from the well, while exploring the possibilities of the mountain-moving atom—a whole country moving at break-neck speed, and yet at a snail's pace—holding out the greatest hopes for the masses, and yet dashing them to the ground every day, every hour—connected and interconnected with a thousand threads to the most distant and most barbarous past, and yet serving as a beacon light for man's future—a vast labyrinthine social complex whose every sinew and muscle is twined and intertwined with the most suffocating and stifling overgrowth of parasitic fat. Such are some of the more obvious aspects of a once isolated and struggling infant state that has now arisen to the stature of a veritable giant.

—Marcy, 1976a (pp. 42–43)

What Marcy is offering is a window into the past, an overture into a dialectical analysis of the historical development of the Soviet Union. That is, the Soviet Union offers a vibrant example of how socialism can only develop out of, and not apart from, existing conditions. Consequently, the history of the Soviet Union is a complex matter that the West has thoroughly exploited to boost its own capitalistic interests. As the center of imperialist power and finance capital shifted from Europe to the U.S., and the center of revolutionary gravity shifted to the East, the process of transforming a backward, conservative, capitalist feudalism into the world's most progressive communist workers' state cannot be disconnected from this larger context. The Soviet Union emerged from not only its own past but also from a definite position within the world stage. As Marcy makes clear in the above passage, this monumental shift could not possibly have been easy or one-sided. Again, because new relations can only ever develop out of existing conditions, the path forged by the Russian people was riddled with complexities and contradictions. Just as the present is always pregnant with the potential to become its opposite, it also carries the DNA of the past.

This is an indispensable insight for a communist pedagogy since it describes, in the most abstract theoretical terms, the world we will always confront. It challenges the revolutionary to avoid unrealistic expectations and romantic, utopian visions of a pure, perfectly worked out social harmony gracefully arising as the sun dawns on a new day, free from all the contradictions of the capitalist past and present. Rather, the tension within the coexistence of the past, present, and future represents an unavoidable, dialectical reality that carries with it the contested curriculum of struggle. It is this complex existence that the imperialist powers exploit to feed the pages of their anticommunist propaganda campaign. It is this purpose of education that has been so consistent in its messaging and pervasive throughout the U.S. that even the Left has been unable to purge itself from, and not contribute to, anticommunist propaganda and indoctrination.

Having been educated in critical pedagogy, it has only been relatively recently that I have come to understand the errors in dismissing the Soviet Union based upon vague, decontextualized claims of authoritarianism. The anti-Soviet position in critical pedagogy is so taken-for-granted, so presupposed, that those of us in the field reproduce it effortlessly like a daily, ritualized routine. I wish my past work were an exception to this betrayal of the most basic norms of the scientific community, but it is not. It was not until I was invited to embark on the process of joining the Party for Socialism and Liberation that I began the long journey of self-reflection and de-indoctrination. *Marx, Capital, and Education: Towards a Marxist Critical Pedagogy of Becoming* (2015), co-written with Derek Ford, is the first major work I co-wrote that completely breaks from imperialism's anticommunist propaganda. Of course, critical pedagogues think they have advanced beyond the assumed oppressive hierarchy and dogmatism of actually existing communism, but, as this book argues, this is a dramatic miscalculation and an example of the crossing of class lines.

For nearly a century, since the success of the Bolshevik Revolution in 1917, this anticommunist propaganda in the U.S. has been so intense and over-the-top that William Blum (2003), in his book on U.S. military intervention since WWII, argues that it has become America's national religion.

Underscoring the severity of bourgeois opposition to communism—and the Soviet Union in particular—mounted by the global imperialist class camp, Brian Becker (2014), of the Party for Socialism and Liberation, situates it in an historical context:

> Karl Marx and Frederick Engels wrote in 1848, "A specter is haunting Europe—the specter of communism." However haunting the specter of communism may have appeared to the European bourgeoisie in the mid-1800s, it would seem mild compared to the undiluted hysteria directed by all the imperialist powers and old ruling classes against the actually-existing Soviet Union throughout the 20th century.

The emergence of an actually existing socialist state, however imperfect, whose ultimate purpose was to serve the interests of the working class and the vast peasantry, Becker goes on to note, was extremely important to the world communist movement. From the outset, the imperialists put all the resources and military might they could muster into stamping out the spread of the infectious idea that workers and peasants could, in fact, defeat their oppressors and begin creating socialism, which the Bolshevik Revolution proved was an actual possibility. Especially within the vast areas of colonization, from China to Vietnam to South Africa, Soviet-inspired youth were becoming politically engaged and were militantly building a serious international communist movement. Within such colonized regions the call for communism became synonymous with national independence from the imperialist occupiers, that is, from the capitalists, foreign and domestic. The working classes and peasants of the world, through communism, experienced many important victories in China, Korea, Vietnam, Eastern Europe, Cuba, and in some African nations, achieving governments that comprised what would become known as the Socialist Bloc. Of course, being the first, the Soviet Union, from the imperialist point of view, was the center of global socialist power and therefore held it all together. While pointing out the advantages for the world's communist movement of the existence of the Socialist Bloc, Becker, as well as Dean, notes that the imperialists lumped them all together, and any shortcoming or mistake committed by any one of the socialist countries and its leadership was used as an indictment against communism in general. The most obvious example is Stalin, who came to represent the evils of communism during the so-called Cold War era. This representation of Stalin here is not Stalin the man, who embodied complex contradictions, but Stalin the caricature, fixed and rigidly essentialized as the archetypical enemy of freedom and democracy.

While the opportunism of the imperialist powers is readily apparent, the anticommunism of the Left is a more complex affair. For example, there continues to be strong debate within the communist movement regarding the legacy of Trotsky. For some socialists Trotsky represents a justified stand against the police state that emerged within the Soviet Union as a response to the external and internal bourgeois counterrevolutionary forces. In other words, there remains strong opposition to the Stalin faction of the leadership for handling the siege by imposing tight discipline on every sector of society, viewing all difference as potentially treasonous (and not just those associated with Trotsky's Left Opposition). Another commonly cited example is the 1917 Bolshevik central committee members, the commanders of arguably the greatest achievement in the history of the working class, and almost half of them were executed under Stalin's leadership. For many communists it seems unlikely that they were all part of a vast fascist fifth column and therefore were correctly dealt with.

For other communists, Trotsky represents another tendency that has proven disastrous for the global Left, as many communist parties throughout the world identify with Trotsky. Harry Haywood (1978), in his text, *Black Bolshevik: Autobiography of an Afro-American Communist*, offers a concise summary of what the Bolshevik Revolution had accomplished. In his brief statement, Haywood makes a point of mentioning the importance of the unity between the working class and the peasantry, which, as we will see, was also instrumental in the Soviet Union's ability to survive the tumultuous years immediately after the Revolution. Consider:

> The Soviet working class, under the leadership of Lenin and the Bolsheviks, had vanquished capitalism over one-sixth of the globe; shattered its economic power; expropriated the capitalists and landlords; converted the factories, railroads and banks into public property; and was beginning to build a state-owned socialist industry. The Soviet government had begun to apply Lenin's cooperative plans in agriculture and begun to fully develop a socialist economic system. This colossal task had to be undertaken by workers in alliance with the masses of working peasantry .(p. 11)

After the October Revolution until 1921 when the civil war had ended and the imperialist counterrevolutionists, including the U.S. military, had been expelled, the Central Committee temporarily shifted the economic policy from complete wartime economic nationalization to relaxing the socialist economic form, allowing free trade between small manufacturers and the peasantry to restore the exchange between rural and urban centers, which had been degraded during the period of crisis (between 1917 and 1921). Lenin's position was that this one-year period would allow the economic base to become restored and expanded in preparation for another socialist leap forward. Making this point, Haywood notes, "It was a temporary retreat from the attack on all remnants of capitalism, a time for the socialist state to stabilize its base area, to gather strength for another advance." (p. 1)

Some communists challenge Trotsky for not supporting this position because he did not believe the rural peasantry to be sufficiently sophisticated or progressive enough to be trusted to advance the communist revolution. Haywood (1978) therefore argues that Trotsky's position against Lenin was defeatist and corrosive to the solidarity the Bolshevik program fostered between the urban proletariat and the rural peasantry, which was literally the foundation of the Soviet Union. Trotsky argued that it could only be the global industrialized proletariat that would bring forth the communist era. However, since the working-class communist movements in Germany, Bulgaria, Italy, and Poland had been severely crushed by 1923, signaling a communist recession in Europe, the Soviet Union had little choice but to build socialism in the USSR until other emerging communist states could be supported.

With Lenin incapacitated in 1923 from a series of strokes, and dead by 1924, Stalin was already in a position to take over, having been elected general secretary in 1922. This was the context from which Stalin announced the dialectical strategy of Socialism in One Country—dialectical, in part, because it was informed by the world as it existed concretely in the twentieth century, not the world confronted by Marx in the nineteenth century. However, the path Stalin chose was not the only option in terms of responding to a tireless, imperialist aggressor. For example, Cuba has usually pursued the other policy path, greater openness in communication between the masses and the Party and more robust control over the state by the grassroots in the face of extreme difficulty. There was a failed effort to massively increase sugar cane production in the early 1970s, which not only didn't reach its goals but also caused serious economic problems because it diverted resources from other sectors. In response the government apologized and held a series of mass consultations that resulted in the neighborhood assembly-based "People's Power" electoral system the country uses today (before that there were no elections for high public office in Cuba). That wasn't nearly as serious a crisis as the Soviet Union faced, but during the special period, which really did lead to extreme suffering (and a consensus in world bourgeois opinion that the revolution would be imminently overthrown), they actually amended the constitution to deepen the role of local people's assemblies and increase the number of delegates they elect to the National Assembly. While this example is not provided as evidence to condemn the former Soviet Union, it is offered to remember that critique is central for advancing proletarian camp of the global class war.

While critique is important, some communists maintain that Trotsky took it too far, arguing that Stalin's position represents a departure from Marx's global conception of communism. To this day, this Trotskyist line has been one of the primary sources of Western Marxists' charges that the Soviet Union was not actually Marxist, especially after the death of Lenin. But Marx's approach was not dogmatic. Marx's dialectical method charged the revolutionary Communist Party to confront the world as it actually is and not make decisions based upon an imagined or bygone reality. One might therefore argue that one of the unfortunate legacies of Trotsky is a tendency toward utopianism. Far from advocating for Soviet isolationism Lenin, Stalin, and the Central Committee understood quite well the threat of imperialism as long as it existed. Advancing this insight with a precise clarity Haywood is instructive:

> Stalin's position did not mean the isolation of the Soviet Union. The danger of capitalist restoration still existed and would exist until the advent of a classless society. The Soviet people understood that they could not destroy this external danger by their own efforts, that it could only be finally destroyed as a result of a victorious revolution in at least several of the countries of the West. The triumph of socialism in the Soviet Union could not be final as long as the external danger existed. Therefore, the success of the revolutionary forces in the capitalist West was a vital concern of the Soviet people. (p. 2)

Haywood goes on to report that during his time in the Soviet Union, when Trotsky was challenging the Central Committee and Stalin's position, Trotsky's writings were widely distributed and read by workers and peasants throughout the country. Rather than being exiled by Stalin without sufficient debate or pretense, Haywood argues it was the Soviet people themselves who had rejected Trotsky's ideas as class collaborationist and ultimately counter-revolutionary because he argued that until socialism was established in the most advanced Western centers of capitalist power, socialism could not be built in the Soviet Union After five years of raging debate, in 1926 Trotsky unsuccessfully defended his position at the Seventh Plenum of the Executive Committee of the Communist International in the Kremlin.

While the Trotsky line tends to be a critique picked up more often by the international Left, including Marxists, and socialist parties such as the

International Socialist Organization (ISO), the caricature of Stalin as a monster and mass murderer is more closely associated with capitalist propaganda. In *Blackshirts and Reds: Rational Fascism and the Overthrow of Communism,* Michael Parenti (1997) investigates the evidence concerning the so-called crimes against humanity Joseph Stalin was directly responsible for. Introducing the topic, Parenti reflects on how "we have heard much about the ruthless Reds, beginning with the reign of terror and repression perpetuated during the dictatorship of Joseph Stalin (1929–1953). Estimates of those who perished under Stalin's rule—based principally on speculations by writers who never reveal how they arrive at such figures—vary wildly" (p. 77). Parenti cites six different writers whose estimates range from five million to one hundred million. If such estimates had any relation to reality, Parenti notes, the gulag system would have been the Soviet Union's "largest enterprise" (p. 78). Having gained access to previously secret Soviet police and prison records, Parenti notes that the total number of people executed between 1921 and 1953 in Soviet Union prisons was around seven hundred thousand, many of which were for punishable crimes, including Nazi collaborators and traitors who facilitated imperialist invaders until their final expulsion in 1921. Offering a summary of what actually seems to have taken place, Parenti notes:

> What we do know of Stalin's purges is that many victims were Communist party officials, managers, military officers, and other strategically situated individuals whom the dictator saw fit to incarcerate or liquidate. In addition, whole categories of people whom Stalin considered of unreliable loyalty—Cossacks, Crimean Tartars, and ethnic Germans—were selected for internal deportation. Though they never saw the inside of a prison or labor camp, they were subjected to noncustodial resettlement in Central Asia and Siberia. To be sure, crimes of state were committed in communist countries and many political prisoners were unjustly interned and even murdered. But the inflated numbers offered by cold-war scholars serve neither historical truth nor the cause of justice but merely help to reinforce a knee-jerk fear and loathing of those terrible Reds. (pp. 78–79)

While Parenti is not denying that mistakes were made and crimes committed, he is absolutely clear that the labor camps in the Soviet Union were not death camps with mass exterminations and gas chambers, such as in Nazi Germany. Parenti does not deny that conditions were harsh, but the vast majority of inmates, he proves, eventually returned to society after serving their terms. What is more, between 12 and 30 percent of gulag inmates had been convicted of counterrevolutionary crimes while many more were serving time for murder, rape, robbery, assault, smuggling, and other crimes punishable in any society. In any given year 20 to 40 percent of inmates were released. During WWII nearly one million inmates were released to serve the Red Army's successful defeat of the Nazi war machine, which cost the Russian people twenty-seven million lives. Parenti notes that more than half of all deaths that occurred in the labor camps were the result of malnutrition due to the same wartime privations that had the same effect on the Soviet people in general.

Parenti does not end his discussion here without failing to mention, "We hear a great deal about the crimes of communism but almost nothing about its achievements" (p. 84). It is therefore important to note:

> During the years of Stalin's reign, the Soviet nation made dramatic gains in literacy, industrial wages, health care, and women's rights. These accomplishments usually go unmentioned when the Stalinist era is discussed. To say that "socialism doesn't work" is to overlook the fact that it did. (Parenti, 1997, p. 85)

Similarly, Sam Marcy (1976a), noting that the class character of the Soviet Union has been a hotly debated topic since its inception, and that despite conservative turns taken by the leadership of its later years (discussed below), it always retained its workers' state–class character. As such, the former Soviet Union achieved a great deal of progress for its people. Writing before the unfortunate fall of the Soviet Union, Sam Marcy (1976a) comments on its superiority compared to capitalism:

> The underlying social system of the USSR is infinitely superior to that of the most developed, the most "glorious," and the most "democratic" of the imperialist states. Whatever the drawbacks of the Soviet Union, whatever its trials and tribulations, whatever false policies have been imposed on the USSR by its leaders, it has nevertheless been able to achieve tremendous social, cultural, and material progress for the masses which no capitalist state could possibly have accomplished in the circumstances under which the USSR was originally founded and developed. (p. 2)

The success of communism and the brilliant self-determination that emerges from workers' independence is precisely why it is such a threat to the capitalist class, and it explains why the imperialist powers have done and will do everything in their power, using every political, diplomatic, military, and economic means, to crush every remaining and emerging workers' state and communist movement. Further elaborating on what he identifies as the four parameters of a workers' state as developed by the Soviet Union, Brian Becker (2008), founding member of the PSL, offers a concise and instructive Leninist-inspired summary:

First, the state and government were created following the smashing of the old state power of the bourgeoisie by a revolution of the workers and peasants. Second, there was public ownership of the means of production. Third, there was centralizing economic planning rather than the commodity market as the engine driving economic production—production for needs instead of private profit. Fourth, the government administered a monopoly of foreign trade, preventing world imperialism from linking up with local Russian capitalists to create a "fifth column" within Soviet society. (p. 10)

While these advances represented a major leap forward for the lives of Russian peasants and workers, in the Soviet Union's seventy-four years of existence it was never able to develop past the initial stage of creating communism due to the strangulation of internal bureaucratic developments driven by the external threats of imperialists and counterrevolutionaries. Despite its own limitations and the perpetual external war waged upon it, the Soviet Union still represented a model for achieving equality and happiness capitalism could never compete with. It is precisely because communism is a superior system to capitalism that the imperialists have had to crush it violently and with extreme ideological manipulation. Again, Marcy (1976a) is worth quoting here:

Indeed, the USSR is rooted in a social system superior to the capitalist system. It is our fundamental political position that, regardless of the Soviet bureaucracy, the USSR contains a new social formation, based on a historically superior mode of production, and is progressive in relation to monopoly capitalism in the same way that capitalism was a superior system in relation to feudalism, as indeed feudalism was a higher social system than slavery. (p. 2)

While I think Marcy is correct in his insistence that communism represents a qualitative advance from capitalism, which, again, has caused great fear and anxiety among the capitalist class, his ontological framework in this document does not account for the existence of Indigenous societies. The fact that many communist parties have based their position on Marx's early writings that suggested that tribal societies are backward and conservative, and thus must move through a bourgeois capitalist phase before advancing to the higher communist society, have led many American Indian activists to view communism as no better than imperialism in respect to hostility toward Indigeneity (Churchill). In chapter 1, I offered a correction to this error through a brief engagement with Native Studies. Despite any mistakes communist states have made, from capital's perspective, the objection is not necessarily the content of the alternative, but its independence from imperialism.

What is more, imperialists also used the fact that socialist revolutions tended to occur in the poorest of countries, rather than in the imperialist countries themselves such as the United States, as evidence for why socialism will only ever offer poverty and suffering. That is, the propagandists of imperialism distorted the fact that capitalist imperialism was the cause of the poverty that led to socialist revolutions in the first place. Socialism, rather than keeping workers in poverty perpetually, offers a way for the working class to begin transcending capitalism and abolishing the perpetual poverty and immiseration associated with capitalist exploitation. Again, communism does not mean the end of Indigenous sovereignty but, rather, the affirmation of it, its reemergence and coming to be situated in the concrete context of the world as it now exists. Of course the U.S. (and other imperialist countries), in hiding or falsifying the actual social gains made under workers' socialist states, argues that it was the wealth and abundance created by the capitalist states that allowed their workers access to resources and services unavailable in the so-called backward communist countries. What is ignored is that in the global capitalist economy the extension of opulence in the direction of the capitalist class is always accompanied by poverty and degradation in the other direction, the side of the working class and peasantry.

The collapse of the Soviet Union and much of the proletarian class camp's states, therefore, was not caused by the inherent defectiveness or authoritarianism of communism but by the imperialist counterrevolutionary offensive. That is, weakened by a U.S.-Chinese alliance, the Soviet Union began to collapse, but, contrary to imperialist propaganda, its fall was orchestrated not by the Russian people themselves, 77 percent of whom supported their communist state at the time of its fall, but by the U.S. and its imperialist allies' anticommunist war they had been waging since the end of WWII, when communism was at its height of influence after the Soviet Union defeated the Nazi war machine, losing almost thirty million Russian people in the process. The global anticommunist war machine has been so corrosive and all-encompassing that it wound up influencing high-level members of the USSR's Communist Party to become opportunistic and counterrevolutionary.

Of course, the counterrevolutionaries from within the Soviet Union (and the Eastern Bloc more generally), adopting the rhetoric of democracy from U.S. capitalists, presented their expulsions and purges of communists from the government, media, universities, the courts, and so on as "democratic reforms" (Parenti, 1997, p. 88). True to the allusions of freedom and equally within capitalism, truly democratic measures would not be able to restore capitalism in the Soviet Union due to the widespread support for communism among the people throughout Russia and the former republics. Repressive measures and "presidential decrees" were required to implement "market reforms" (p. 88). In classic capitalist fashion, the Communist Party officials who resisted the subversion of the people's Soviet workers' state were labeled "hardliners" and "holdovers," dogmatically impeding progress.

Parenti notes that the suppression of communists was not just something that happened after the fall of the Soviet Union, but was part of the process leading up to it. For example, a few years after Stalin's death in 1953 Khrushchev delivered a speech where he adopted the imperialist position that Stalin was a criminal. This move has proven devastating to the legacy of the Soviet Union in the eyes of much of the global Left. Negatively impacting the Black radical tradition in the U.S., W. E. B. Du Bois's support for Stalin has been dismissed since it occurred before Khrushchev's expose. Even in a relatively recent world history book titled *A People's History of the World*, by Chris Harman (2008), the Khrushchev line is reproduced uncritically:

> In February 1956 Khrushchev, the Communist Party general secretary, decided to reveal some home truths to party activists in order to strengthen his hand in the leadership struggle. He told the 20th party congress in Moscow that Stalin had been responsible for the murder of thousands of innocent people and the deportation of millions of members of national minorities. What is more, he said Stalin had been incompetent and cowardly at the time of the German invasion of Russia in 1941. The impact of these revelations on tens of millions of people across the world who had been taught to regard Stalin as a near-god was shattering, even if many tried to close their minds to them. (p. 563)

It is, therefore, not surprising that the end was near for the world's first dictatorship of the proletariat, the first workers' state. Consequently, according to Parenti (1997), months before the official dissolution of the Soviet Union, Gorbachev announced that the "Communist Party of the USSR no longer had legal status. The Party's membership funds and buildings were confiscated. Workers were prohibited from engaging in any kind of political activities in the workplace. Six leftist newspapers were suppressed" (p. 88). In the U.S. these moves were praised as advancing democratic reforms. Gorbachev then demanded that the Soviet Congress disband itself, claiming it was a barrier to democracy even though democratic elections and debates were already in practice. The problem with the Soviet Congress, from a counterrevolutionary perspective, was that through democratic measures, it was firmly positioned against free market reforms. What gave Gorbachev justification for the repression of communism was what Parenti (1997) characterizes as a poorly planned coup against him that fell apart before it really even materialized. The emerging Russian capitalist class was the primary opponent of the workers' state and repeatedly expressed their bewilderment at why so few Soviet workers embraced so-called democratic reforms.

It is argued that the real coup came when Boris Yeltsin "used the incident to exceed his constitutional powers and dismantle the Soviet Union itself, absorbing all its powers into his own Russian Republic" (Parenti, 1997, p. 89). In 1993 the resistance of the Soviet people, outraged at the subversion of their workers' state, led Yeltsin to take further anticommunist steps as he "forcibly disbanded the Russian parliament and every other elected representative body … and launched an armed attack upon the parliamentary building, killing an estimated two thousand resistors and demonstrators" (Parenti, 1997, p. 89). For these and many other crimes Yeltsin was highly praised among the U.S. bourgeois media and politicians for defending democracy and never wavering in his support for the privatization of the former Soviet Union. Yeltsin, Parenti reports, had political rivals assassinated and what remained of the people's Communist Party suppressed. With the aid of International Monetary Fund and World Bank money and the most sophisticated U.S. electoral advisors, and a heavy-handed monopoly control over Russian television, Yeltsin was able to secure the reelection of his presidency. While Yeltsin was prepared to declare election results null if the Communist Party won, he was advised such a move would cause too much outrage and threaten the free market reforms with outright rebellion. Part of the Yeltsin campaign's rhetorical strategy was the use of fear bombarding the public with the message that a communist victory would cause civil war. The subtext here was the threat of violence that Yeltsin was clearly not afraid to employ to ensure capitalism triumphed over the peoples' desire for communism.

Perhaps one of the greatest arguments for communism can be found within what emerged in its absence. With the fall of the Soviet Union and the Eastern Bloc, the communist ethic that sought to "provide a better life for all citizens" vanished and was replaced with the drive "to maximize the opportunities for individuals to accumulate personal fortunes" (Parenti, 1997, p. 106). The capitalist restorationists, cheered on by the Western capitalist press, immediately began reprivatizing ownership of production and dismantling the vast network of social programs that had provided a guaranteed standard of living to its people. The Eastern Bloc was quickly transformed into a series of third world countries providing capitalist investors from within the imperialist centers of capitalist wealth with sources of cheap labor and all manner of economic extraction. The once vibrant trade between former communist states ground to a halt as foreign investment worked to ravage and exploit workers of former communist workers' states. With public coffers and programs obliterated and with production thrown into the global economy, production rates plummeted, leading to skyrocketing unemployment and poverty (Parenti, 1997). The dramatic austerity measures further degrading Eastern Europe can best be understood within this context of capitalist restoration.

The end of communism also brought with it a return to dramatic gender inequality in the former Soviet Union. Because the reigning caricature of the former Soviet Union and the Eastern Bloc more generally portrays them as male-dominated, hypermasculine, rigid dictatorships, it is worth quoting Parenti (1997) at length, summarizing the lost progress that had been made concerning gender equality:

> The new constitution adopted in Russia eliminates provisions that guaranteed women the right to paid maternity leave, job security during pregnancy, prenatal care, and affordable daycare centers. Without the former communist stipulation that women get at least one third of the seats in any legislature, female political representation has dropped to as low as 5 percent in some countries. In all communist countries about 90 percent of women had jobs in what was a full-employment economy. Today, women compose over two-thirds of the unemployed. … Instances of sexual harassment and violence against women have increased sharply. … The Communist party committees that used to intervene in cases of domestic abuse no longer exist. (pp. 114–115)

The high rates of sexual abuse and gender inequality in capitalist democracies should shed new light on just how progressive the former Soviet Union actually was. For critical pedagogues interested in challenging sexist oppression, a new, objective look at communism might just be in order.

While capitalist cheerleaders argued that the period of hardship after the communist fall was only temporary, as it would take some time for the redistribution of wealth upward and outward to trickle back down and into the working classes, it should now be clear to anyone who did not believe Marx that capitalism induces immiseration and that only communist restoration will improve the lives of the Russian people. Growing inequality is one of the capitalist system's contradictions it cannot escape without a qualitative change from capitalist production relations to socialist ones. Shifting from an economy designed to meet people's needs, as highlighted in the above quote, to an economy designed to maximize accumulation has severe implications that can only be resolved through communist restoration.

This point has not been lost on the Russian people. For example, it has long been noted that Russians of all ages, whose suffering since the fall of the Soviet Union has not abated, tend to hold a deep sense of patriotic nostalgia for their communist past. For many Russians, communism does not represent an outdated authoritarianism but a society based on the genuine pursuit of equality and freedom and the end of all oppression and exploitation, which is quite appealing given the devastation brought on by capitalist restoration (i.e., the privatization of industry and agriculture for the accumulation of surplus-value for an elite capitalist class, built off the backs of exploited laborers). Russians remember the Soviet Union as a world communist leader endowed with a military rivaling that of the U.S., thereby keeping imperialist aggression at bay for the proletarian class camp of the global class war. Public opinion polls have consistently found that more than 60 percent of Russians view the collapse of the Soviet Union as a negative event (Weir, 2016).

While it was believed that Soviet nostalgia would eventually dissipate as the immediate hardships of the transition from communism to capitalism also faded away, the intensification of both has pressured the Kremlin to more closely align itself to the Soviet past, even if in rhetoric alone. However, these trends offer the proletarian camp in the global class war a sign of hope for what may come (i.e., communist restoration and expansion) (Weir).

As opportunistic as they are, it comes as no surprise that when the Soviet Union fell, imperialist propagandists proclaimed the end of communism and even the end of history. This proclamation, of course, is unsubstantiated, but the impact on even the Left within imperialist nations, such as the U.S., has been devastating. As mentioned above, even critical pedagogy, for example, is not based on the most rudimentary insight that communism actually does represent the interests of the world's diverse working classes. The position I am taking here in this book, therefore, remains a controversial position within the critical pedagogy community, especially in the centers of imperialist power, such as the U.S. Whereas communism identifies the peasantry and proletarian labor base as the global subject of historical change, critical pedagogy tends to disregard the global class war in favor of a diversity of subjectivities whose equally diverse desires constitute a democracy of possibilities that the monolithic communist end-point subverts and ignores.

Within bourgeois critical pedagogy, unconscious of its own indoctrination, the interests and desires of people of color are incorrectly believed to be subverted by the economics of Western communist ideology and practice. From a Marxist reading of the history of the world's Communist Parties and workers' states, on the other hand, the socialist project emerges as the true representative of the expressed interests and desires of millions of the world's people of color. It is within a worker-controlled state that the world's working classes, peasants, and oppressed peoples have come to see the possibility of complete emancipation. This is the dangerous realization bourgeois propagandists have dedicated themselves to preventing.

This negative anticommunist dogma is so thoroughly saturated within every pore of foreign and domestic U.S. policy, that is, within nearly every avenue of popular media production and every piece of official public school curriculum, that when Paulo Freire brought the movement of radical pedagogy to North America in the early 1970s, receptive educators brought their American anticommunism to the field. Even the first real U.S. Marxist education text, *Schooling in Capitalist America*, by Bowles and Gintis (1976), reproduces capitalist imperialism's rejection of not just top-level Soviet leadership but also the workers' state (i.e., the Soviet Union) itself, while advocating for socialism in the abstract, as demonstrated in the previous chapter. We might understand this to be an antisocialist socialism. This tendency exists right up to the present moment. The democratic socialist alternative advocated for by today's U.S. educational Marxists is based upon an incorrect assessment of actually existing socialism. The purpose of this chapter, as indicated above, is to offer a communist correction to the aforementioned error. With this spirit of solidarity in mind, let's now turn to the example presented by the People's Republic of China.

The People's Republic of China

When the Soviet Union emerged as the first workers' state, it assumed an important international role, supporting, defending, advising, and inspiring communist movements. For example, almost immediately after the success of the October Revolution in 1917, the new Soviet Union immediately lent its support to the center of China's progressive gravitational force, which, for two years, was the Kuomintang, the National People's Party, led by Chiang Kai-shek, which would eventually become a point of contention after 1949 (Ruíz, 2008). In 1921 the Communist Party of China (CPC) was formed with Mao Zedong named as secretary of the Hunan Province receiving Soviet guidance. In 1923 CPC members, as individuals, combined with the Kuomintang, forging a united front against Japanese colonialism. Between 1925 and 1927, a revolutionary advance emerged, marking the beginning of the suffering and death of millions of Chinese people that would last until 1949, when the CPC finally seized state power with the birth of the People's Republic of China.

Again, the road to victory was a long and tumultuous one in which the Soviet Union offered critical assistance. For example, in 1925 advisors from the Communist International (the Comintern) in Moscow were sent to assist Chiang Kai-shek in establishing the Whampoa Military Academy to train Chinese officers. However, by 1927 Chiang Kai-shek's forces attacked the urban-based CPC in an anticommunist coup, decimating nearly 80 percent of its membership. Mao and the remaining CPC would retreat to the country-side, continuing their struggle, surviving four more attempted exterminations led by Chiang Kai-shek's forces, leading to the Long March between 1934 and 1935, ending in Yenan where the CPC would establish a new base of operations. In 1937 imperialist Japan launched a massive invasion into China, leading to another temporary alliance between the CPC and the Kuomintang against the Japanese forces. While the war with Japan lasted until 1945, Mao's truce with Chiang Kai-shek would break down between 1940 and 1941 (Becker, 2008; Hrizi, 2008; La Riva, 2008; Mills, 2008; McInerney, 2008).

Whereas the Kuomintang would turn to the U.S. for aid, the CPC continued to expand its guerilla operations and remained connected to the Soviet Union. Between 1937 and 1945, the CPC grew from one hundred thousand to nearly one and a half million members. In 1948 the CPC and the recently renamed People's Liberation Army defeated the heavily U.S.-funded and -supported forces of Chiang Kai-shek in Manchuria. Eventually, in 1949, the People's Republic of China was formally declared. Mao was elected chairman, a position he used to move the People's Republic of China toward the path of communism, following the example of the Soviet Union, including the use of five-year plans and agricultural communes or collectives. Toward these ends a massive land redistribution program was instituted, transferring the agricultural means of production from landlords to the peasantry. Greater gender equality was also institutionalized through reforms to marriage laws. Consequently, the membership of the CPC climbed to nearly five million (Becker, 2008).

Like the Soviet Union, China did not build communism from an advanced capitalist economy with a large and powerful proletariat, but from an impoverished nation of peasants that continued to reel from the long legacy of opium addiction that dated back to British imperialism and the Opium Wars of the 1840s. As outlined above, the country also suffered from twenty-two years of civil war and fifteen years of Japanese imperialist occupation (Becker, 2008).

What the Chinese people were able to achieve, in an utterly complex and difficult context, under the leadership of Mao Zedong, was truly remarkable. Key to the success of the workers' state was the creation of a class instrument of coercion, suppressing the bourgeoisie's ability to continue to exploit the peasantry and working class. This dictatorship of the proletariat is one of the most thoroughly demonized and distorted aspects in the West of what is required when the poor and oppressed take state power and reconstitute society in the interests of workers and peasants.

Abolishing private property, collectivizing agriculture, and creating a monopoly on foreign investment so capitalist interests could not use the imperialist method of exporting capital to control and dominate Chinese markets, thereby subverting an emerging workers' state are some of the measures employed by successful proletarian revolutions to transform capitalist production relations to socialist ones. It is precisely these tactics that a bourgeois education seeks to demonize and distort, convincing workers in capitalist societies that communist notions of collectivity require the negation of the individual to be enacted (Spring, 2007). Rather, the collective individuality of the masses represents the strength of the people, whereas individualism isolates and divides those who rely on a wage to survive. A communist pedagogy must, therefore, challenge bourgeois illusions and refuse to cross class lines. A communist pedagogy celebrates and defends, for example, what the 1949 Chinese revolution was able to achieve through the dictatorship of the proletariat.

Armed with this new dictatorship of the peasantry and the proletariat, the People's Republic of China, guided by the CPC, between 1949 and 1955, was able to eradicate starvation, prostitution, and drug addition, and make impressive gains in providing health care to millions, combatting illiteracy and eliminating unemployment among the urban proletariat (Becker, 2008; Puryear, 2008). With landlordism done away with in the countryside and key industries nationalized, impressive progress was being made toward organizing the economy around use-value rather than exchange-value. The gross domestic product and the standard of living made the most impressive gains during this period of socialist progress. The most noticeable gains were among the urban working class, but this segment of society represented a minority of the population. While the industrial working class grew as the Chinese communist revolution aimed to increase productivity, the standard of living for the vast peasantry also saw major improvements. As a result of the turn toward socialism, in 1950, China signed a treaty with the Soviet Union, the Sino-Soviet Treaty of Friendship, Alliance, and Mutual Assistance (Ruíz).

However, despite the tremendous significance of the Sino-Soviet Treaty, Ruíz notes that their shared commitment to "proletarian internationalism" was hindered by "the perceived national interests of the respective ruling parties" (p. 132). The choice of the word "perceived" here is key. That is, the perception that a national interest supersedes an international communist interest plays into the imperialist hand of divide and rule. This is no minor point. Whereas the Soviet Union provided China with much needed assistance and aid during much of the 1950s, by the 1960s, after Stalin's death, Khrushchev's turn rightward signaled a fracturing of relations. Arguing that the military might of the Soviet Union had rendered war with imperialists no longer an inevitability, Khrushchev took the position that socialist development could be advanced through bourgeois alliances and, therefore, without revolution. Khrushchev's break from Marxist-Leninism led to China's partial isolation from the proletarian class camp in the global class war.

As if this position were not bad enough, Khrushchev then traveled to the U.S. for a summit with the anticommunist Eisenhower administration, leaving China feeling betrayed. China maintained its Leninist position that revolutionary movements against imperialism must be defended unconditionally to avoid the crossing of class lines. After a clear divergence in position had been established, in 1960 the Soviet Union withdrew its economic and technical support in China, leveling a substantial blow to the Chinese economy. While relations were strained, the Sino-Soviet split had not yet occurred, although Ruíz notes that for all practical purposes China had been pushed out of the proletarian class camp. Throughout the 1960s tensions escalated to a point where the CPC accused the CPSU of revisionism and finally socialist imperialism, although "there was no objective evidence for the allegation that the USSR had somehow become capitalist, much less imperialist. … There was no sign of the dismantling of the socialized core of the economy" (Ruíz, p. 137).

One of the major charges against the former Soviet Union is that it had imperialist ambitions with respect to its relationships with other countries, such as China, which were aspiring toward socialism. However, as a workers' state, the Soviet Union never benefited from, or exploited, other socialist or independent states that they offered support and assistance to, and the same can be said of China (Mills, 2008). Nonetheless, as relations between China and the Soviet Union continued to deteriorate, tensions along the long Chinese-Soviet border escalated with hundreds of thousands of troops amassing on both sides of the border. While an all-out senseless war was adverted, tragically, there were human casualties on both sides—comrades killing comrades. Again, the ultimate benefactor of the Sino-Soviet split has been imperialism.

Capitalist Reforms in China

After the death of Mao in 1976, and the subsequent imprisonment of his remaining supporters in the CPC, the People's Republic of China was taken in the opposite direction of communism, toward capitalism. Contrary to the path toward communism, China has since legalized and encouraged private property, that is, the private ownership of the means of production and the exploitation of human labor power. What is more, the state monopoly on foreign investment gradually has been relaxed, opening the door for the domination of Western capitalists and bankers over the flow of capital and productive forces within China (Becker, 2008; Mills, 2008).

Contrary to Marx and Engels' prediction that feudalism would give way to capitalism, and then capitalism would create the conditions for socialism, China's development progressed from feudalism, to socialism, and then in a capitalist direction, even though it continues to retain fundamental elements of socialism worth defending. However, like all revolutions, developments in China have always emerged out of existing conditions. In this way, the example of China followed Marx's dialectics in that its new social arrangements did not emerge in a vacuum, isolated and disconnected from the world as it existed, but emerged from the concreteness of its contradictions.

For example, whereas the vanguard of the bourgeoisie in Western Europe played the revolutionary role in destroying the European nobility of medieval feudalism, in China it was the peasantry and urban working class that played this revolutionary role by bringing forth the bourgeois liberal advances, such as free speech and literacy, associated with bourgeois revolutions (Becker, 2008). The bourgeois class in China was too weak and underdeveloped to play this revolutionary role. One of the reasons why Marx and Engels believed that socialism could only develop out of capitalism was based on their developmental analysis applied to the only concrete example they had to study—the British and Western European example.

That is, capitalism in Europe had developed out of feudalism as the advances of feudalism reached their structural limits, making new arrangements a necessity. The restrictions of feudal relations that tied specific workers to specific branches of industry focused on their use-value. Money in feudalism facilitated the equal exchange of different commodities so the farmer could exchange a portion of his crop for an equivalent in money to access other use-values. Disconnecting the peasant from specific types of labor allowed the merchant to begin trading and investing in human labor power, disconnecting it from the use-values it produced and allowing the new capitalists to accumulate exchange-values like never before. The extreme dehumanizing and degrading efficiency of productivity of an economy focused on the production of exchange-value, or capital, leads to massive economic growth and correspondingly exaggerated rates of exploitation. Marx believed that the economic growth of capitalism was creating a society that was able to meet the material needs of all people, thereby creating the material conditions for socialism. If the high level of productivity under capitalism could be put to the task of satisfying human need or use rather than the accumulation of exchange-value, great humanitarian strides could be made.

In other words, the fact that the accumulation of capital—or the creation of all new value—comes only from the exploitation of human labor power, and the higher the rate of exploitation, the more capital the capitalist accumulates, therefore, the growing capitalist economy tends toward working-class immiseration and revolution. Since China did not go through a sustained capitalist period of development before communism, Mao's forces not only had to seize the existing means of production, but they also had to modernize and expand what existed as of 1949, producing new industrial means of production. Whereas capitalist development in Britain emerged from feudal relations and developed through technological advancements revolutionizing the methods of cooperation where many isolated laborers are brought together with the further development of the division of labor. This movement would eventually give way to the machine factory, further dividing the tasks of labor separating manual labor from mental labor. With the advent of communism in feudally based capitalist societies, such as China, the knowledge of modern, industrial, highly efficient, production relations developed within capitalist societies could be imported, thereby subverting the long process of creating this knowledge.

Whereas the leadership within the CPC agreed that the implementation of such modern methods of production were necessary for economic expansion, there was disagreement on the methods to achieve this goal. On one side, Deng Xiaoping argued for a more capitalist, free-market approach while espousing a commitment to the social justice goals of socialism. Mao, on the other hand, advocated for a move toward the Soviet style of socialism including "nationalized public property in the core industries and banking, centralized planning, collectivized agriculture, mobilization of the workers and peasants, and a monopoly on foreign trade (Becker, 2008, pp. 13–14). The Cultural Revolution in 1966, contrary to imperialist propaganda that portrays it as an attack on diversity, was a campaign led by Mao designed to encourage the working class and peasants to dislodge Deng and his allies—known as the "capitalist roaders"—from power and subvert the capitalist path of development and the inequality that accompanies it. With the success of the Cultural Revolution, the Soviet approach to socialist development in China proved effective, facilitating massive economic growth while simultaneously improving the lives of the working class and peasants rather than degrading them.

Becker (2008) points to a number of factors that contributed to Deng's eventual subversion of the socialist path in China. First, the failure of the revolution in Indonesia in 1965 weakened the proletarian camp of the global class war while simultaneously strengthening the Sino-Soviet split. Second, Mao's death in 1976 further opened the door for Deng's subversion of much of the remaining Leftist elements in the Chinese Communist Party. Deng incorrectly referred to his eventual collaboration with the U.S. and the imperialist class camp as market socialism, opening up, as it were, the Chinese economy to Western banks and corporations, which has proven to be devastating to Chinese labor, despite the corresponding influx of massive amounts of capital investments, leading to a wave of strikes and work actions in the present era (Chen, 2003).

Under the Deng reforms the collective, commune approaches to agriculture were also dismantled, leading to the restratification and immiseration of the Chinese peasantry. For example, Becker (2008) reports that while millions of more privileged peasants saw substantial gains in their wealth as a result of the capitalist reforms, millions more lost everything, that is, all direct access to the means of production (i.e., land), thereby being forced to migrate to work in the new cities producing commodities for foreign capitalist markets. Within twenty-five years the world's largest industrial workforce had been established and China was fully integrated into the world capitalist economy. A new bourgeoisie has therefore been established in China with interests distinct from both China's proletariat and Western and Japanese imperialists.

However capitalist the economy of the People's Republic of China has become, the CPC continues to retain administrative and economic control over the country, enabling them to restrict foreign investment and economic development when necessary, which is always met with cries of outrage and discrimination by the West. While the capitalist class in the West certainly won a major victory with the Deng reforms, the fact is that the communist core represents a constant threat of recommunization, making it an ongoing target for imperialism. In other words, no matter how much the Chinese Communist Party capitulates to imperialism, U.S. imperialists in particular will not rest until it is completely dissolved and a puppet regime takes its place (La Riva, 2008).

Denationalized branches of industry have proven disastrous for Chinese workers, leading to widespread strikes and some working-class victories. Chen notes that China's working class responded to the initial privatization of State-Owned Enterprises (SOE) with patience, anticipating no real change to their conditions. As more and more SOEs became privatized, it became increasingly clear to Chinese labor that capitalization was detrimental to the Chinese working class. Chen explores the complexity of China's economic reshuffling. First, some workers are employed by corporations that were never SOEs while other workers have experienced "deprivation of benefits, ruthless labor rights abuses, and brutal working conditions" as a direct result of their SOEs being "converted into shareholding companies with mixed private and public ownership, sold or leased to private individuals" (pp. 237–238).

Chen's study of working-class resistance in China found that protests by workers in restructured SOEs had a significant advantage that workers in the private sector did not have. That is, because SOEs are still under the direct authority of the state, the state is able to intervene on behalf of labor to ensure social stability. SOE workers have Workers' and Staff Councils (WSC) that are normally ignored by management because their decisions, under normal circumstances, do not have enforcing power, their demands are nothing more than recommendations. However, when workers take to the streets and shut down branches of industry, the WSCs mediate between management and the government, often securing state mandates favoring the interests of workers. As long as workers' demands are not counterrevolutionary and follow the mandates of the CPC regarding workers' rights, labor tends to benefit from the ongoing existence of the People's Republic of China. Countering the imperialist rhetoric that the CPC is an oppressive force in relation to China's working class, Chen explains:

> Suppressing workers who make no political demands and whose claims are often derived from the official rhetoric on working-class interests would place to government in a morally and politically indefensible position. (p. 254)

However degraded the CPC has become, there clearly remains a progressive element within its existence, alluded to by Chen, that would represent a major historical setback if the CPC as a whole were overthrown. Any remaining potential for further communist advancement would abruptly end if the CPC was overthrown by capitalist interests. Immiseration would surely skyrocket if the Chinese people lost the protection of the People's Republic of China, which, as a national entity, would likely be dissolved as was the case with the Soviet Union, Czechoslovakia, and Yugoslavia. With the CPC in power the possibility that capitalist restoration could be slowed or halted, however remote, remains a possibility.

The Democratic People's Republic of Korea

Current imperialist propaganda tends to characterize the DPRK as an isolated totalitarian state that oppresses its people's political liberties and exploits their labor power for the benefit of its ruling class. Perhaps even more so than either the Soviet Union or the Peoples' Republic of China, the Democratic People's Republic of Korea is especially demonized. As much as the Left, especially in the U.S., has embraced the caricature of Stalin as an almost alien monster, the debasement of North Korea and its leaders is especially bitter and malicious. Perhaps one of the West-known counterrevolutionary attacks in the field of education comes from Joel Spring's (2007) widely used foundations of education text, *Wheels in the Head*. Spring's primary attack is centered on the DPRK's focus on nationalism as a form of indoctrination or *wheel in the head*.

While Spring acknowledges Korea's difficult history, having had to fight off both Japanese colonialism and U.S. imperialism, he does not seem to understand what it takes to defeat the counterrevolutionary global forces of imperialism. Spring's critique of authoritarianism falls within Lenin's (1917/2015) critique of anti-authoritarians as either naïve or class collaborators. Spring's objection to North Korea's education system as a form of indoctrination is hardly worth engaging when one really considers how the DPRK is under the constant threat of and danger of being the next victim of U.S. foreign policy. Writing Kim Il-Sung's approach to education off as a form of backward patriotism because he believed in Marx's polytechnic approach to education where manual labor and mental labor were reunited, thereby countering the alienation of capitalism and fostering a form of patriotism or loyalty to communism and the dictatorship of the proletariat, can be understood as nothing less than counterrevolutionary.

However, it is not my intention here to suggest that there are no contradictions within the DPRK's state apparatus or that its process of creating socialism is complete or perfectly worked out. Lenin's insistence that the dictatorship of the proletariat must persist until all internal and external capitalist threats are neutralized, however, offers a window into why workers' states have not progressed faster or farther than they have. Again, workers' states do not exist in a vacuum but are situated within a global context dominated by the anticommunist foreign policy of U.S. imperialism, which forces countries like the DPRK into defensive positions and compels them to consume growing portions of their total social product on defense spending as a necessary deterrent. This is a challenge to resist contributing to the imperialist propaganda demonizing the DPRK by exaggerating its struggles decontextualized from the larger context of global capitalism and imperialist aggression. The correct communist position is, therefore, to express a deep objection to imperialism's policies of isolation, economic sanctions, ideological distortions, military hostility, and racism toward the DPRK. Positively, the correct position here in regards to the DPRK is one of solidarity and support for its right to exist and an affirming of the socialist nature of its society and economy. In this regard perhaps the best way to demonstrate support for the DPRK and challenge imperialist propaganda is to provide a brief history of the DPRK and how it came to develop the organizational form that it has.

The story here begins in 1905 when Japan colonized the entire Korean peninsula, subjecting the Korean people to the most vicious treatment and oppression. Korean families living in Manchuria were equally victimized, leading to Korean communists living in Manchuria playing a particularly decisive role after WWII and the defeat of Japan. At this time Korean communists throughout the peninsula, side-by-side with Chinese comrades, agreed among themselves to unite around the leadership of General Kim Il-Sung. While he was only thirty-two years old at the time, he was selected due to the effectiveness of his guerilla units in Manchuria while fighting the Japanese occupying forces under the most difficult circumstances. The significance of Kim Il-Sung's leadership cannot be exaggerated. This is important because a common distortion is that when the Soviet Union and the United States, allies during WWII, divided Korea at the 38th parallel, the Soviet Union handpicked Kim Il-Sung to be North Korea's puppet dictator. This might have been the case when the U.S. selected South Korean leader Syngman Rhee, but the DPRK chose a more independent path. While Rhee was spending decades in the U.S. attending Princeton University and then developing close relationships with both Republican and Democratic leaders in Washington, D.C., Kim was leading cadres of guerilla fighters against Japanese imperialist colonizers in Manchuria and Korea.

As the central gravitational force of the global class struggle after WWII was between the U.S. and the Soviet Union, until the fall of the latter, Marcy is clear that the struggle in Korea was connected to this larger context. However, as suggested above, Marcy also rejects the suggestion that Korea was nothing more than a pawn in the match between U.S. President Harry Truman and Stalin. At the same time, Marcy refuses to accept the equally incorrect position that the Korean scene operated in isolation and was unaffected by the influence of the two great powers of class antagonism. Making this point, Marcy (1976a) notes, "While it is incontestably valid to affirm that the revolutionary ferment of the Korean workers and peasants was the most indispensable social ingredient in the composite interplay of class forces in that corner of the Asiatic crucible, it would be entirely wrong to regard it as a unique phenomenon divorced from the historic process of our time" (p. 35).

For example, the division of Korea into northern and southern states subverted what was a unified communist offensive against imperialism throughout the entire peninsula. This division was a Soviet compromise to the U.S.-led imperialist class camp of the global class war. The division of Germany into an East and a West, and the division of Vietnam into two states, all represent the concessions to global capitalism. While capitalist propaganda portrays the communist portions of these divided states as losses to so-called democracy despised by the people living within them, it was actually Kim Il-Sung's communist politics that led to his widespread popularity among Korea's working class and peasantry. In South Korea, on the other hand, no popular leader existed. When Japan surrendered in 1945 and gave up its grip on Korea, the U.S. took over South Korea to maintain the colonial control and domination instituted by Japan. From 1945 it was therefore clear that the U.S. did not support Korean independence. Between 1945 and 1950 more than one hundred thousand communist supporters in South Korea were executed by the U.S.-backed Rhee regime. Kim Il-Sung, therefore, came to represent independence and socialism on the Korean peninsula. The repression against Kim supporters in South Korea was intense for fifty years. Thirty- to forty-year prison sentences awaited anyone found guilty of supporting Kim and the DPRK.

Following in the communist footsteps of the Soviet Union, China would lend support to Korean communists after an invasion by U.S.-led United

Nations forces in 1950, when the People's Republic of China was still new. Just as China sent troops to fight on the side of the DPRK, the U.S. obviously fought on the side of bourgeois interests in South Korea. While the center of the proletarian class camp in the global class war was universally recognized as the Soviet Union, being the first Socialist state, of which national communist parties around the world, in theory at least, were supposed to be branches, in practice, Kim Il-Sung and the Korean Communist Party were more closely aligned with the Chinese Communist Party. This alliance stemmed from their collective struggle in not only the war against the invading U.S. military between 1950 and 1953 that ended with the near complete destruction of North Korea, and against Japanese imperialism before then, but also from the Korean Workers' Party sending thousands of troops to China between 1945 and 1949, which provided decisive support for the PLA's victory over the nationalist forces and the establishment of the People's Republic of China. However, North Korea's remarkable rebuilding effort after the U.S. bombed the country nearly out of existence between 1950 and 1953 was made possible by the generous aid and support of the Soviet Union, and by their close connections with the socialist countries of Eastern Europe. The international solidarity during this time was remarkable and continues to inspire communists today the world over.

When the relationship between China and the Soviet Union broke down, the DPRK was pulled in multiple directions with both pro-Soviet and pro-China factions within the DPRK leadership. Ultimately, the DPRK maintained its own independent path. What continues to warrant support in the DPRK today is its status as a sovereign nation and right to self-determination, as well as its socialist structure, including its full employment and free universal education, healthcare, and housing. The workers' state of the DPRK, in other words, should be supported just as any other workers' state or any union should be supported when under attack from the capitalist class. The aforementioned resources the DPRK is forced to dedicate to defense spending places tremendous strain on its economy already weakened by U.S. economic sanctions. The resulting periodic privations and hunger that strike pain at the working class and peasantry of the DPRK is used as evidence by imperialist propagandists for the failure of communism in general, and to paint the DPRK communist leadership as particularly cruel, and living a luxurious existence off of the backs of workers in particular. So successful has this propaganda been that not even the Western Left has been able to offer much resistance in terms of reproducing it.

The Black Panther Party

Now I want to examine an important communist group that operated on the understanding that has been articulated thus far in this book. As politically engaged African American community college students in Oakland, California, during the 1960s when American Blacks were gaining inspiration from African independence movements, Huey P. Newton and Bobby Seale, searching for a path toward Black liberation in America—especially after the murder of Malcolm X in 1965—drafted the Black Panther Party (BPP) for Self-Defense's Ten-Point Program in 1966 and organized and directed its rapid expansion during 1967. Reflecting on the strengths of Newton, the revolutionary Mumia Abu-Jamal (2000) recounts, "He was a youth of rare brilliance, who molded mass militancy into a national Black political movement that lit an age into radical incandescence" (p. 137). While it is most common to focus on the cultural influences of African freedom fights on African American radicals, including the BPP, perhaps the most significant influence was communism. However, accepting the communist influence of African freedom fighters was not something that was automatic for Newton or the thousands of African Americans who joined the BPP and started chapters across the U.S.

For example, in her autobiography, *Assata: An Autobiography*, Assata Shakur (1987) recounts how she was raised to be suspicious of communism because of its image in the Black community as just another European imposition and also due to its demonization in U.S. society in general. In her book Shakur reflects on how her engagement with the works of African communists transformed her misperceptions. The fact that every anticolonialist struggle in Africa from the 1950s through the 1970s was fighting for socialism offered her compelling evidence for the relevance of Marxism-Leninism.

In her discussion of the International Section of the Black Panther Party, Kathleen Cleaver (1998), echoing Harry Haywood, notes that the Party understood that "Black self-determination was not feasible under American imperialist domination" (p. 212). Cleaver notes that while the BPP's membership was exclusively Black, their message and practice were geared more toward the communist ethic of power to the people and the unification of all anti-imperialist movements and workers' states rather than on the more isolationist practice of Black nationalism and Black Power. Regarding the revolution in Algeria, which the CIA was concerned would pave the way for the rise to power of communists through the National Liberation Front (NLF) (Blum,

2003), Cleaver notes, "The Panthers admired the Algerian revolution and considered its victory a powerful example of the ability of oppressed people to attain power over their destiny" (p. 213). Black Panther Party members would be represented at the Organization of African Unity conferences hosted in Algeria and had visited and established relationships with workers' states such as Cuba and the DPRK. The BPP, therefore, struggled to extend the communist movement in the U.S., which was difficult given the limitations of the CP-USA and the SWP as demonstrated by Marcy (1976b).

Huey P. Newton was not only the BPP's co-founder, he was also its revolutionary theoretician and, as such, was continuously engaged in the process of developing the party's tendency, the influences of which were wide ranging, including Marxist-Leninism. Newton (1995) would eventually come to adopt what is obviously Lenin's (1917/2015) framework outlined in *The State and Revolution*. For example, Newton, in a creative twist on Lenin, argues that U.S. imperialism had negated the conditions for states to exist, such as economic and territorial sovereignty. Newton, therefore, argues that the world consisted not of states or nations, but of imperialists, on one hand, and dominated or colonized oppressed communities on the other. From this point of view, Cuba, China, the Soviet Union, and the DPRK were examples of liberated communities. Oppressed communities within the U.S., such as the Black community, from this perspective, should follow the example of liberated communities, adopting their revolutionary goals as adapted for the American context. The Panthers therefore argued for a unified struggle of all oppressed communities the world over aimed at destroying imperialism and the capitalist system in general and replacing them with communism. Under communism, in accordance with Lenin's model, Newton was adamant that oppressed communities would retain their right to self-determination, realized under the protection of democratic centralism dedicated to fighting the counterrevolutionaries of the capitalist class. Newton also understood that racism and all manner of bigotry would also have to be eradicated through education in order for the proletarian state to be able to wither away and for communism to be able to flourish freely.

The BPP's first campaign was the establishment of a regularized armed patrol targeting the state's Oakland Police Department due to its history of terrorizing and murdering members of the Black community, the vast majority of which represented some of the highest concentrations of unskilled, super-exploited workers. The BPP understood that the role of the police was to employ deadly force to create an intimidation-based consent to extreme exploitation. At the height of his popularity, Huey Newton, who has been described as a youth of rare brilliance, commanded the respect and commitment of the African American community across the country, leading to the establishment of BPP chapters from coast to coast.

A fundamental component of why Newton was so dangerous in the eyes of the U.S. bourgeoisie was because he understood that the global proletariat was a great chain, and each conglomeration of workers around the world can be thought of as links in the great chain. What happens to workers in England affects workers and the price of their labor in the U.S. Lenin applied this insight to unions and the role of the strike (see chapter 4). When one shop strikes and wins victories, it affects the average price of labor within the whole branch of industry and can also inspire workers in the same region to take similar actions, thereby affecting other branches of industry. Newton, familiar with the work and tradition of Harry Haywood, employed this concept in the U.S. to understand how racism was used to push down the price of labor among Black and Brown workers and, in turn, their communities, and because all workers are links in the same chain, the overall price of labor within the whole country is suppressed. From this view it makes little sense to hold on to colonial structures and pressure more privileged white workers to paternalistically support more oppressed and exploited workers as a moral act because it is far more revolutionary for more privileged workers and less privileged workers to dissolve their class differences through revolutionary struggle as comrades. Again, following Haywood, this requires an engagement with racial differences within the labor market rather than pretending they do not exist.

Again, the anticommunism of the American Left is so deep-seated that it is uncommon in retrospective discussions of the BPP to acknowledge that they were a party in the communist sense and stood in solidarity with workers' states. For example, as a U.S. political prisoner, BPP leader George Jackson found inspiration in the political writings of imprisoned Palestinians in Israel (Pierce, 2015). The BPP not only was a descendant of Malcolm X, it was also following in the communist footsteps of Harry Haywood, adopting much of his analysis and practice. The BPP regularly sent delegations to workers' states and routinely distributed Maoist literature at rallies.

Perhaps the internal contradictions of the BPP were too great to overcome, as some commentators suggest. However great their errors were, the evidence seems to suggest that the FBI's Counter Intelligence Programs (COINTEL-PRO) operations played the most decisive role in the destruction and elimination of the BPP. The same can be said of the SWP and the CP-USA who had been subjected to COINTELPRO operations since the 1940s (Churchill & Vander Wall, 1990). The goal of COINTELPRO was to disrupt, discredit, and neutralize communism and the political Left in general. Churchill and Vander Wall describe this war as secret because it was. The FBI, for example, would employ agent provocateurs who would infiltrate the ranks of the BPP in order to foment internal dissent within the organization, as well as provide authorities with critical intelligence that could be used against the radicals.

William O'Neal was such a character who joined the BPP as an undercover FBI agent. O'Neal would eventually work his way up the ranks of the BPP and become Fred Hampton's personal security guard. Hampton was of interest to the FBI because he was the chairman of the Chicago chapter of the BPP and a dynamic, influential revolutionary leader who had made great strides in fostering working-class solidarity across racial lines. O'Neal seems to have drugged Hampton and provided the FBI and the Chicago PD with a floor plan of Hampton's apartment, making it much easier to carry out his assassination, which occurred on December 4, 1969, at approximately 4:30 A.M. (Churchill & Vander Wall). Among the tactics employed by COINTELPRO operatives to neutralize the BPP nationwide included eavesdropping, sending bogus mail, "black propaganda" operations, disinformation or "gray propaganda," harassment arrests, infiltrators and agent provocateurs, "pseudo gangs," bad-jacketing, fabrication of evidence, and assassinations (Churchill & Vander Wall). While most of these tactics require explanations and examples to develop a full understanding, suffice it to say that the FBI's efforts to destroy the communist movement within America's Black working class were limited only by the creative deviancy of COINTELPRO agents.

At the first Black Radical Tradition conference at Temple University in early January 2016, Mumia Abu-Jamal, phoning in from prison to deliver a keynote presentation, argued that the FBI's secret war to exterminate and neutralize the BPP was designed to not only obliterate them but also to replace them. That is, the goal was to remove the Black community's organic leadership and replace it with a puppet leadership no different than the way the imperialist U.S. military has instituted regime changes across the globe, such as in Iraq and Afghanistan and as is the current goal for Syria. The Black bourgeois leadership class that has emerged in the U.S. might be understood as serving this purpose.

Globally, the Soviet Union—and the communist movement more generally—has suffered the same fate at the hands of the imperialist counterrevolutionaries. Whether operating within the U.S. through federal and state police agencies or outside the U.S. through the military and the CIA, the physical bourgeois assault on the communist horizon has been fundamental. This imperialist threat is also another link in the chain of the global class war.

Becoming Communist

The coalescing of the revolutionary center of gravity with that of the economic center will be the great turning point in ... history. The first truly revolutionary outburst on the social soil of the American continent will light the flames of a new revolutionary conflagration which is sure to envelop the entire globe. It will graphically demonstrate how "East meets West" not by the construction of new and more tortuous artificial, boundaries, but by the revolutionary destruction of all of them. It will be the supreme and ultimate alliance of the great truly progressive classes of the East and West in a final effort to accomplish their own dissolution. This in turn will terminate the first great cycle of man's development from sub-man—man—to Communist Man, and set him on the path to new and higher syntheses.

—Marcy (1976a, p. 41)

What Marcy describes here began to take place in 1966 with the birth of the Black Panther Party. Rather than realizing its global revolutionary vision, its leaders were murdered, imprisoned, and demonized. Despite this and other setbacks, the ultimate unification of the world's proletarian masses, united around a shared vision of communism, remains possible. However, even though it is changing, the communist vision is still stigmatized as incomplete. As previously argued, the communist coming-to-be informing this book should not be interpreted as the violent imposition of a European conception of being forced onto non-European and Indigenous subjectivities. Rather, communism offers a global economic structure where Indigenous subjectivities can be reformulated after centuries of physical, biological, and cultural genocide.

Lenin's conception of Oppressed Nations offers a more complete picture of how the sovereignty of the world's Indigenous peoples would be an integral component of a socialist future. Marx's notion of each according to her ability and each according to her need offers a more philosophical approach to understanding the inclusiveness of a communist ethic. Marcy's work is crucial because he is absolutely clear that the threat of U.S. imperialism, situated in a world forever at war, makes all states dedicate such a large portion of their national productive capacity to the military as to render serious efforts for socialist planning nearly impossible. For this reason, Marcy (1976a) argues that the center of global capitalist economic power, which is the U.S., must develop into the center of global revolutionary gravity. Marcy, therefore, suggests that only through the defeat of U.S. imperialism can the unification of the global proletarian class camp be realized. This, perhaps, remains true today. Each day, then, Lenin (1917/2015) grows more relevant and more urgent.

Ironically enough, there is a strong tendency within the U.S. Left, and the educational Left in particular, to argue that the actual communists, communists in China, the former Soviet Union, and the DPRK, are not the real communists, but state capitalists betraying the spirit and intent of Marx. The arrogance of such positions is absurd, even taking into consideration the imperfections of real existing communism. Given the anticommunist nature of U.S. society, I believe that other potential communists, people like myself who have been involved in Marxism and/or critical pedagogy for decades, might struggle with the necessary solidarity with the aforementioned communist states. This is important because members of communist parties cannot pick and choose which aspects of the party's platform to support and defend. Party members, correctly in my view, must support and defend the entire platform. To clarify what a Communist Party program entails, I will briefly turn to the PSL as an example. The purpose here is not to provide a complete overview, but to spark the reader's interest.

A Party for Socialism and Liberation

The first two lines of *Socialism and Liberation in the United States: The Program of the PSL* (2011) provides a succinct summary of the overall purpose and vision of the PSL:

> The Party for Socialism and Liberation exists to carry out the struggle for socialism inside the United States, the center of world capitalism and imperialism. The PSL stands in solidarity with our sisters and brothers around the world who are resisting capitalist exploitation and imperialist domination. (p. 3)

Toward these ends the PSL, while agitating for the difficult transition from capitalism to socialism in the U.S. and beyond, stands with all movements fighting for progressive reforms, from lesbian, gay, bisexual, transgender, and queer (LGBTQ) rights, the struggle to increase the minimum wage, to the reemergence of the Black community's historic role as the vanguard of the freedom struggle in the U.S., to workers' states, parties, and unions throughout the world. As a critical pedagogue, I can say with confidence that the PSL consistently not only verbalizes its support for the full emancipation of all workers and oppressed communities, but it daily and consistently fights for it in the streets through an effective party system of organization necessary in the struggle against the extremely organized bourgeoisie.

Consequently, the PSL does not treat social class as a separate and unrelated form of oppression from racism, sexism, homophobia, xenophobia, and so on. Rejecting the analysis that treats racism, sexism, and classism as separate forms of oppression, the PSL is grounded in a Marxist analysis of capitalism, that is, the process of expanding value through the exploitation of labor power, as the larger context and motivation to understand, for example, the centrality of racism to capitalism. As a result, the PSL is truly the people's party, a party for all workers, not just some of the workers. This is crucial since there tends to be an assumption within critical pedagogy that Marxists do not believe that race, for example, is relevant (or as relevant as class, for example) for a proletarian revolution. While some Marxists might make this mistake, the PSL does not, and its organizational structure provides a pedagogical model that demands an educated membership.

The competitive drive among capitalists for progressively greater and cheaper sources of labor power, raw materials, and new markets led to a series of stages or eras identified by V. I. Lenin in his globally influential pamphlet, *Imperialism: The Highest Stage of Capitalism*, and recently updated in a book by the Party for Socialism and Liberation (2015), *Imperialism in the 21st Century: Updating Lenin's Theory a Century Later*. Summarizing this movement of capital, Lenin argues that during Marx's time capitalists competed among themselves nationally in leading capitalist nations, the U.S., England, France, and Germany in particular, which led to national monopolies. The General Law of Accumulation (see chapter 5) identified by Marx (1867/1967) then led capitalist nations to face each other in competition over the dividing up of Africa and East Asia in particular. The imperialist nations, argues Lenin, underwent significant shifts such as exporting capital rather than products of labor, which was made possible by the merging of bank capital with industrial capital, giving way to financial capital. These shifts occurred during capital's earlier monopoly phase of development. Imperialist capital was becoming a more globalized and dominating force (PSL, 2015).

Lenin emphasizes how such imperialist tendencies emerged within competing capitalist nations not as the product of particular policy choices, but as a result of the internal laws of capitalist accumulation, which Marx (1867/1967) repeatedly points out, acted upon individual capitalists as an external coercive force (PSL, 2015). In fact, in every stage of the development of capital the laws of accumulation compel capitalists to act in particular kinds of savage ways or be driven out of business by their competitors. This tendency remains true today. In other words, U.S. imperialism is not the product of a group of evil Republicans and corrupted Democrats who have subverted the "democratic" process, but rather it reflects the current stage in the historical development of capital, which can only be temporarily slowed down, it cannot be reformed out of capital. Only a worldwide working-class revolution can transcend imperialist capitalism, and only the dictatorship of the proletariat will ensure that all remnants of counterrevolutionary capitalist forces will be crushed once and for all time. The PSL stands with China, the DPRK, Cuba, and all nations independent of imperialist control, such as Syria, as the BPP had in an earlier era, and this stance is, therefore, the correct position for the U.S. proletarian camp in the global class war.

However, while the PSL stands with workers' states, for bourgeois nationalist governments like the Ba'ath government in Syria, the PSL defends the right to self-determination, which is a project of the whole nation and not just the Ba'athist state. Sometimes their state acts to defend national sovereignty, as in the case of the current civil war, but other times the PSL would have to be critical of it (and not in a comradely way), like when they suffocated the Lebanese revolution in 1975–1976. When the Left condemned British aggression, they certainly weren't defending the state that was literally waging war on the Argentine communist movement but, rather, were defending the Argentine nation's right to self-determination over the entirety of its territory. We can think about the dilemma of the Iranian communist movement when it comes to this question. It is opposing U.S. hostility toward a regime that came to power by massacring tens of thousands of their comrades—but they're defending the Iranian nation, not the Iranian state.

Once the world was divided up into colonies controlled by the imperialist nations, the only path to the ongoing expansion required by capital's laws of accumulation, beyond revolutions in production, was for nations to encroach on each other's colonial territories, which Lenin correctly predicted would lead to the World Wars. After World War II the Soviet Union emerged stronger than ever, giving way to a global working-class socialist camp with Soviet-supported socialist countries all over the world. The so-called Cold War consisted of the U.S. and its supporting countries waging a global class war on the Socialist Bloc. Once the Soviet Union fell, the U.S. emerged as the world's single capitalist superpower, targeting independent peripheral capitalist nations that had been able to survive under the protection of the Socialist Bloc. Today's global communist movement is correctly targeting U.S. imperialism by attacking capitalism and all of its divisive and oppressive mechanisms such as homophobia, sexism, xenophobia, and racialization. A communist pedagogy not grounded within this fundamental position has not yet developed political maturity.

· 4 ·

RIGHT-TO-WORK LAWS AND LENIN'S COMMUNIST PEDAGOGY

Introduction

This chapter examines so-called Right-to-Work (RTW) laws as a nearly seventy-year push by the capitalist-state machine to not only dislodge restrictions on capital's ability to increase the rate of exploitation of labor power as one of many measures to counter falling rates of profit, but as an attack on communism as well. This focus is markedly different from the analysis generally offered by the educational Left in the U.S., which tends to focus exclusively on the privatization of public education and the devastating restrictions on public sector unions as attacks on the public sphere and democracy. These notions suggest that neoliberal policies can be rolled back for a kinder, more egalitarian capitalism.

The analysis articulated within this chapter is therefore based on the assumption that the struggle against RTW laws should be understood, expressed, and engaged as part of the global, anticapitalist movement itself. In the process, following Lenin more directly, the case is made that the only realistic way to defeat capitalism is through an organized movement, or through the Party-form (i.e., a Communist Party). Within this discussion we point to some of the ways Lenin's discussion on the Communist Party offers pedagogical insights. Finally, this chapter does not provide a systematic analysis of Lenin or RTW but, rather, offers an introductory discussion.

Right-to Work Propaganda and Lenin's Communistic Optic

If you are working on a degree in the education field, or any number of social services, your future will likely entail joining a public sector union. Such unions not only come with certain protections and benefits, they also tend to set high standards of pay and working conditions for non-unionized workers. However, it is not just unions or their achievements that are of particular importance to Lenin concerning what we might call a *communist pedagogy*. Rather, it is the effect of the process of those victories, such as strikes, on workers' collective consciousness. Reflecting on the tendency of unionized shops to reduce the rate of exploitation within both specific branches of industry and within the space of a region or town, Lenin (1924/1970) notes:

> See what a tremendous effect strikes have both on the strikers themselves and on the workers at neighboring or nearby factories or at factories in the same industry. … Workers of neighboring factories gain renewed courage when they see that their comrades have engaged themselves in struggle. (p. 62)

This tendency to radicalize is the result of workers sharpening their awareness of the true nature of the relationship between themselves as labor power and the capitalist and its state as personified capitalists. That is, the relationship is one of oppressed and oppressor or exploited and exploiter, which cannot be reformed but only destroyed and replaced. In other words, because labor power is the only commodity endowed with a self-expansive property, the capitalist as such, as augmenter of capital, cannot exist without exploiting labor power. Without the exploitation of labor power, on an extending and deepening scale, the capitalist does not exist because no new capital will have been created. This insight leads the workers to gain a collective consciousness that their true class enemy is the capitalist class. This, of course, is our first insight into understanding why unions—these legal assemblies of workers— are, and have been since their emergence, under attack. However, unions in the U.S. are still being harassed, having been terrorized by the capitalists' private and public militia and police forces, ideological machine, and legal apparatus. Consequently, the labor movement in the U.S. has been beaten and duped into largely abandoning its former militancy. However, a new gen-eration of teachers and teacher union radicals is returning unions to their necessary militant past (Weiner, 2015). This new/old social movement model of unionism, outlined by Lois Wiener, is beginning to challenge the official position of many public and private sector unions in the U.S., thereby chal-lenging the bourgeois myth that harmony between labor and capital is possi-ble (Lenin, 1912/1970).

Many teachers and faculty unions today, in response to the trend of cutting state education budgets, still continue to argue that creating more educated workers enables individual states to attract employers offering "better" jobs, thereby bolstering their local economies. However, if economists are correct that nearly 80 percent of all new jobs created in the U.S. in the next twenty years will be low-skill level, service-oriented, minimum-wage jobs (Marsh, 2011), then these unions, whether they realize it or not, are contributing to competition among workers for a scarcity of well-paying jobs (i.e., between states). The competition for a reduced number of manufacturing jobs due to technological advancements and greater access to foreign labor markets have led states to a race to the bottom. Ultimately, the competition has spawned special tax breaks for corporations, leaving communities with depleted public coffers. This contributes to the cutting of school budgets and the deteriora-tion of school districts and the opening up of schooling as a market service that is publicly funded. There is little evidence in the U.S. that unions are adequately challenging this competition among workers instigated by capi-tal's current dominance and manipulation over the market in labor. That is, the organization of the economy around exchange-value at the expense of use-value.

While Marx (1866/1990) recognizes that capitalism fosters an unavoid-able competition among workers, "trades' unions originally sprang up from the spontaneous attempts of workmen at removing or at least checking that com-petition" (p. 33). The fact that working conditions and the power of unions have deteriorated to such an extent that many of them betray the spirit from which they originally sprang is further evidence that a Marxist-Leninist inter-vention is needed. Again, the developing social movement model of teacher unionism is evidence that a new communist movement is developing in the U.S.—and well beyond.

Of course, the situation of trade unions consenting to both the com-petition between workers and the myth of fairness within capital, and the fact that the capitalist state machine continues its relentless attacks against unions, despite this long legacy of accommodation to the reification of wage labor, are not new. In other words, workers' unions have been targeted at every stage in capitalism's historical development, even when they capitulate to the demands of capital. If the trade unions are currently not an immediate threat to capital by radicalizing workers, they are always a potential threat, and they always stand as a barrier of more or less effectiveness to capital's ability to freely increase the rate of exploitation. Workers' unions continue to hold the greatest potential of realizing labor's potential to become its collective communist opposite organized together, across unions and across nations, through the Party-form.

Perhaps the biggest threat to the ongoing existence of public (as opposed to private) sector labor unions in the U.S., outside of their accommodationism or opportunism, are Right-to-Work (RTW) laws, which have been passed in twenty-five states. Because RTW laws prevent unions from employing fair share dues (explained below), membership in public sector unions in RTW states has declined significantly, degrading the ability of workers to collectively defend their professions, working conditions, and quality of life. What I argue below is that RTW laws reduce workers' collective, material, and concrete power as a result of states enacting laws, made possible, in part, from the employment of bourgeois ideology through schooling and the mass media that spreads disinformation about the true nature of trades' unions.

While recent national antilabor momentum has propelled RTW into the spotlight across the U.S., it is not widely known that the first RTW laws were actually passed in the mid- and late 1940s in Florida, Arkansas, and Texas. Unsurprisingly, the history of RTW has deep racist roots fueled by anticommunist and race-mixing propaganda. In the 1930s Vance Muse, a Texan capitalist, began conceptualizing anti-union legislation informed not only by his desire to retain the high rates of exploitation unions threatened but also by his deep belief in white supremacy. Muse reasoned that unions foster a form of comradery between white and Black workers, which led to race mixing and coalition building. He correctly viewed communism as antiracist, but as a racist himself, this was not viewed as progressive but as threatening. Thus, while some unions, such as the American Federation of Labor and Congress of Industrial Organizations (AFL-CIO) began to adopt antiracist positions ahead of federal policy, other unions, such as the Industrial Workers of the World (IWW), were strongly internationalist and antiracist. Muse's position on race was reflected in organized labor where histories of discriminatory practices kept Black and Brown workers, as well as women, out of their organizations.

The racism of American unions was so entrenched that even as recently as the 1960s, teachers' unions in New York City resisted a working-class, African American movement for community control of the curriculum. The teachers went as far as blocking entrances to particular schools to prevent African American students from entering. The unions' move was interpreted as another example of the racism of white teachers operating as an external, bourgeois force in Black communities (Kohl, 1999; Perlstein, 1999). However, from a capitalist perspective, unions were still the representatives of the white working class.

It is no coincidence that the RTW movement emerged in the U.S. during the Great Depression when massive unemployment, poverty, starvation, and general immiseration led to the radicalization of U.S. workers and the explosion of the numbers of workers joining Socialist and Communist Parties (Becker, 2015; Parenti, 1997). For example, in 1929 the CP-USA had eight thousand members. A decade later, toward the end of the Great Depression, the Party swelled to more than one hundred thousand members. This coincided with massive increases in trades unions, which occurred more than sixty years before Fair Share. Fair Share is now being threatened in states such as Pennsylvania by so-called Paycheck Protection legislation. Lenin (1924/1970) explains the logic of working-class momentum as infectious. He notes the rise of radicalization among workers when "study circles and associations become more widespread among them and more workers become socialists" (p. 63). The dispersion of radicalism certainly took place during the Great Depression, which brought on deadly state repression aimed at destroying and demonizing socialism in the U.S. Just as unions lead to strikes, victories such as higher wages and the potential for subsequent radicalization led to an attack against unions. Accordingly, the focus of anti-union organizations became increased exploitation and reduced wages. Most damaging to union progress was the attack and demonization of the party as well as a movement to downplay capitalism. A necessary component of the communist movement, unions required that capitalism be the center of the global proletariat's revolution.

Lenin reminds us that it is when workers become class conscious and begin to organize, strike, and thus flex their collective strength that they start to realize that the state is a tool of capital and its laws tend to be designed to serve their interests. In this way Lenin (1924/1970) describes the strike as "a school of war" (p. 65). This conceptualization of change within Marx's Hegelian dialectic is seen as developmental.

Lenin adopts a new concept, where new conditions can only emerge directly from, and not separate from, old ones (Malott & Ford, 2015). That is, by describing the strike as a school, Lenin draws upon the workers' collective ability for learning and creating a knowledge base needed to transform capitalism into socialism. Lenin's (1924/1970) insights are instructive:

> Every strike strengthens and develops in the workers the understanding that the government is their enemy and that the working class must prepare itself to struggle against the government for the peoples' rights. Strikes, therefore, teach the workers to unite; they show them that they can struggle against the capitalists only when they are united; strikes teach the workers to think of the struggle of the whole working class against the whole class of factory owners and against the arbitrary, police government. This is the reason that socialists call strikes "a school of war," a school in which the workers learn to make war on their enemies for the liberation of the whole people, all of who labor, from the yoke of government officials and from the yoke of capital. (p. 65)

While this insight is crucial in understanding the development of working class critical consciousness, Lenin critiques the tendency of trades' unions, and even some socialists, to believe that full emancipation can be achieved for workers in capitalism through the strike. For this reason, Lenin is clear that while the strike might be a school of war, it is not a war itself. That is, the strike must be conceptualized as a tool to not only enhance the material conditions of workers' lives, but it also must be strategically employed to increase the number of class conscious workers as a way to seize state power and socialize the means of production.

To this end, the economy is organized and planned around meeting workers' needs rather than augmenting capital (i.e., perpetually expanding capital). The workers' school is consciously forged in the practice of organizing and carrying out a strike. In practice a strike can be defined as the collective refusal of workers to work, thereby abruptly stopping the bringing together of variable capital (i.e., labor power) and constant capital (i.e., raw materials and machinery) in the production of commodities, including both physical items, such as books, and immaterial services, such as teaching and waiting tables in a restaurant. In other words, this refusal to labor blocks the process of extracting surplus labor time from laborers, which is the sole incentive the capitalist has for entering the labor market as purchaser of this unique human commodity. In fact, the consumption of human labor power is the only way the capitalist can expand his money and create new value and, thus, the only way the capitalist can exist as such. Refusing to work retards the capitalist's ability to exist as such, self-expansively. Only when the conflict is resolved can the capitalist continue the self-expansive process. Again, because of the importance of human labor power to the capitalist, the state is controlled by capital to discipline this human, and, thus, always potentially rebellious source of capital's self-expansion.

For the communist the purpose of spreading working-class, revolutionary consciousness is necessary because the experience of exploitation alone is not enough to develop a scientific understanding of the capitalistic process of perpetually expanding capital, the heart and internal drive of bourgeois society—nor is it enough to understand that there is an alternative to capitalism. Such insights are crucial because they challenge the bourgeois myth that the exchange between labor and capital is fair, or ever could be fair. If some degree or rate of exploitation is a requirement for capitalism to exist, then it becomes clear that it is, by definition, impossible to ever strike a fair agreement between labor and capital. The only path to justice is, therefore, to transform capitalist production relations into socialist ones. The strike as the school of war has as its purpose the creation of the Communist Party, and the purpose of the Party is also to engage the war against the capitalist class and the ultimate establishment of the workers' state and the management of the planned economy—planned for the purpose of meeting human needs rather than planned for the management of the market and for the maintenance of the capitalist class, as is the case within the capitalist state. Rather than repressing the self-determination of oppressed nations, both inside and outside of imperialist states, the workers' state represses the old capitalist class from exploiting and oppressing workers.

Again, the state's attack on unions is done both to prevent short-term gains in wages and also to subvert the long-term goal of overthrowing capitalism in general. It is within this context that we can best understand the passage in 1947 of the Taft-Hartley antilabor legislation that mandated unions use their own resources to defend all workers, even those workers who did not pay union dues (Kahlenberg & Marvit, 2012). This law led to the disempowerment of public sector unions in states that have passed RTW laws by draining their economic base (i.e., the collection of fair share compulsory union dues). As a result of this legislation, fourteen states passed RTW laws by 1947. In 1961, even as Martin Luther King Jr. spoke out against RTW laws, his commitment to the equal treatment of all workers moved him further and further toward the rational conclusion of anticapitalism (Kahlenberg & Marvit).

On average, workers in states that have adopted RTW laws earn close to $6,000 less a year than workers in states without such laws (Kahlenberg &

Marvit). In addition, RTW states spend nearly $3,000 less per student for elementary and secondary education than free bargaining states (Kahlenberg & Marvit). The record of workplace safety is considerably worse in RTW states as well. For example, the rate of workplace deaths in RTW states is nearly 53 percent higher than in Fair Share states (Kahlenberg & Marvit). Consequently, RTW is not only economically devastating and disempowering, but it can also be deadly. States with "normally" functioning unions with less interference of RTW laws also have better records of keeping racialized compensation discrimination at bay. For example, RTW states pay Latino/a workers 50 percent less and African American workers nearly 30 percent less, on average, as compared to states without RTW (Kahlenberg & Marvit). These differences in compensation and workers' treatment echo the previous discussion on racist capitalists and their indignation toward people of color.

Since the U.S. Supreme Court has decided to take on the case of RTW through the *Friedrichs v. California Teachers Association* case, the threat of the whole capitalists' state machine could have negative consequences for current students' future earning power—especially teachers, social workers, nurses, and other graduates who will seek employment in commonly unionized public-sector occupations. The petitioners in the *Friedrichs* case are supported by the conservative legal collective, the Center for Individual Rights. If RTW passes at the federal level, public sector unions across the country, and the workers they represent, will be threatened. Consequently, public sector unions across the country are currently ramping up their membership drives, attempting to restore and reenergize the old spirit of union militancy and commitment. In today's antilabor, anti-union conservative climate, this is an uphill battle, but an indispensable one. Individuals who are a part of public-sector unions are, therefore, joining multiple organizations' efforts to build collective power. Current trends are also accompanied by many teachers and professors engaging with Marx and Lenin. While the internal tendencies and dynamics of capital are counterintuitive, complex, and vastly more expansive than is typically assumed, the conclusion that the only real path to more permanent stability and human fulfillment is through the success of the Party's establishment of a communist state and a use-value-led economy is more readily apparent. In other words, capitalism is an economy designed to maximize profit, thereby focusing on a commodity's exchange-value, which often compromises their use-value or useful effect. For example, turning education into a profit-making enterprise has led to a situation where its useful effect has been through many tactics, such as the development of labor-saving technologies like online education. A focus on use-value, on the other hand, directs production toward the maximization of use with no regard for profit because exploitation has no use according to human (i.e., socialist) values. Examining RTW laws a little more closely offers an even more concrete understanding.

As previously suggested, RTW laws subvert labor unions from safeguarding themselves against workers refusing to pay their dues, often the result of employee intimidation tactics and the aforementioned multigenerational, long anti-union propaganda campaign. According to RTW advocates (i.e., propagandists), forcing workers to pay union dues is an attack on "personal freedom," but because unions are obligated by law to represent all workers regardless if they join the union or not, the National Labor Relations Board allows unions to negotiate safeguards against freeloaders and intimidation.

For example, if your union negotiates a contract, and you receive healthcare benefits, others who work there should also have to pay their fair share to support the work that brought you those benefits. The logic is simple: all workers in an organized shop should pay their union dues because all workers benefit from the union in terms of wages, benefits, and legal protections. What is less known, however, are Lenin's (1924/1970) insights regarding the strategic role of unions in pushing for the complete emancipation of labor from the yoke of capital. The most common critiques directed at RTW, for example, lack an analysis of capitalism itself and, therefore, suggest that the role of unions is to maintain a perpetual harmony between labor and capital. Again, ignored is the deepening crisis within capitalism itself, and the need for and possibility of a communist alternative. As previously argued, the unstillable drive to expand capital cannot be content with a bourgeois model of labor unions and, therefore, will not rest until unions are gone completely.

It is within this anti-union context that the ceaseless barrage of assaults constantly emerges. To illustrate: a common myth about unions, such as teacher unions, is that they protect bad teachers. In reality, however, teachers' unions protect the due process by which faculty members are evaluated and then retained or fired. Teachers' unions ensure that those in power do not arbitrarily dismiss workers. Consequently, rather than posing a challenge to capital, unions tend to function to maintain the appearance of a harmonious relationship between labor and capital. This might be considered one of the contradictions of capitalism. That is, the capitalist impulse will target any barrier to profit, even labor organizations that ultimately maintain capitalist legitimacy. Capitalists also tend to oppose unions not because they are anticapitalist, but because they are an obstacle to unfettered exploitation. Another common myth is that unions are driven solely by self-interest. In reality, teachers and faculty unions, for example, have a long history of advocating for student needs by defending the mission of providing working people an affordable, high quality public education (Perlstein, 1999). This purpose of unions is also not inherently antithetical to capitalism, but has actually proven useful to capital. With the rise of the educational marketplace, public education is now a barrier to educational capitalists who have a direct economic incentive to privatize public education.

If RTW laws were genuinely informed by the true class interests of wage earners, then you would expect the initiative to have emerged from workers themselves—this is not the case. One of the primary groups advocating for anti-union measures is the National Right to Work Committee (NRTWC). Some of the more well-known contributors to the NRTWC are the Koch family, the Walton Family Foundation, and the American Legislative Exchange Council (ALEC), which have gained reputations for throwing millions of dollars behind antilabor efforts (Kahlenberg & Marvit). Among their initiatives, the NRTWC has spent more than $33 million since 1999 lobbying the U.S. Congress (Kahlenberg & Marvit). Demonstrating their true class interests, the NRTWC lobbied against the Employee Free Choice Act, which would have made it easier for workers to organize, while supporting initiatives that would reduce the power of the National Labor Relations Board over employers.

Again, unions have historically protected worker safety, advocated for benefits like sick days, and supported employment conditions that we all take for granted, like the concept of the weekend. It is important to note that unions have allowed workers an ability to strike, which, as Lenin argues, is necessary for the development of class consciousness and proletarian revolutions. However, as suggested above, unions can also serve more reactionary, counterrevolutionary purposes. Understood in the context of growing poverty, suffering, and imperialist aggression of the contemporary era, Lenin's insights regarding trade unions and the building of the anticapitalist Socialist Party are indispensable.

Rising Poverty and the Party

As RTW legislation advances and as attacks on workers continue, the conditions for wage labor continue to deteriorate. With the expanding degradation of workers, as we will see below, the frequency of spontaneous uprisings increases and with them, the potential for communist organizing and communist revolution becomes more fertile. However, this potential is not likely to mate-rialize without conscious socialist intervention. Lenin (1924/1970) therefore describes one of the primary purposes of the Party as increasing the number of socialist workers

> in order to make the working-class cause known to the masses of workers and to acquaint them with socialism and the working-class struggle. This is a task the social-ists and class-conscious workers must undertake jointly by organizing a socialist work-ing-class party for this purpose. (p. 66)

The task of the Socialist Party to challenge counterrevolutionary measures of the state is measured by several realities: increased poverty, a widening wealth gap, elitism and excess, and the antagonism between labor and capital. However, this is not to suggest that short-term reforms that alleviate some of this suffering should be rejected. On the contrary, any achievable reform, such as the current movement led by fast food workers for increasing the minimum wage to $15 an hour, should be supported. Marx (1866/1990) notes that "this activity of the trades' unions is not only legitimate, it is necessary" (p. 34). The task of the unions in this context is, therefore, to "look carefully after the interests of the worst-paid trades" in order to "convince the world at large that their efforts, far from being narrow and selfish, aim at the emancipation of the downtrodden millions" (p. 35).

Marx (1867/1967), of course, understood all too well the larger context in which these struggles have been situated. As predicted, the world has increas-ingly been divided into two oppositional class camps—the capitalist class on one side and the working class on the other. The task of the communists and of the class-conscious trades' unions is therefore to agitate toward the unifi-cation of the world's workers, which entails being sensitive to not only the similarities between workers but their differences as well. For example, in a recent essay, Dave Hill, Christine Lewis, Alpesh Maisuria, Patrick Yarker, and Julia Carr (2015) note that in the aftermath of the 2007 recession, the rich in Britain are 64 percent richer and the poor are 54 percent poorer. Similarly, in the U.S., the amount of total wealth going to the top 1 percent has more than doubled since 1979. Of course, such growing inequality not only disrupts the lives of workers, it is also disruptive to capitalism itself—one of the many counterintuitive laws or tendencies of the capitalist system.

Honing in on the contradictory tendency of how the process of capitalist production leads to the growing immiseration of laborers is also disruptive to the process of capitalist production by disrupting realization. Hill et al.

(2015) cite an acknowledgment by the International Monetary Fund that notes the negative consequences of income inequality on "account deficits." What this refers to is one of the central contradictions of capital that Marx (1992) outlines in the second volume of *Capital*. That is, the central drive of capital to expand accumulation on an unlimited extending scale, manifesting in efforts to push down wages below what is socially necessary, resulting in the premature exhaustion and death of the laborer unless regulated by the state or slowed down or stopped by working-class resistance, will lead to periodic disruptions in realization because of the negative effects on workers' ability to access and consume articles of their daily need. When the capitalist returns to the market as a seller of goods and services but is unable to find a sufficient number of workers entering the market as buyers of products to meet their immediate and leisure consumer needs, the circuit of capital is not completed and crisis ensues. In other words, as wages are driven down through a multitude of mechanisms from antitrade union legislation, to labor-saving technology and intensification, to the export of capital and imperialist expansionism, laborers' socially necessary access to consumption funds is subverted, and if a welfare system is not in place, rebellion will likely ensue. Increasing the credit economy and creating new markets in luxury goods, for example, have temporarily displaced such crises.

As global capitalism continues to descend into deepening crisis, imperialist countries, such as the U.S. and Britain, also continue their attacks on public education. Many teachers' and faculty unions argue that investing in public education makes economic sense. By ensuring that local school districts and universities are properly funded, local economies are directly supported. So how should this be understood beyond my previous discussion on competition? Are capitalists just not smart enough to see the obvious? I think there are many interrelated answers to this conundrum. First, the aforementioned education capitalists have a direct interest in turning the public against publicly controlled education so they can take control of the tax monies appropriated for public education in order to attempt to make a profit off of them. Second, technological developments have changed capital's needs in terms of the level of education or skill level of laborers. However, there is much more to this story than what first appears.

To provide an example from the nineteenth century, the advent of the machine factory in the mid-1800s shifted the knowledge base of workers to command the tools of industry. For the first time in history, the workers did not control the means of production; the machines controlled the workers. In the place of the artificial divisions of labor created by manufacture stepped the natural division of age and sex. Where the skill level required by industry was lowered and the efficiency of production was greatly enhanced, rather than freeing workers from labor as they reproduced the value of their own existence in a much shorter time, this revolution in production was used by capital to extend the length of the workday beyond its natural limits and increase the immiseration and degradation of the laborer to new levels of barbarity. The previous leverage the workers had in advocating for better wages embodied in the necessary knowledge they possessed concerning the operation of their tools was swept away. The resulting suffering and debasement led to a new militancy and movement for socialism from the U.S. to England and beyond. It was within this context of increased alienation and intellectual degradation that mass schooling emerged. Thus, common schooling emerged not because capitalists needed more-educated workers, but because they were convinced education could be employed to create more obedient workers, adding another front of struggle in their fight against communism.

As poverty and suffering escalate in the U.S., and as U.S. imperialism dominates, it is not surprising that we are witnessing a renewed emphasis on flag education and blind patriotism. But what is happening in the schools where we have witnessed recent rebellions such as Ferguson, Missouri, and Baltimore, Maryland? Are teachers joining the movement? Are radical teachers being marginalized? Are there ramped-up efforts to pacify Black and Brown students in these oppressed communities? We know that in Baltimore there is currently a proposal to cut funding to the city's schools by $35 million, where schools are already $2,000 per pupil below what the state says is adequate. The proposed cuts put four hundred teachers and seven hundred support staff in jeopardy of losing their jobs (Campbell, 2015). If national trends are any indication, these proposed cuts were already in the works before the uprising. The question, however, is what effects might the ongoing rebellion have on who or what gets cut?

Of course, the larger context is a capitalist economy whose changing composition is driven by such factors as military intervention, the imperialist export of capital, and the digital advancements in the machine factory, which are leading to a situation where capital requires smaller pools of skilled and unskilled laborers. As always, who wins and who loses, or who loses first and the most, is racially mediated. While education is being downgraded in this context, patriotic education and ideological management, as mentioned above, are being enhanced. The role of the socialist educator is, therefore, to intervene in both the classroom and in teachers' and professors' unions. Lenin's work and legacy should take center stage among today's communist pedagogues.

The Communist Challenge

Lenin's communist challenge here is for trade unionists and radicalized workers—including teachers—to resist and expose bourgeois unionism. In his comments on the rising tide within the U.S. working class of socialism, as opposed to an accommodationist trade unionism, Lenin (1912/1970) makes the communist position absolutely clear:

> Strange as it may seem, in capitalist society even the working class can carry on a bourgeois policy, if it forgets about its emancipatory aims, puts up with wage-slavery and confines itself to seeking alliances now with one bourgeois party, now with another, for the sake of imaginary "improvements" in its indentured condition. (p. 231)

For example, the push within much of the educational Left in the U.S. for expanding the public sphere or the democratic impulse and resisting neoliberalism, while informed by the best of intentions, leaves the underlying cause unaddressed. And that is, of course, the true spirit and intent of capital itself. Marx's (1867/1967) metaphor of the werewolf remains a powerful way to begin understanding this spirit and intent. The capitalist drive to accumulate as much surplus-value as possible will always lead to the premature death and exhaustion of the laborer. Unless, that is, the rate of exploitation is regulated by the state through restrictions, such as minimum wage laws or minimized by working-class resistance through such tactics as the strike. When capital is deregulated and the power of trades' unions is restricted through RTW laws, the true spirit and intent of capital will always surface, as is currently happening throughout the world. Like the werewolf, who always emerges given the proper conditions (i.e., a full moon), so too will the barbarism of capital emerge given proper conditions (i.e., the deregulation of capital or the restriction of the trades' unions and the destruction of workers' states). Lenin therefore insists that the role of the Communist Party is to educate all workers of the true nature of capitalism and, thus, the only path to full emancipation, which is the revolutionary transformation of capitalist relations to socialist ones.

Given the unreformable characteristic of capital, as well as its current ascendancy, we can expect greater frequency of spontaneous uprisings and rebellions, desperate acts of random violence, and monstrous perversions of humanity. If an organized antiracist progressive movement does not take a leadership role in the frustrated bursts of outrage, then the frequency of uprisings and hate crimes will surely increase. Even more, potential opportunities for progress will be missed and white supremacist groups could strengthen their foothold, taking leadership of disenfranchised poor whites.

In this context of uncertainty, oppression, exploitation, and contradiction, organized communist struggle also seems to be growing. The resistance is developing not only outside of the U.S., but within the U.S. as well. With the Soviet Union unfortunately gone and the bigotry of anticommunism in the U.S. slowly dissipating, a new socialist and anticapitalist movement is taking hold. Despite some significant socialist critiques of the Occupy Movement and the 2016 presidential campaign of Vermont senator Bernie Sanders, these moments of resistance and support have been contextualized as harbingers of reform.

What might these movements signify for the future? It means we have to fight harder than we ever have. It means we have to be more disciplined and organized than we ever have. It means we have to be smarter than we ever have. It means we have to be fiercer and more committed than we ever have. The future is not guaranteed, by any means. While it may be hard to imagine, things could take a turn for the worse, and it is up to us to ensure they do not. Now is the time to put our academic pride and egos to the side and join a movement for socialism (i.e., a party), and get involved.

· 5 ·

COMMUNIST PEDAGOGY

Centering Marx's General Law of Capitalist Accumulation

In this chapter, I turn to Marx's insights on capitalist accumulation, his theory of becoming, and his writing on the necessity of the planned economy. This chapter, then, returns us explicitly back to the U.S. context, detailing the causes of the crises of capitalism and how we can—through the Party-form—overthrow capitalism and institute socialism. This chapter contributes to Marxist educational theory not by doing the important work of summarizing and building upon the contemporary body of existing Marxist pedagogy, but by offering a systematic analysis of Marx's (1867/1967) General Law of Capitalist Accumulation, as outlined in chapter 25 of the first volume of *Capital*. Underscoring this analysis is the beginning of a systematic examination of the second volume of *Capital*, which takes the circuit of capital as a whole as its object of examination. This unique focus pushes the Marxist revolutionary pedagogy advanced here, as we will see, toward the unnecessarily controversial concept of the *planned economy*. The form such a Marxist pedagogy takes is necessarily the *Party*, a conclusion, which follows the work and practice of Derek Ford (2013; 2015; forthcoming).

***

Central to Marx's many thorough critiques of political economy, and his resulting discoveries regarding the many counterintuitive laws and tendencies of capitalist accumulation, is his correction of the Hegelian concept of *becoming*. Marx's subsequent concept of becoming (discussed below), contrary to popular belief, is grounded in a firm rejection of economic determinism and all forms of oversimplified, vulgar reductionism and predetermination. For Marx, becoming is complex, theoretically rigorous, and, while firmly grounded in the immaterial ideological aspects of capitalism, based on the concrete objectivity of the global system as it actually exists in the world and the many ways it is mediated by the conscious social actors, personified as labor and capital, antagonistically and internally related.

The Moving and Generating Principle

For Marx, it is contradiction that is at the heart of all movement and historical development. All entities change because all entities are contradictory. For example, the conditions that allow all living things to grow simultaneously lead them to their own negation. If life and death are opposites, they each embody and imply the other. Without life, there can be no death; without death, its prerequisite, life, could not have been. Similarly, the conditions required for capital to develop according to its own internal laws simultaneously create the conditions for its own demise. However, the end of capitalism, an inorganic set of manmade laws and practices, is not as guaranteed as the end of capital personified (i.e., the capitalist), an organic entity whose life implies an inevitable death. This is so because the existence of capitalism is not dependent on a single individual but rather on the reproduction of society as a whole. Capitalism's life existence therefore rests on the will and consciousness of labor power personified and capital personified in laborers and capitalists, respectively.

However, the internal laws and tendencies of capitalist accumulation compel, but do not determine, capitalists and laborers to make particular choices or to act in specific ways as buyers and sellers in an unequal relationship falsely assumed to be based in fairness or the exchange of equivalents. This complex interaction between the historical development of capitalism and the accompanying historical development of the capitalist and the laborer, and the intervention of these individuals in the production process, is the primary focus of the communist pedagogy advanced here. It is the collective of individuals that either will or will not create communism and, in the process, create or not create the conditions for becoming. In the process of more explicitly outlining the details of Marx's (1867/1967) concept of becoming, I will turn to a detailed discussion of his General Law of Capitalist Accumulation (p. 612), highlighting relevant connections to this Marxist pedagogy (Malott, 2014; Malott & Ford, 2015). Ultimately, it is the general law of capitalist accumulation that must be grasped if it is to assist student–laborers in conceptualizing and enacting a movement to, as we will see, abolish surplus labor time, the material substance and lifeblood of capital itself, which is now a global system dominated by an imperialist uni-power. The dominance of this system is being challenged by not only its own internal limitations but also by a growing global opposition movement. The uprising in Baltimore, Maryland, the movement to stop school closures, and the national opt-out movement against high-stakes testing and the privatization of public education more generally might be understood as examples of the most recent manifestation of this movement within the U.S. However, as the global movement develops one of its major challenges is to overcome the fractured and disconnected nature of its existence. Before exploring Marx's discussion of the General Law of Accumulation, I will briefly outline Marx's (1844/1988) concept of becoming.

Marx's Concept of Becoming

As suggested above, Marx developed his concept of becoming through a correction of Hegel's dialectic (see Malott & Ford for a discussion of this critique). Summarizing Marx's conclusions here, as they relate to a Marxist critical pedagogy of becoming, we might observe that essence is more than consciousness and, thus, the transcendence of estrangement or alienation, that is, oppression and exploitation, is more than a mere mental act. Marx's position here is grounded in the fact that humans are sensuous beings that are in and of the natural, concrete world, and thus endowed with "natural powers of life" (p. 154) that compel and drive us. The species' natural biological endowments simultaneously enable and limit the human life as it engages objects external to it, "objects of his *need*—essential *objects*, indispensable to the manifestation and confirmation of his essential powers" (p. 154).

Contrasting this concreteness to what we might take as the abstractness of absolute knowledge, which, in the most progressive sense, is self-consciousness, that displaces the object for the idea of the object, Marx notes that "a being which does not have its nature outside itself is not a *natural* being, and plays no part in the system of nature" (pp. 154–155). Marx (1844/1988) then makes the point that because humans are objective and sensuous beings, they suffer, and because humans feel what they suffer, they are passionate beings. Consequently, "passion is the essential force of man energetically bent on its object" (p. 155). A Marxist critical pedagogy of becoming, therefore, celebrates the indispensable work of the passionate revolutionary party intervening in spontaneous insurrections and thus directing the working class, the global proletarian class camp, against the General Law of Accumulation and against the racism, sexism, and the ongoing process of colonial domination and subjugation of the world's Indigenous communities. Together, this represents the primary barriers to becoming and, for Marx, the goal was to become communist through mass militant organization.

I now turn to a discussion of Marx's (1867/1967) concept of the General Law of Accumulation to demonstrate that Marx's notion of becoming is not utopian. That is, qualitative changes in social relations never just emerge or magically appear. Becoming is always a process that can only develop out of existing conditions. Capitalism may be driven by its own internal laws, but those laws are mediated by people who make choices and are, therefore, not just determined by social structures. There is no guarantee that capitalism, once having reached a certain point in its own quantitative development, will deterministically transform into socialism. The capitalist class will continue to fight with every fiber of its being against the objectives of a proletarian revolution. To facilitate the proletarian process of becoming, and to transcend its capitalistic barriers, the working classes, and working people in general, need an education that does a better job at facilitating a deeper understanding of capitalism.

The General Law of Accumulation

In chapter 25 of the first volume of *Capital*, one of the final chapters and one that consumes approximately one-seventh of the book, Marx begins by revisiting the dual nature of the composition of capital. That is, capital is made up of a value side and a material side. On the value side, "capital consists of constant capital or the value of the means of production and variable capital or the value of labor power, the sum total of wages" (p. 612). On the material side of capital's composition, "as it functions in the process of production," capital consists of "means of production" and "labor power" (p. 612). Each component of capital, means of production and labor power, has, in other words, a material basis, which directly influences its value basis. The percent of each component is determined by the amount of labor needed to transform a given quantity of means of production into useful products. Marx identifies the total composition of capital as consisting of the "value composition" on one side and, on the other, the "technical composition" (p. 612). Marx notes that the value composition of capital is determined by, and changes with, the technical composition—this relationship is referred to as the "organic composition" of capital. Following Marx from here on, when referring to the composition of capital, I will be implying the organic composition. Marx notes that each individual capitalist has an average composition; likewise, each branch of production taken together has an average composition, and each country, combining all branches of production, yields a national average composition of capital. The general law of capitalist accumulation investigated by Marx refers to this national average.

The fluid and fluctuating composition of capital is due to its sole driving and motivating force, that is, the necessity of perpetually expanding surplus-value. If the variable component of capital (i.e., labor power), the component, unlike constant capital (i.e., the means of production), endowed with the unique ability to produce a surplus-value, must increase, so too must the capital "invested in labor power" (p. 613). Situated in the context of the cycle of production, Marx notes, "A part of the surplus-value turned into additional capital must always be re-transformed into variable capital, or additional labor-fund" (p. 613). Knowing that changes in such production factors as productivity and intensity alter the composition of capital, Marx makes it clear, in order to isolate the aspect of the general law he is explaining, that assuming no changes in the composition of capital occur, increases in variable capital "increase in the same proportion as the capital, and the more rapidly, the more rapidly the capital increases" (p. 613).

In other words, given Marx's assumption, as profits increase so too does capital's investment in variable capital, and as variable capital increases so too does surplus-value. Without importing new reserves to swell the pool of the reserve army of labor, the perpetually expanding and flexible nature of capital often leads to a situation where "the demand for laborers may exceed the supply, and, therefore, wages may rise" (p. 613). Just as simple reproduction reproduces the labor-capital relationship itself, so too does "reproduction on a progressive scale, i.e., accumulation, reproduce the capital-relation on a progressive scale" (p. 613). From this perspective, the system of public or common education itself might be viewed as part of expanding production, or part of the changing price of reproducing labor, along with labor's necessary consumption fund, for capital in general requires a workforce educated with basic literacy and numeracy skills, and an ideology or worldview favorable to the perpetuation of the labor-capital relationship. However, because of constant advancements in technology and subsequent revolutions in production, capital's needs in terms of the general level of education of their workforce also always change.

While the specific content and quantities of education are forever shifting with the perpetually shifting nature and composition of capitalism itself, what is clear from volume 2 of *Capital* (Marx, 1992) is that all value, including the value transmitted to students from educators, school buildings, books, digital and computerized technology, and so on circulates. That is, even if the labor of the educator does not produce new direct value capitalistically, a point of debate within Marxist educational theory (Malott & Ford), education, through the educational process, transfers its value to the students it educates or schools.

Again, we can consider whether or not the transmission of information to students creates new products, that is, the creation of the skilled laborer. The educated student, regardless of how the educational process is interpreted, is therefore loaded with more value than before the schooling was administered. Of course this level of abstraction does not take into account many factors, such as racialized, gendered, and class-based cultural capital, that impacts the actual quality of education and the perceived value transmitted as a result of students being educated. However, when successful at selling their educated labor on the labor market, and set into motion through the labor process, they transfer their value to the goods or services they participate in producing. Through this circuit, the value of education circulates. We might summarize this process as the metamorphoses from money capital, to the educator's labor power and means of production (i.e., school buildings, curriculum, computers, etc.), to the education of students, to the educated students' labor power mixed with means of production, to the production of new goods and services, to realization after said goods and services are sold on the consumer market.

Despite the specificities of the circulation (Marx, 1992) of educational value and despite structural inequalities and fluctuations in capital's required skill levels of the workforce, topics beyond the scope of this particular chapter (see Malott, 2012), ideological consent might shift in content, but it remains relatively constant in terms of capital's need. If the labor-capital relationship reproduces the enslavement of the laborer and is "concealed" only "by the variety of individual capitalists to whom it sells itself" (Marx, 1867/1967,

p. 614), capital, since Marx's time, has increasingly relied on education's unique ability to manufacture consent to the idea that capitalism is inevitable and, ultimately, based in fairness and justice. However, capitalist production relations themselves make it seem as though every hour of work is requited, leaving surplus labor hours, or the unpaid portion of the workday, hidden beneath the surface of the money relation, creating the appearance of a system based on fairness and equality.

However, as capital expands, its alienating and immiserating tendencies deepen and become more complete, rendering the need for ideological indoctrination through schooling and culture a growing and necessary, but unproductive, cost of production and circulation. Of course, this unacknowledged purpose of education is masked, however shabbily, through abstract conceptions of learning that privilege outcomes over process and content and legitimized through a seemingly never-ending series of performance standards or high-stakes examinations. However, with the expansion and development of capital, it not only becomes more productive, it also renders greater segments of the world's peoples desperate, suffering, and potentially ungovernable, rebellious, or even revolutionary. Marx (1867/1967) explains this immiseration in volume 1 as the result of capital's quest for exchange-value. In volume 2 Marx (1992) focuses on the "constant disruptions" (p. 390) that stem from this focus on exchange-value.

Capital Realization, Imperialism, and the Planned Economy

What we might call overaccumulation among the capitalist class leads to the degradation of workers' ability to consume what they need to survive, thereby disrupting realization. David Harvey (2014) examines a host of interventions the capitalist employs to counter this tendency, such as the creation of new markets of luxury consumption for elites and the capitalist class and the expansion of the credit system, temporarily displacing looming crises that, from time to time, emerge, sending shock waves throughout working-class communities. One such example that Harvey explores is the housing market crash of 2007, which was created by and based upon the advancement of credit to home builders, and then the advancement of credit to home-buying consumers. When the fictitious basis of this growth in the housing market began impacting realization through a wave of mortgage defaults, the bubble, as it were, burst.

On the other hand, the focus on producing for the sake of producing for exchange-value, at the expense of use-value, leads to a situation where capitalist enterprises are constantly throwing workers out of work and back on the job market, creating constant disruptions. To resolve this ongoing capitalist contradiction between production and realization, Harvey argues, "Realisation should be replaced by the discovery and statement of the use-values needed by the population at large and production should then be orchestrated to meet these social needs" (p. 85). It is interesting that Harvey is, in essence, describing a planned economy, but he does not call it that, nor does he provide any examples of actually existing socialism. For Marx (1992), a planned, communist economy can be thought of in the following way:

> If we were to consider a communist society in place of a capitalistic one, then money capital would immediately be done away with, and so too the disguises that transactions acquire through it. The matter would simply be reduced to the fact that the society must reckon in advance how much labor, means of production and means of subsistence it can spend, without dislocation. (p. 390)

The primary disguise here is the appearance of the exchange of equivalents, which conceals the inherent exploitation within capitalist production. The planned economy alluded to by Marx (1992) is driven by the satisfaction of human need, thereby subverting accumulation. Many contemporary North American Marxists, however, unlike Harvey, do not avoid their critiques of planned socialist economies. For example, Peter Hudis (2012), in a unique work on Marx's vision of the alternative to capitalism, argues that the notion of a planned economy represents a simplified vulgarization of Marx and is discredited by the "dismal failures" of "societies that called themselves 'socialist' or communist'" (p. 3). However, Hudis fails to contextualize the experience of the Soviet Union, as was done in chapter 3 of this text. As a result, Hudis faults the structure of the Soviet Union's planned economy itself. One of Hudis's primary arguments is that the Soviet Union's planned economy did little to transform production relations toward reuniting mental labor and manual labor. While this is undoubtedly a central desire of Marx's vision of communism, his concept of becoming was developmental and not necessarily linear or black and white, and making progress toward the ethic of each according to her ability and each according to her need has been an extremely difficult task situated in the aforementioned context of the global class war. To assume socialist progress could proceed smoothly or immediately in such an environment is, at best, utopian.

While examining actually existing socialist countries in detail is beyond the scope of this chapter, I clearly situate my position here within the proletarian camp of the global class war (Marcy, 1976a). Marcy describes this global class war as driven by a "fundamental antagonism" between imperialist countries, including the U.S. and Japan, on one side, and all socialist countries and the proletariat within imperialist countries on the other. The approach to understanding imperialist capitalism that focuses on the circuit of capital is significant because "the capitalist production process is conditioned by circulation" (Marx, 1992, p. 140), which compels the capitalist to push outward and into conflict with the workers' states that had experienced some initial successes at breaking free from the global capitalist system. In other words, production does not occur independently of realization, which must be considered when looking at working-class resistance and agency situated within the larger context of capitalist crises and contradiction.

Looking inward, within imperialist countries, those bourgeois educational spaces and their testing apparatuses, as well as the use of and over the physical space of the city itself have been and continue to be targeted for working-class resistance (Ford, forthcoming). Capitalist education is, therefore, guided by exchange-value rather than use-value. Advancing a critical educational resistance must therefore also include an understanding of the ways in which the value of education circulates capitalistically. Otherwise, educational activism will fail to grasp the full role that education plays in the circuit of capital as a whole.

The contemporary role of the Socialist or Communist Party, especially within the time and space of North America, is to therefore agitate toward these ends and build its membership and prepare for embryonic rebellions and assume leadership positions within them in order to direct their destructive energies toward socialism, within the classroom and in the streets. Without a full understanding of the circuit of capital, such work will remain partial and, thus, limited. Without progressive, working-class organization, there is a real possibility that white supremacists and reactionaries could seize control of emerging rebellions and unleash new waves of terrorism across imperialist countries such as the U.S., again, in the classroom and in the space of the city in general (Ford, 2015). More commonly, however, rebellions are suppressed and reabsorbed into the capitalist totality.

This tendency can be observed the world over. In the U.S., uprisings from Ferguson, Missouri, to Baltimore, Maryland, represent the most recent and dramatic examples of how the most oppressed and exploited segments of bourgeois society are rebelling, and how socialists from within those communities are codirecting and facilitating the resistance, which is rapidly learning to fight back, and connect the ways police departments across the country routinely murder Black youth with near impunity to a crisis-ridden capitalist system. While it is important to remember that all workers in capitalist society, from the most privileged to the most excluded and impoverished, have a vested interest in fighting capitalism for communism, the extreme differences between white and Black workers in particular must take center stage in the movement for becoming communist.

For example, there has been a world health study circulating that found that the more unequal a society or country is, the unhappier it tends to be, even among the most privileged, and I assume that includes the capitalist class. Predictably, the U.S. is the unhappiest country because it is the most unequal. This is one in a long list of indictments against capital (see below). While such studies are important, it must be acknowledged that being unhappy is far different from living under the threat of constant state terrorism combined with crushing, relentless poverty. We cannot lose sight of the fact that working-class whites have good reason to fight for communism, but we also cannot forget that impoverished whites are more likely to get out of poverty than their Black and Brown counterparts, and under capitalism, workers do not have a choice but to take their human commodity to the market in hopes of exchanging it for a decent wage. While this is increasingly difficult for all workers, it is especially desperate for African American, Latino, and Native American communities. The enslavement of the worker is only masked by the number of masters and by fluctuations in the price of labor. To the capitalist, as argued below, labor is a natural resource he or she is entitled to, and black and brown workers' devaluation has provided capital with a cheaper source of labor and a more disposable source. This source can be scapegoated, murdered, impoverished, imprisoned, disrespected, miseducated, and made the floor mat of a dying and decaying global capitalist system as an almost permanent reserve pool of unemployed communities that function to keep the price of labor low and to keep white workers clinging to their capitalist masters. Many of today's Communist Parties are taking this approach to anticapitalist global revolution as a core insight as they intervene in spontaneous uprisings and rebellions.

Seizing Negation

As capital creates the conditions for its own negation, the capitalist (i.e., personified capital) must intervene to preserve the labor-capital relationship, to which he is the sole beneficiary. As the example just provided indicates, such intervention increasingly includes the use of a highly militarized police force to beat back rebellions and brutalize people of color, which seems to simultaneously serve as a media spectacle desperately attempting to placate and scare the increasingly alienated labor force of a decaying capitalist society marked by a long legacy of antiblack and -brown white supremacy. The situation outlined by Marx (1867/1967) here offers a clear incentive for why capital has actively supported means by which they may socially control labor as a form of insurance on their property. While it is true the price of labor fluctuates around a common average, the enslavement of labor is in no way threatened by the periodic rises in its price and, therefore, does not indicate the liberation of labor from the production of surplus-value. Consider: "A rise in the price of labor, as a consequence of [the] accumulation of capital, only means, in fact, that the length and weight of the golden chain the wage-worker has already forged for himself, allow of a relaxation of the tension of it" (p. 618).

Capital's consumption of this labor power, to be sure, is not motivated by the usefulness of the products of labor themselves, but by the surplus labor contained in them and the profit realized when sold on the market. Again, Marx (1867/1967) notes that the "production of surplus-value is the absolute law of this mode of production" despite lofty bourgeois rhetoric insisting that capital has allowed laborers the freedom to elevate their status with hard work and thriftiness. Summarizing capital's true view of labor, Marx (1867/1967) argues that labor power is a commodity worth investing in only when it is able to preserve the means of production, "reproduce its own value as capital" (p. 618), and produce a surplus-value in the form of additional capital through unpaid labor. However, as indicated above, capital's drive to shift the ratio between necessary labor time and surplus labor time to the latter creates major problems for realization and social control for personified capital.

Labor power, to capital, is thus nothing more than a natural resource or a gold mine of value that it believes it has a right to. The student, to capital, is therefore nothing more than a depository of value awaiting future productive consumption and hopeful realization as labor power. The student as future worker is increasingly a depository of crushing student debt and burdened with the anxiety of a jobless labor market. However, the contradiction here resides in the fact that the reproduction and extension of capital requires the perpetual reselling of labor power to the capitalist. Wages themselves, regardless of their periodic increase or decrease, imply an unpaid portion of labor time, that portion of the workday labor expends itself beyond the time necessary for its own reproduction. The limit to the rise in wages is set by capital's need for a surplus portion of the workday. If no portion of the workday goes unrequited, then no surplus labor time is available for accumulation, and no capital would, therefore, have been augmented. Without surplus labor time, without exploitation, the capitalist, as such, cannot exist—and if the laborer has a right not to be exploited, to be sure, then the capitalist has no right to be a capitalist and must, therefore, join humanity in the collective reproduction of social existence.

The abolition of surplus labor time would therefore mean the end of capitalism and consequently must be one of the central goals, along with the seizure of the state apparatus, of a global anti-imperialism. Such a conscious movement is needed because it is a development that will not emerge spontaneously from capital's own internal movement, playing itself out deterministically like a mechanical clock winding itself down. Rather, as capital has expanded and encapsulated the planet, leaving no major regions to dominate, its investment trends fluctuate through cycles of de-investment and re-investment, surviving as such in perpetuity. Because capital's ongoing existence here depends, to an extent, on working-class consent, it must be regarded with some degree of legitimacy, which, as suggested above, rests on the myth of equivalents. As a result, a working-class movement, organized through the Party-form against surplus labor time, must first reveal the hidden exploitation of labor power operating below the surface and behind the backs of not just laborers but capitalists as well, who tend not to be aware of the existence of unrequited labor hours. While Marx (1867/1967) is keenly aware of the human choices and actions continuously intervening in this process of expansion, he does not fail to pinpoint, with precise accuracy, the internal check against rising wages and declining accumulation built into the logic of capital itself:

> Either the price of labor keeps on rising, because its rise does not interfere with the progress of accumulation. ... Or, on the other hand, accumulation slackens in consequence of the rise in the price of labor, because the stimulus of gain is blunted. The rate of accumulation lessens; but with its lessening, the primary cause of that lessening vanishes, i.e., the disproportion between capital and exploitable labor-power. The mechanism of the process of capitalist production removes the very obstacles that it temporarily creates. The price of labor falls again to a level corresponding with the needs of the self-expansion of capital. (p. 619)

Challenging classical political economy Marx then argues that it is not a shrinking population that causes capital to be in excess but, rather, it is the excess of capital that makes the availability of exploitable labor insufficient, and, as noted above, the contraction of capital creates the conditions for renewed expansion on a progressive scale. Herein resides another major factor contributing to the "constant disruptions" (p. 390) that Marx (1992) refers to in volume 2 in making the case for a planned economy and the organization of the party required for the seizure of state power. Today, as in Marx's time, economists explain away this cycle of boom and bust as the product of the interaction between two unrelated variables, population and capitalistic wealth. For Marx (1867/1967), however, the connection between the "magnitude of capital" and the size of the laboring population is nothing more than "the relation between the unpaid and paid labor of the same laboring population" (p. 620). Again, because it is the sole focus of capital to expand unpaid labor and reduce paid labor, at a certain point in capital's development, "the development of the productivity of labor becomes the most powerful lever of accumulation" (Marx, 1867/1967, p. 621).

Up to this point in chapter 25, Marx's discussion of the law of accumulation is based on an assumed unchanging and thus consistent level of productiveness of labor through revolutions in the means of production. Marx now re-introduces us to the role of increasing productivity in the expansion of capital through progressive accumulation. In chapter 15, "Machinery and Modern Industry," another chapter consuming well over one-seventh of the first volume of *Capital*, Marx (1867/1967) painstakingly lays bare the magnitude of how productive the advent of the nineteenth-century machine factory made the laborer and, in the process, diminished the value of his commodity, rendering a great deal more complete the subjugation of labor to capital.

Changes in the productiveness of labor do not immediately alter the value of labor. Rather, it allows labor to reproduce the value of its own existence in a shorter period of time, thereby increasing the surplus portion of the workday. However, because productivity does not automatically alter the value of labor, the value it transmits to what it produces is simply spread out over a greater number of products, thereby lowering their individual value. Because advances in productivity do not immediately affect the price of commodities, the capitalist is able to sell his product for an inflated price, yet still lower than his competitor, giving him a competitive advantage until the lower average time it takes to produce said commodity becomes the universal norm, at which point the competitive process begins anew, in theoretical perpetuity, but as nature (i.e., the earth) has physical limits, so, too, does the physical expansion of capital. Does immaterial labor and cognitive capitalism remove this barrier? It might temporarily displace said physical limits, but it is not likely that the physical limits of the earth itself can be artificially extended. Similarly, the credit economy, too, has limits, as we have seen, in displacing the looming crises of realization the process of perpetually expanding accumulation engenders.

That is, through the productiveness of labor the composition of capital undergoes a dramatic transformation as the variable component lessens in relation to the constant component, as a given quantity of labor power is able to transform greater sums of means of production into useful products. Because labor power is the only commodity endowed with the ability to produce a surplus-value and, therefore, the historical objective of capital has been to set more of it into motion, it seems a contradiction that productivity would diminish the variable component, the surplus-value creating element, and simultaneously increase the constant component, the means of production, such as raw materials, that creates in itself no new value but, rather, serves as a depository of value transferred into it by labor in motion. However, rather than throwing laborers into the street when displaced by machines, the immediate effect of increasing productivity was actually the more rapid expansion and intensification of production, consuming labor power on an intensified progressive scale. With the machine factory and the displacing of the human muscle and intelligence needed to operate or command the tools of manufacturing, the length of the working day, and the intellectual degradation of the laborer were pushed to their natural limits, leading to working-class push-back and regulations on the length of the workday. Almost immediately, the capitalist responded to regulations by intensifying production by speeding up the machines and minding ever more closely the movements of labor, further mangling and prematurely exhausting the laborer. Marx (1867/1967) refers to these results, driven by the insatiable appetite for surplus-value, as the product of capital's "cynical recklessness" and "terrorist energy," which he identifies as the capitalist mode of production's true spirit and intent. As argued above, this is also the force that has led capital to its imperialist stages zigzagging across the planet, amassing absurd fortunes out of human flesh and leaving mass graves and misery in its wake. It is also the impulse that causes periodic crises in realization.

Marx (1867/1967) then takes us back to chapter 13, "Co-operation," noting that "the development of the productiveness of social labor presupposes co-operation on a large scale" (p. 623) for maximum efficiency, and profitability requires a high degree of uniformity in operations to make possible the centralization cooperation implies. Cooperation is the result of the expansion of capitalism into all branches and means of "social production" and "subsistence are transformed into the private property of the capitalist" (Marx, p. 624). Marx argues that this process may be referred to as a form of "primitive accumulation" because "it is the historic basis, instead of the historic result of specifically capitalist production" (p. 624). Cooperation, like the machine factory that manufacturers created the conditions for, is a method for increasing the "social productive power of labor," which is simultaneously one of the ways to increase the "production of surplus-value or surplus product, which in its turn is the formative element of accumulation" (Marx, p. 624). The capitalist needs to forever expand his capital and the resulting contradictions and working-class resistance propel the historical development of this mode of production. The objective of a communist pedagogy is to expose this internal and hidden logic, hoping to lead and inspire global embryonic rebellions into a coordinated, organized communist movement bent on seizing state power and planning the economy around the creation of use-values, not for the realization of exchange-value but for the satisfaction of human needs. The objective is therefore to move toward a communist horizon full of all the unrealized potential embodied within the dehumanization accumulation leaves in its wake of extending alienation and the division between manual labor and mental labor.

Summarizing accumulation, identified as the driving force of the capitalist mode of production, Marx (1867/1967) argues that it "presents itself on the one hand as increasing concentration of the means of production, and of the command over labor; on the other, as repulsion of many individual capitals one from another" (p. 625). However, the competition that causes the repulsion between capitals is counteracted by their attraction. In other words, the expansive nature of capital leads to the dominant capitalist consuming his competitors, thereby creating a monopoly, which Marx calls "centralization proper" (p. 626) and, eventually, to imperialism, and today a uni-power imperialism, as previously mentioned. As indicated above, "the battle of competition is fought by cheapening of commodities. The cheapness of commodities depends ... on the productiveness of labor, and this again on the scale of production. Therefore, the larger capitals beat the smaller" (Marx, p. 626). This tendency of the General Law of Accumulation has held true through all of the subsequent stages of capitalist development. That is, while the relationships between capitalists, nationally and globally, and between labor and capital undergo periodic shifts, the basic drive to accumulate surplus-value to the point of crises in realization has remained consistent. Just as the shift from manufacture proper to the machine factory changed production relations, capital's drive for accumulation remained the same, which is the driving force propelling capital to progressively expand, quantitatively leading to said qualitative transformations after having reached a certain point in their development (i.e., from manufacture to the machine factory). Not only competition, but the credit system also has historically served as one of the primary levers of centralization and of ensuring the ongoing completion of capital's circuit. Consider:

> The credit system, which in its first stages furtively creeps in as the humble assistant of accumulation, drawing into the hands of individual or associated capitalists, by invisible threads, the money resources which lie scattered, over the surface of society, in larger or smaller amounts; but it soon becomes a new and terrible weapon in the battle of competition and is finally transformed into an enormous social mechanism for the centralization of capitals. (Marx, 1867/1967, p. 626)

For Marx (and Lenin) centralization has been fundamentally important in accelerating the process of accumulation globally, because the process of expanding capital tends to be a very slow process. Centralization, which entails the rearrangement of the "quantitative groupings of the constituent parts of social capital," can happen "in the twinkling of an eye" (Marx, 1867/1967, p. 628), simultaneously speeding up the impulse for global expansion since larger capitals have greater absolute expansion needs. Consequently, centralization "intensifies and accelerates the effects of accumulation," speeding up the cycle through which old capitals and advancements become the basis of new forms of exploitation and thus subsumed by new techniques and processes stemming from advances in technology and science. Each advancement both negates a previous period of development and also creates the conditions for its own eventual negation. This process of change is of special interest because working-class resistance, organized through the Party, embodies the potential to negate the process of progressive accumulation, which is built off of the changing methods of augmenting the surplus labor time of productive laborers, the primary barrier to becoming. Put another way, the competition among capitalists for surplus-value does not include concern for the products of labor, for their usefulness, or of the well-being of the producers beyond whatever happens to be necessary for the continued expansion of capital.

Consequently, Marx again returns to the topic of the reserve army of laborers situated in the context of the shifting composition of capital through the historical development of the process of accumulation. As capital expands, its composition progressively shifts toward the diminution of the variable component. As capital grows, its need for more labor power also grows, but in increasingly smaller proportion as compared to constant capital. Eventually, "the social capital in its totality" (Marx, 1867/1967, p. 630), in all branches of production, is subjected, as a whole, to periodic fluctuations in capital's labor-power needs, rendering each individual labor component relatively disposable and thus disempowered. Making this point Marx notes, "The laboring population therefore produces, along with the accumulation of capital produced by it, the means by which itself is made relatively superfluous, is turned into a relative surplus-population; and it does this to an always increasing extent" (p. 631). Again, a globally integrated system here is implied where segments of labor are continuously thrown out of the circulation of capital. An economy organized around use-values rather than exchange-values as a solution to this constant chaos and instability is the Communist Party's historic object of desire. A communist pedagogy brings attention to the fact that the taken-for-granted social totality of labor is subjected to the often violent fluctuations in the production process developed over time and is, therefore, not a natural state of existence, thereby exposing the potential of negation and encouraging the general humanization implied within the Hegelian concept of becoming.

Underscoring, again, this potential to become, Marx (1867/1967) makes absolutely clear that the law of population under capitalism is unique to capitalism alone, noting, "Every special historic mode of production has its own special laws of population, historically valid within its limits alone" (p. 632). Consequently, a new law of population must exist within the current capitalist law of population as a potential, as the negation of what is, as its opposite, and, therefore, part of the objective of a communist pedagogy. The capitalist law of population situates laborers as a reserve army that belongs to the capitalist as a resource cultivated by its laws of accumulation. The elasticity of capital requires an equally flexible army of laborers that can be absorbed, expelled, and reabsorbed continuously without disrupting the whole system and movement of progressive accumulation. As noted above, this tendency toward expansion and contraction now operates on a global scale. Summarizing this cyclical or spiraling process as it affects the lives of laborers, Marx (1867/1967) argues, "The whole form of the movement of modern industry depends, therefore, upon the constant transformation of a part of the laboring population into unemployed or half-employed hands" (p. 633). This swelling of the reserve army, as suggested above, encourages the intensification of labor's productiveness magnifying accumulation, which, as noted above, is further intensified by racialization and the devaluing of Black lives within the cultural logic of the imperialist nation-states. The inherent insecurity of laborers within the circuit of capital, as stated within this chapter over and over again, drives the party's analysis and understanding of why capitalist barbarity cannot be reformed and, thus, must be overthrown through the seizure of the capitalists' state machine.

However, like capital and its historic drive for accumulation more generally, this tendency is not static, but developmental. For example, William Robinson (2014) makes a strong comparison between African Americans and Palestinians in an article outlining how recent immigration in Israel has led to the displacement of Palestinian workers as Israel's primary source of super-exploited labor, leading to new threats of genocide against rebellious colonial subjects no longer needed for accumulation by Israeli capitalists. Robinson notes that in postslavery America, African Americans, already devalued and discriminated against, served the role of the super-exploited labor force, keeping the price of labor in the U.S. suppressed. As if this era was not bad enough, the situation for African Americans, like their Palestinian counterparts, has deteriorated. That is, as neoliberal restructuring has led to new waves of Latin American immigration, African American working-class communities are being reduced from the status of super-exploited laborers to no longer needed and, thus, redundant. Offering another comparison, Robinson then points to the genocide of Native Americans whose land was needed to expand industrial capitalism in the nineteenth century, but whose labor was not, which led to the physical, biological, and cultural genocide of Native Americans. This is another example of how capitalism operates. The goal of the system is to expand value through the production process. Producing is done for the sake of producing. What is produced, how it is produced, and what was done to ensure production could take place are irrelevant from the perspective not of personified capital, but for capital itself. The genocide of Native Americans, Palestinians, and African Americans, from this perspective, is not the result of white supremacy but, rather, genocide and white supremacy are the result of how the laws of capitalist accumulation compel capitalists to act in certain barbaric ways. With the labor power of African Americans being replaced by new immigrants, African American communities face heightened state terror, mass incarceration, and growing exclusion or marginalization from the circuit of capital. Again, I argue this is the barbarism and savagery of capitalism personified in the actions of capital and its state apparatus. Summarizing this crucial point, Marx (1867/1967), again, points to the destructiveness that these processes always exert upon the life of the laborer:

If the means of production, as they increase in extent and effective power, become to a less extent means of employment of laborers, this state of things is again modified by the fact that in proportion as the productiveness of labor increases, capital increases its supply of labor more quickly than its demand for laborers. The over-work of the employed part of the working-class swells the ranks of the reserve, whilst conversely the greater pressure that the latter by its competition exerts on the former, forces these to submit to over-work and to subjugation under the dictates of capital. (p. 636)

Marx's insights here regarding the role of unemployment in fostering competition between laborers, thereby creating a race to the bottom, is an indispensable insight that students must understand if they are to be fully informed regarding their value and purpose from the perspective of capital. That is, students, whether they are being trained or certified to be able to sell their labor capacity as teachers, or some other job, must realize that the very logic of capital and the function of the reserve army of labor foster a situation where labor is increasingly forced to accept wages that are below what is necessary, or below their market value, forfeiting more and more of their necessary consumption fund and, as a result, risks premature exhaustion, and today in so-called free-trade zones often in the so-called third world, even death. The creation of consumer credit and luxury markets for elites can only displace the pending crises such tendencies foster. The work of the party, within this context, therefore takes on a sense of urgency that cannot be exaggerated. Consequently, a communist pedagogy seeks to engage students and workers of all sorts to critically reflect on the implications of the following situation:

Taking them as a whole, the general movements of wages are exclusively regulated by the expansion and contraction of the industrial reserve army, and these again correspond to the periodic changes of the industrial cycle. (Marx, 1867/1967, p. 637)

Again, what this points to is another way that capital internally pushes toward crisis, immiseration, and the mangling of the laboring body, not necessarily out of any bias or prejudice on the part of capital toward labor but due to the cold, calculating pursuit of surplus-value. While capital as an economic system is not able to be racist, capital personified is. This statement is not meant to contradict the previous discussion concerning the way racism (and sexism, etc.) has historically played a central role in accumulation. Rather, it is meant to point out that the accumulation of capital is the driving force behind capitalism, and if racism serves that end, then the capitalist (i.e., capital personified) will employ it. Having employed it for so long, white supremacy has taken on a relatively independent existence within the cultures of working- and middle-class whites. An antiracist education connected to Marx's work is therefore central to this pedagogical project of becoming and the work of the Communist Party more generally. This position is not the same as the belief that white supremacy is a political system determined by the drive to privilege whites over all others. In other words, the Marxist position here is that the quest to expand value is the primary determining factor, even if culture and ideology enjoy a semi-autonomous existence in capitalist society. As long as the law of supply and demand of labor suppresses wages below their market value, capital will defend it as sacred, especially against organized working-class resistance. However, where a stable army of surplus labor is not able to be established, as was the case in the American colonies when the abundance of cheap land kept the labor markets thin and wages as much as three times higher than in England, capital wages war on the law of supply and demand of labor through such government interventions as artificially inflating the cost of land, thereby restricting immigrants' access to the means of production and keeping them dependent on wage labor, thereby creating an artificial labor dam, swelling the ranks of capital's army of reserve labor in the colonies. After WWII this was accomplished by waging war on the global Socialist Bloc. Summarizing his indictment of capital, pulling from previous chapters, Marx's (1867/1967) depth and contemporary relevance are difficult to ignore:

> Within the capitalist system all methods for raising the social productiveness of labor are brought about at the cost of the individual laborer; all means for the development of production transform themselves into means of domination over, and exploitation of, the producers; they mutilate the laborer into a fragment of a man, degrade him to the level of an appendage of a machine, destroy every remnant of charm in his work and turn it into a hated toil; they estrange from him the intellectual potentialities of the labor-process in the same proportion as science is incorporated in it as an independent power; they distort the conditions under which he works, subject him during the labor-process to a despotism the more hateful for its meanness; they transform his life-time into working-time, and drag his wife and child beneath the wheels of the Juggernaut of capital. (p. 645)

A pedagogy of becoming, spearheaded by the Communist Party, could not be more important considered within this reckless context of capital's social universe and internal driving intent and spirit that will always lead to the premature exhaustion and death of the laborer unless regulated or resisted by working-class organization. The increasing alienation of the intellectual and creative powers that are arguably at the center of the human species' biological endowments (needed to operate tools), and the physical strength needed to move them, is made more complete with the machine factory, and has been extended yet further with robotics and computerization, contrary to popular arguments based on loose economic concepts such as cognitive capitalism. Marx (1867/1967) makes clear that the methods of increasing productivity, from co-operation, to the machine factory, to robotics and computerization are at the same time the methods of expanding accumulation. Similarly, the alienation of creativity and immaterial labor from unskilled labor and deskilled labor (i.e., teaching and education) represent the same movement toward efficiency of production and maximization of surplus labor time operating from cooperation to computerization. Today it has just developed to a more exaggerated extreme. Completing his indictment of capital, making clear the connection between productivity and accumulation, Marx (1867/1967) explains:

> All methods for the production of surplus-value are at the same time methods of accumulation; and every extension of accumulation becomes again a means for the development of those methods. It follows therefore that in proportion as capital accumulates, the lot of the laborer, be his payment high or low, must grow worse. The law, finally, that always equilibrates the relative surplus-population, or industrial reserve army, to the extent and energy of accumulation, this law rivets the laborer to capital ... firmly. ... It establishes an accumulation of misery, corresponding with accumulation of capital. Accumulation of wealth at one pole is, therefore, at the same time accumulation of misery, agony of toil, slavery, ignorance, brutality, mental degradation, at the opposite pole, i.e., on the side of the class that produces its own product in the form of capital. (p. 645)

To become is, therefore, to disrupt this globalized, imperial process of accumulating misery, made the more difficult because it is not just a misery of material existence, but a misery of intellectual debasement. This project cannot be accomplished by the individual but can be realized only through the collective, disciplined will of the proletarian Party-form. Consequently, the knowledge and development of intelligence that the laborer's command over work tools requires, which was passed over to the machine factory, and now made more complete with the motherboard and hard drive, have negatively affected working-class organization for becoming. In other words, as working-class schools operate at an increasingly low cognitive level as a result of the era of high-stakes testing and conservative, bourgeois curricula, our capacity to uncover the hidden logics and tendencies of capital and the ideological role of white supremacy and sexism, for example, has been degraded. Despite these serious limitations, most negatively impacting the aforementioned African American communities under threat of genocide as Black labor power becomes increasingly excluded from the market in labor, new cadres of impoverished, battle-worn Black revolutionary leaders, many of whom are women, are emerging from the uprisings against the homicides police officers are committing with near impunity against African Americans (Van Gelder, 2015). These uprisings, from Ferguson to Baltimore, represent the reemergence of the Black revolutionary in the U.S. who has historically served as the revolutionary vanguard from the abolitionist movement against slavery to the socialist Black Panther Party leading the struggle against global capitalist imperialism in the 1960s and 1970s. A communist pedagogy must therefore not only support the opt-out Movement working to counter the generalized mental degradation and developmental debasement represented most starkly and obviously in high-stakes testing, operating at a very low cognitive level of factual recall, dominating American schooling for the past couple of decades, and showing no signs of reversing (Au & Ferrare, 2015), but it must also resist school closures and support and contribute to Black Lives Matter. The Party's role has been to intervene in these struggles, channeling their energies against not just the visible consequences of capital but against capital itself.

Conclusion: Marx and Becoming

Becoming, to be sure, is not mere caprice of labor but also is grounded in an organized movement leading in the opposite direction of intellectual alienation, degradation, hero worship, self-hatred, and prejudice, which we might call the general intellectual advancement that is best developed within a workers' state and the necessary form of education for a planned economy. That is, under capitalism, workers are a resource to expand value and, therefore, are subjected to varying degrees of debasement and redundancy. In socialism, on the other hand, the goal is to satisfy human need, which is best served by intellectual advancement. A revolutionary pedagogy for becoming therefore privileges a critical thinking grounded not only in the well-developed reasoning and analytical skills of the scientific mind, but also in the critical theories that unearth the hidden structures of a global capitalist system deeply entrenched in white supremacy, patriarchy, homophobia, xenophobia, and all manner of bias and prejudice.

The goal of a pedagogy of becoming is therefore the abolition of capitalism and the eradication of both systemic racism and sexism and individual racism and sexism. The form a pedagogy of becoming takes is the Party. A related goal of this critical pedagogy of becoming is the self-governance of all oppressed nations, including all North American First Nations. That is, all treaty agreements and stolen lands must be returned to American Indian Nations, and if said lands have been destroyed beyond use, said nations must be compensated. In short, a critical pedagogy of becoming seeks the complete emancipation of all laborers and all peoples in all corners of the world. If one of the first steps, after the Party's seizure of state power, includes the abolition of surplus labor time through an international movement against the capitalist imperialist uni-power, the current racialized and gendered division of labor will likely not change completely in the beginning stages of communism. The Black Lives Matter movement and the Native American Idle No More movement must continue to serve as leaders in a postcapitalist situation.

One of the first major changes in a postcapitalist society would be to nationalize the means of production and abolish unrequited labor hours, not withstanding deductions for a necessary reproduction fund. One of the first orders of business might also be to dramatically expand the education fund not only for school-aged children and adult learners but for educators as well. An inquiry-based education could serve the purpose of expanding general intelligence by ensuring that one set of dogmas does not replace another. A socialist or postcapitalist pedagogy of becoming might therefore rethink the pursuit of knowledge and the advancement of science away from methods of accumulation and toward the benefit of all of humanity and the preservation of the earth's vital ecosystems (that have been all but obliterated in a few hundred years from rapid global capitalist expansion). This postcapitalist pedagogy must also take an antiracist and antisexist position as one of its central purposes—as the Party currently does. A firm grounding in the internal logics and workings of capital provide the possibility of facilitating the negation of capital and the communist future its well-developed levels of productivity makes possible. In the hands of capital, advancements in productivity provide the leverage to further dominate and degrade laborers. In the hands of labor, it can provide the basis for the general satisfaction of needs and provide the freedom to unite personal, human needs with collective, social needs, and the material basis for enactment.

What this points to is a critical pedagogy of becoming where a communist horizon (Malott & Ford) implies a mode of production that does not include processes that result in the permanent and extending intellectual degradation and mangling of individual laborers and, collectively, society as a whole. A mode of production that does not dehumanize both laborers and capitalists but, instead, compels individuals to collectively pursue their unique interests and abilities situated within the context of a means of production that is highly advanced, mechanized, and thus highly productive. It also implies an economy that is not plagued by constant disruptions and perpetual insecurity as the circulation of capital is always at risk of crisis. As the ratio of constant capital to variable capital has been shifting with ongoing developments in productivity since the beginning stages of the capitalist era, a communist future based on the value of humanization could dramatically reduce the length of the workday or the amount of labor time required to reproduce the value of society's necessary consumption fund. The laborer would then possess large portions of the day to pursue her or his own interests and passions.

Destroying the basis of the capitalist mode of production where one person's labor provides the substance for another's enrichment, a communist future removes the capitalist barriers to becoming and allows society's collective labor to provide the basis for society's free development. Marx (1875/2002) summarizes this in his *Critique of the Gotha Programme* as embodied in the sentiment, *each according to her ability, each according to her need.*

REFERENCES

Abu-Jamal, M. (2000). *All things censored.* New York: Seven Stories.

Allman, P. (1999). *Revolutionary social transformation: Democratic hopes, political possibilities and critical education.* New York: Bergin & Garvey.

Anderson, K. (2010). *Marx at the margins: On nationalism, ethnicity, and non-Western societies.* London: University of Chicago Press.

Aronowitz, S. (1989). *Crisis in historical materialism: Class, politics and culture in Marxist theory.* St. Paul: University of Minnesota Press.

Au, W., & Ferrare, J. (2015). *Mapping corporate education reform: Power and policy networks in the neoliberal state.* New York: Routledge.

Becker, B. (2008). What do socialists defend in China today? In A. McInerney (Ed.), *China: Revolution and counterrevolution.* San Francisco: PSL.

Becker, B. (2014, January 14). 6 ways socialism is superior to capitalism. *Liberation.* Retrieved from https://www.liberationnews.org/why-socialism-is-superior-to-capitalism-html/

Becker, B. (2015). How the ideas of "The State and Revolution" changed history. In B. Becker (Ed.), *Revolution manifesto: Understanding Marx and Lenin's theory of revolution* (pp. 7–30). San Francisco: Liberation.

Becker, R. (2009). *Palestine, Israel, and the U.S. empire.* San Francisco: PSL.

Blum, W. (2003). *Killing hope: U.S. military and C.I.A. interventions since World War II.* Monroe, ME: Common Courage.

Boers, D. (2007). *History of American education primer.* New York: Peter Lang.

Bowles, S., & Gintis, H. (1976). *Schooling in capitalist America: Educational reform and the contradictions of economic life.* New York: Basic.

Button, H. W., & Provenzo, E. (1983/1989). *History of education & culture in America* (2nd ed). Englewood Cliffs, NJ: Prentice Hall.

Callinicos, A. (1989). *Against postmodernism: A Marxist critique.* Oxford: Polity.

Campbell, C. (2015, February 15). Baltimore students, parents protest state budget cuts proposed for city schools. *The Baltimore Sun.* Retrieved from http://www.baltimoresun.com/news/maryland/education/bs-md-ci-build-protests-cuts-20150219-story.html

Carr, E. H. (1961). *What is history?* New York: Vintage.

Chen, F. (2003). Industrial restructuring and workers' resistance in China. *Modern China, 29*(2), 237–262.

Churchill, W. (Ed.). (1983). *Marxism and Native Americans.* Boston: South End.

Churchill, W., & Vander Wall, J. (1990). *Agents of repression: The FBI's secret wars against the Black Panther Party and the American Indian Movement.* Boston: South End.

Cleaver, K. (1998). Back to Africa: The evolution of the international section of the Black Panther Party (1969–1972). In C. E. Jones (Ed.), *The Black Panther Party reconsidered.* Baltimore: Black Classic.

Cole, M. (2007). *Marxism and educational theory: Origins and issues.* New York: Routledge.

Coulthard, G. S. (2014). *Red skin, white masks: Rejecting the colonial politics of recognition.* Minneapolis: Minnesota University Press.

Cremin, L. (1957). Horace Mann's legacy. In L. Cremin (Ed.), *The republic and the school: Horace Mann on the education of free man.* New York: Teachers College Press.

Cubberley, E. (1919). *Public education in the United States: A study and interpretation of American educational history.* New York: Houghton Mifflin.

Darder, A. (2009). Teaching as an act of love: Reflections on Paulo Freire and his contributions to our lives and our work. In A. Darder, M. Baltodano, & R. Torres (Eds.), *The critical pedagogy reader* (2nd ed.). New York: Routledge.

Darder, A. (2014). *Freire and education.* New York: Routledge.

Dean, J. (2012). *The communist horizon.* New York: Verso.

Deloria, V., Jr. (1969). *Custer died for your sins: An Indian manifesto.* New York: Macmillan.

Du Bois, W. E. B. (2001). *The education of Black people: Ten critiques, 1906–1960.* New York: Monthly Review.

Elton, G. R. (1967/2002). *The practice of history.* Oxford, UK: Blackwell.

Engels, F. (1885/1972). Preface. In K. Marx, *The eighteenth brumaire of Louis Bonaparte,* 2nd ed). New York: International.

Engels, F. (1891/1993). Introduction. In K. Marx, *Civil war in France: The Paris commune.* New York: International.

Evans, R. (2000). *In defense of history.* New York: W. W. Norton.

Foner, E. (2009). *Give me liberty!: An American history: Vol. 2. From 1865* (2nd ed.). New York: Norton.

Ford, D. (2013). Butler goes to work: A political economy of the subject. *borderlands e-journal, 12*(1), 1–19.

Ford, D. R. (2014). Spatializing Marxist educational theory: School, the built environment, fixed capital, and (relational) space. *Policy Futures in Education, 12*(6), 784–793.

Ford, D. (2015, September 15). Baltimore protest leaders targeted as movement continues. *Liberation*. Retrieved from http://www.liberationnews.org/baltimore-protest-leaders-targeted-for-repression-as-movement-continues

Ford, D. (forthcoming). A pedagogy for space: Teaching, learning and studying in the Baltimore rebellion. *Policy Futures in Education.*, 1–18. First published online October 6, 2015.

Ford, D. (in press). Joining the party: Critical education and the question of organization. *Critical Education.*

Foster, J. B. (2012). Education and the structural crisis of capital. *Monthly Review, 63*(3), 1–19.

Freire, P. (1970/1998). *Pedagogy of the oppressed.* London: Continuum.

Gaither, M. (2012). The revisionists revived: The libertarian historiography of education. *The History of Education Quarterly, 52*(4), 488–505.

Giroux, H. (1981). *Ideology, culture, and the process of schooling.* Philadelphia: Temple University Press.

Giroux, H. (1983). *Theory and resistance in education: A pedagogy for the opposition.* Amherst: MA: Bergin & Garvey.

Giroux, H. (2004). *The terror of neoliberalism.* Boulder, CO: Paradigm.

Glazebrook, D. (2013). *Divide and ruin: The West's imperial strategy in an age of crisis.* San Francisco: PSL.

Grande, S. (2015). *Red pedagogy: Native American social and political thought* (10th anniversary ed.). Lanham, MD: Rowman & Littlefield.

Gutek, G. (1970). *An historical introduction to American education.* New York: Cowell.

Hall. G. M. (2012). Introduction. In H. Haywood, *A Black communist in the freedom struggle: The life of Harry Haywood.* Minneapolis: University of Minnesota Press.

Harman, C. (2008). *A people's history of the world.* New York: Verso.

Harvey, D. (2014). *Seventeen contradictions and the end of capitalism.* New York: Oxford University Press.

Haywood, H. (1958). *For a revolutionary position on the Negro question* (P. Saba, Ed.). Retrieved from Encyclopedia of Anti-Revisionism On-Line, https://www.marxists.org/history/erol/1956-1960/haywood02.htm

Haywood, H. (1978). *Black bolshevik: Autobiography of an Afro-American communist.* Chicago: Liberator. Retrieved from Marxist Internet Archive, https://www.marxists.org/archive/haywood/black-bolshevik/ch06.htm

Haywood, H. (2012). *A black communist in the freedom struggle: The life of Harry Haywood.* London: University of Minnesota Press.

Hill, D. (2013). *Immiseration capitalism and education: Austerity, resistance, and revolt.* Brighton, UK: Institute for Education Policy Studies.

Hill, D., Lewis, C., Maisuria, A., Yarker, P., & Carr, J. (2015). Neoliberal and neoconservative immiseration capitalism in England: Policies and impacts on society and on education. *Journal of Critical Education Policy Studies, 13*(2), 38–88. Retrieved from http://www.jceps.com/archives/2618

Holt, T. (1992). *Thinking historically: Narrative, imagination, and understanding.* New York: College Board.

Hoop, D. (2015, September 17). Seattle teachers can fight for what they deserve. Socialist-Worker.org. Retrieved from http://socialistworker.org/2015/09/17/seattle-teachers-can-fight-for-more

Howitt, W. (1838/2012). *Colonization and Christianity: A popular history of the treatment of the Natives by the Europeans in all their colonies*. London: Longman.

Hrizi, N. (2008). Behind the U.S. smears against China. In A. McInerney (Ed.), *China: Revolution and counterrevolution*. San Francisco: PSL.

Hudis, P. (2012). *Marx's concept of the alternative to capitalism*. Leyden & Boston: Brill.

Kahlenberg, R., & Marvit, M. (2012, December 20). The ugly racial history of "Right to Work." *Dissent*. Retrieved from https://www.dissentmagazine.org/online_articles/the-ugly-racial-history-of-right-to-work

Katz, M. (1975). *Class, bureaucracy, and schools: The illusion of educational change in America*. New York: Praeger.

Katz, M. (1987). *Reconstructing American education*. London: Harvard University Press.

Kohl, H. (1999). Facing tough decisions. In B. Peterson & M. Charney (Eds.), *Transforming teacher unions: Fighting for better schools and social justice* (pp. 93–96). Milwaukee, WI: Rethinking Schools.

Kozol, J. (2012). *Savage inequalities: Children in America's schools* (Rep. ed.). New York: Broadway.

Kumar, R. (2012). *Education and the reproduction of capital: Neoliberal knowledge and counterstrategies*. New York: Palgrave.

James, G. (1954/2005). *Stolen legacy: Greek philosophy is stolen Egyptian philosophy*. Drewryville, VA: Khalifah's.

La Riva, G. (2008). Is China's appeasement policy sustainable? In A. McInerney (Ed.), *China: Revolution and counterrevolution*. San Francisco: PSL.

Le, P. (2015). Seattle teachers' tentative deal tackles issues beyond pay. AP. Retrieved from http://bigstory.ap.org/article/be440091c2534f3f9fb332c226c023ff/seattle-teachers-tentative-deal-tackles-issues-beyond-pay

Lenin, V. I. (1912/1970). *On trade unions: A collection of articles and speeches*. Moscow: Progress.

Lenin, V. I. (1917/2015). The state and revolution. In B. Becker (Ed.), *Revolution manifesto: Understanding Marx and Lenin's theory of revolution*. San Francisco: Liberation.

Lenin, V. I. (1924/1970). On strikes. In Vladimir Lenin (Au.). *On trade unions: A collection of articles and speeches*. Pp. 57–67. Moscow: Progress Publishers.

Loewen, J. (1995). *Lies my teacher told me: Everything your American history textbook got wrong*. New York: Touchstone.

Macedo, D. (1994). *Literacies of power: What Americans are not allowed to know*. Boulder, CO: Westview.

Malott, C. (2008). *A call to action: An introduction to education, philosophy, and native North America*. New York: Peter Lang.

Malott, C. (2012). Rethinking educational purpose: The socialist challenge. *The Journal for Critical Education Policy Studies, 10*(2), 160–182.

Malott, C. (2013). Questioning the American dream: An essay review of *Class dismissed: Why we cannot teach or learn our way out of inequality* by J. Marsh. *Educational Review, 16*(3), 1–17. Retrieved from http://www.edrev.info/essays/v16n3.pdf

Malott, C. (2014). Contributions to a Marxist critical pedagogy: Revisiting Marx's humanism. *JCEPS*, *12*(2). Retrieved from http://www.jceps.com/wp-content/uploads/2014/08/1-JCEPS122-cuma-FINAL-11aug2014.pdf

Malott, C., & Ford, D. (2015). *Marx, capital, and education: Towards a critical pedagogy of becoming*. New York: Peter Lang.

Marcy, S. (1976a). *The class character of the USSR* (2nd ed.). New York: World View.

Marcy, S. (1976b). *Global class war*. New York: Workers & Oppressed Unite.

Marsh, J. (2011). *Class dismissed: Why we cannot teach or learn our way out of inequality*. New York: Monthly Review.

Marx, K. (1843/1978). On the Jewish question. In R. C. Tucker (Ed.), *The Marx-Engels reader* (2nd ed.). New York: W. W. Norton.

Marx, K. (1844/1988). *Economic and philosophic manuscripts of 1844* (M. Milligan, Trans.). Amherst: Prometheus.

Marx, K. (1852/1972). *The eighteenth Brumaire of Louis Bonaparte* (2nd ed.). New York: International.

Marx, K. (1857–1858/1973). *The grundrisse*. New York: Penguin.

Marx, K. (1866/1990). *Trade unions: Their past, present, and future*. New York: Path Finder.

Marx, K. (1867/1967). *Capital. Vol. 1*. New York: International.

Marx, K. (1875/2002). *Critique of the Gotha program*. New York: International.

Marx, K. (1992). *Capital: A critique of political economy. Vol. 2*. New York: Penguin.

Marx, K. (2007). *Dispatches from the New York Tribune: Selected journalism of Karl Marx*. New York: Penguin.

Marx, K., & Engels, F. (1846/1996). *The German ideology: Part 1*. New York: International.

McInerney, A. (2008). Capitalism and socialism in China today. In A. McInerney (Ed.), *China: Revolution and counterrevolution*. San Francisco: PSL.

McInerney, A., & Thompson, I. (Eds.) (2010). *The program of the PSL: Socialism and liberation in the United States*. San Francisco: PSL.

McLaren, P. (2004). *Teaching against global capitalism and the new imperialism: A critical pedagogy*. Lanham, MD: Rowman & Littlefield.

McLaren, P. (2005). *Capitalists and conquerors: A critical pedagogy against empire*. Lanham, MD: Rowman & Littlefield.

McLauren, P. (2007). *Life in schools: An introduction to critical pedagogy in the foundations of education* (5th ed.) Boston: Pearson/Allyn & Bacon.

McLaren, P., & Farahmandpur, R. (2001). Teaching against globalization and the new imperialism: Toward a revolutionary pedagogy. *Journal of Teacher Education*, *52*(2), 136–150.

McLaren, P., & Jaramillo, N. (2007). *Pedagogy and praxis in the age of empire: Towards a new humanism*. New York: Sense.

McLaren, P., & Jaramillo, N. (2010). Not neo-Marxist, not post-Marxist, not Marxian, not autonomous Marxism: Reflections on a revolutionary (Marxist) critical pedagogy. *Cultural Studies↔Critical Methodologies*, *20*(10), 1–12.

Mills, C. (2008). Independent development versus imperialist domination. In A. McInerney (Ed.), *China: Revolution and counterrevolution*. San Francisco: PSL.

Mohawk, J. (1992). *Utopian legacies: A history of conquest and oppression in the Western world.* Santa Fe, NM: Clear Light.

Newton, H. P. (1995). *To die for the people: The writings of Huey P. Newton.* (T. Morrison, Ed.). New York: Writers & Readers.

Parenti, M. (1997). *Blackshirts and Reds: Rational fascism and the overthrow of communism.* San Francisco: City Lights.

Parenti, M. (2001). Rollback: Aftermath of the overthrow of communism. In G. Katsiaficas (Ed.), *After the fall: 1989 and the future of freedom.* New York: Routledge.

Party of Socialism and Liberation. (2011). *Program of the PSL: Socialism and liberation in the United States.* San Francisco: Author.

Party for Socialism and Liberation. (2015). *Imperialism in the 21st century: Updating Lenin's theory a century later* (B. Becker, Ed.). San Francisco: Liberation.

Perlstein, D. (1999). If not now, when? In B. Peterson & M. Charney (Eds.), *Transforming teacher unions: Fighting for better schools and social justice* (pp. 86–92). Milwaukee, WI: Rethinking Schools.

Pierce, R. (2015, December 15). How the sun of Palestine reached a Black Panther in jail. *Electronic Intifada.* Retrieved from https://electronicintifada.net/content/how-sun-palestine-reached-black-panther-jail/15069

Puryear, E. (2008). From liberation to Thermidor: Phases of China's socialist revolution. In A. McInerney (Ed.), *China: Revolution and counterrevolution.* San Francisco: PSL.

Puryear, E. (2012). *Shackled and chained: Mass incarceration in capitalist America.* San Francisco: PSL Publications.

Robinson, W. (2014, September 19). The political economy of Israeli apartheid and the specter of genocide. Truthout.org. Retrieved from http://www.truth-out.org/news/item/26254-the-political-economy-of-israeli-apartheid-and-the-specter-of-genocide

Ruíz, M. (2008). The Sino-Soviet split: From revolutionary potential to tragic consequences. In A. McInerney (Ed.), *China: Revolution and Counterrevolution.* San Francisco: PSL.

Rury, J. (2013). *Education and social change: Contours in the history of American schooling.* New York: Routledge.

Ryan, W. (1976). *Blaming the victim.* New York: Vintage.

Shakur, A. (1987). *Assata: An autobiography.* London: Zed.

Small, R. (2005). *Marx and education.* Hampshire, UK: Ashgate.

Spring. J. (1986/1994). *The American school 1642–1993* (3rd ed.). New York: McGraw-Hill.

Spring, J. (2007). *Wheels in the head: Educational philosophies of authority, freedom, and culture from Confucianism to human rights.* New York: Routledge.

Urban W., & Wagoner, J. (2009). *American education: A history* (4th ed.). New York: Routledge.

Van Gelder, S. (2015, July 24). Rev. Sekou on today's civil rights leaders: "I take my orders from queer women." Truthout.org. Retrieved from http://www.truth-out.org/news/item/32039-rev-sekou-on-today-s-civil-rights-leaders-i-take-my-orders-from-23-year-old-queer-women

Vassar, R. (1965). *Social history of American education: Vol.1. Colonial times to 1860.* Chicago: Rand McNally.

Venables, R. (2004). *American Indian history: Five centuries of conflict & coexistence: Vol.1. Conquest of a continent 1492–1783.* Santa Fe, NM: Clear Light.

Vygotsky, L. S. (1978). *Mind in society: The development of higher psychological processes* (M. Cole & S. Scribner, Eds.). Cambridge, MA: Harvard University Press.

Weiner, L. (2015). Teacher unionism reborn. In Mark Abendroth and Brad Porfilio (Eds.). *Understanding neoliberal rule in K–12 schools: Educational fronts for local and global justice.* *Volume 1.* PP. 271–284. Charlotte, NC: IAP.

Weir, F. (2016, January 29). Maybe the Soviets weren't so bad? Russian nostalgia for USSR on the rise. *The Christian Science Monitor.* Retrieved from http://www.csmonitor.com/World/ Europe/2016/0129/Maybe-the-Soviets-weren-t-so-bad-Russian-nostalgia-for-USSR-on-the-rise?cmpid=gigya-fb

Woodson, C. (2013). *The mis-education of the Negro.* New York: Tribeca.

INDEX

W

Y

EDUCATION and STRUGGLE

Narrative, Dialogue and the Political Production of Meaning

Michael A. Peters
Peter McLaren
Series Editors

To submit a manuscript or proposal for editorial consideration, please contact:

Dr. Peter McLaren
UCLA Los Angeles
School of Education &
Information Studies
Moore Hall 3022C
Los Angeles, CA 90095

Dr. Michael Peters
University of Waikato
P.O. Box 3105
Faculty of Education
Hamilton 3240
New Zealand

WE ARE THE STORIES WE TELL. The book series Education and Struggle focuses on conflict as a discursive process where people struggle for legitimacy and the narrative process becomes a political struggle for meaning. But this series will also include the voices of authors and activists who are involved in conflicts over material necessities in their communities, schools, places of worship, and public squares as part of an ongoing search for dignity, self-determination, and autonomy. This series focuses on conflict and struggle within the realm of educational politics based around a series of interrelated themes: indigenous struggles; Western-Islamic conflicts; globalization and the clash of worldviews; neoliberalism as the war within; colonization and neocolonization; the coloniality of power and decolonial pedagogy; war and conflict; and the struggle for liberation. It publishes narrative accounts of specific struggles as well as theorizing "conflict narratives" and the political production of meaning in educational studies. During this time of global conflict and the crisis of capitalism, Education and Struggle promises to be on the cutting edge of social, cultural, educational, and political transformation.

Central to the series is the idea that language is a process of social, cultural, and class conflict. The aim is to focus on key semiotic, literary, and political concepts as a basis for a philosophy of language and culture where the underlying materialist philosophy of language and culture serves as the basis for the larger project that we might call dialogism (after Bakhtin's usage). As the late V.N. Volosinov suggests "Without signs there is no ideology," "Everything ideological possesses semiotic value," and "individual consciousness is a socio-ideological fact." It is a small step to claim, therefore, "consciousness itself can arise and become a viable fact only in the material embodiment of signs." This series is a vehicle for materialist semiotics in the narrative and dialogue of education and struggle.

To order other books in this series, please contact our Customer Service Department:

(800) 770-LANG (within the U.S.)
(212) 647-7706 (outside the U.S.)
(212) 647-7707 FAX

Or browse online by series:

www.peterlang.com